✕ ✕ ✕ THE ✕ ✕ ✕ CROSS STITCHER'S BIBLE

THE CROSS STITCHER'S BIBLE

Jane Greenoff

David & Charles

Contents

✕✕✕✕✕

×××××

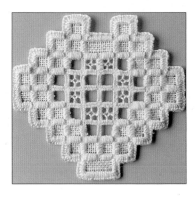

To my husband Bill, whose love makes it all possible!

The Cross Stitch Guild

The Cross Stitch Guild was formed in March 1996 and quickly became a worldwide organisation with a committed and enthusiastic body of members – over 2,000 in the first six months of operation. As word spreads it is clear that many cross stitch and counted thread addicts around the world are delighted to have a Guild of their own. The CSG has received an extraordinary level of support from designers, retailers, manufacturers and stitchers. Guild members receive a full-colour magazine bi-monthly, including free counted cross-stitch designs and technical advice and information.

For more information contact: CSG HQ, Pinks Barn, London Road, Fairford, Gloucestershire GL7 4AR England. Tel: 0800 328 9750.

A DAVID & CHARLES BOOK

First published in the UK in 2000, reprinted 2001
First published in paperback 2003; reprinted 2003
Text and designs Copyright © Jane Greenoff 2000, 2003
Photography and layout Copyright © David & Charles 2000, 2003

Stitch Library artworks © David & Charles 2000, 2003 adapted from originals supplied by the Cross Stitch Guild

Jane Greenoff has asserted her right to be identified as author of this work in accordance with the Copyright, Designs and Patents Act, 1988.

A catalogue record for this book is available from the British Library.

ISBN 0 7153 1470 X

Photography by Alan Duns and David Johnson
Book design by Casebourne Rose
Printed in Italy by STIGE
Graphic and Printing Ltd
for David & Charles
Brunel House   Newton Abbot   Devon

(Page 1)
Poppy and Daisy Posy – see page 15
for instructions.

(Page 2)
Hardanger Flower Chatelaine, Scissors
Keeper and Needlecase – see page 74
for instructions.

❋ Bow Band Sampler ❋

Stitch Count: 29 x 137
Design Size: 7.5 x 35cm (3 x 14in)
Fabric Selection: Zweigart Cork linen
20 threads to 2.5cm (1in)
Tapestry Needle Size: 24 and 22

This delicate sampler has been stitched in
rows using a variety of different stitches,
working from top to bottom as follows:
cross stitch, half Rhodes stitch with bar,
cross stitch with a small Hardanger
section, queen stitch, Rhodes stitch,
Hardanger with eyelet stitches, Bullion
stitch roses and Rhodes stitch. The band
sampler is charted on page 164 of the
Motif Library. You might find it easier to
photocopy the two parts of the chart and
tape them together. See Working the
Projects page 126.

Introduction

xxxxx

I have been asked over and over again 'for a book giving the tips, hints and technical know-how of cross stitch' – and here it is. Pure cross stitch, worked perfectly, is beautiful to look at and simple to do but does require detailed explanations of some of the techniques. So I hope that this unique book will provide the useful, accessible information in an easy-to-use format that so many of you have been seeking.

Cross stitch is usually our first love but I hope that by referring to this book you will be able to add to and enhance your cross stitch patterns and perhaps design for yourself. It is hoped that *The Cross Stitcher's Bible*, with its clear, definitive instructions, computer-generated charts and exciting motif library, will become your essential manual, and that you will not only perfect existing techniques, but also explore exciting companions to cross stitch, such as the use of beads and ribbon, embellishment with charms and buttons, and other decorative counted stitches like blackwork and Hardanger.

✛ How to Use This Book ✛

The book has been divided into sections with colour-coded pages to enable you to find the information you require easily and to provide a clear and comprehensive approach to all aspects of cross stitching.

• Getting Started is colour coded green and tells you all you need to know about choosing and using equipment, fabric and threads plus all the practical aspects of how to cross stitch on Aida and evenweave.

• Creative Options is colour coded yellow and describes cross stitching techniques using some of the many different fabrics and threads available.

• Exploring Choices is colour coded blue and features exciting designs that show you how easy it is to combine cross stitch with many other counted embroidery techniques.

• In Getting Started, Creative Options and Exploring Choices, I have included boxes called Stitch Perfect, which focus on the important points in each section.

• In Creative Options you will see illustrations of worked designs, many of which combine a number of techniques fully explained elsewhere. For example, the Birdhouse (page 54) includes working cross stitch on linen, creating French knots in stranded cotton (floss) and silk ribbon and using a charm for embellishment.

• The extensive Stitch Library includes all the stitches you need to work any of the designs in the book, each with clear, colour diagrams, colour pictures of the completed stitches and explanatory text.

• There is a short section called Working the Projects (page 126). This should be particularly useful for the less experienced stitcher, helping to guide you through the early stages of any project you choose to stitch.

• All of the designs featured in the book are charted in the Motif Library starting on page 127. I have chosen colour charts with black symbols so that you can identify the charts you need but may still photocopy and enlarge them if you wish.

• Most of the designs in the Motif Library may be stitched on Aida or evenweave. Where evenweave is essential it is indicated in the picture caption. All the cross stitch designs have been stitched with DMC stranded cotton (floss) unless otherwise stated.

• Measurements are given in metric with imperial conversions in brackets. Use either metric or imperial when working, do not combine them.

Getting Started

You should find this section very useful as it contains a great deal of invaluable information on cross stitch basics, including how to choose equipment, use charts, manage threads and all the instruction you'll ever need on creating beautiful cross stitch on Aida and evenweave fabric.

✕✕✕✕✕

✳ *Yellow Flower* ✳

Stitch Count: 24 x 43
Design Size: 4.5 x 7.5cm (1³/₄ x 3in)
Fabric Selection: Cream Aida 14 blocks to 2.5cm (1in)
Tapestry Needle Size: 24

This simple design has been cross stitched using two
strands of stranded cotton (floss). The chart for this design
is part of a larger chart in the Motif Library on page 129.
See Working the Projects page 126.

Using Charts

The designs are worked from charts and are counted designs. The charts and keys for all the projects are contained in the Motif Library (pages 127–181) and are illustrated in colour with a black and/or white symbol to aid colour identification.

• Each square on a chart, both occupied and unoccupied, represents two threads of linen or one block of Aida unless otherwise stated. Each occupied square equals one stitch.

• The church in winter shown here could have been worked from a black and white chart, a coloured chart or a combination of both, as shown opposite.

• Cross stitch charts generally consist of whole squares representing complete cross stitches, but you will see additional stitches added to some charts in the Motif Library indicating three-quarter cross stitches (sometimes called fractional stitches), French knots and so on. These stitches will be clearly labelled in the key or included on the chart.

• The count of a fabric (the number of stitches to 2.5cm or 1in) affects the size of a finished piece even when worked from the same chart, whether a coloured chart or a black and white one. This is shown clearly on page 16, where a rosebud has been worked on different counts.

• Traditionally cross stitchers begin to stitch from the middle of the chart and the middle of the fabric thus ensuring that the design is centred when it is mounted and framed. To prevent serious counting errors, use a coloured pen to rule a line on the chart from arrow to arrow to find the centre and then add a line of tacking (basting) to the fabric. This can act as an early warning system!

• When looking at a chart, try to plan the direction in which you are going to stitch. If you count across the shortest distances of empty fabric each time you will avoid making counting mistakes. This may sometimes mean that you are counting diagonally, vertically or horizontally across a pattern, which may seem a peculiar route but is one which will actually help prevent counting mistakes. Mistakes most often occur when counting across long sections of blank fabric.

❋ *A Church in Winter* ❋
Stitch Count: 88 x 48
Design Size: 16 x 19cm (6^1/$_2$ x 3^1/$_2$in)
Fabric Selection: Grey Aida 14 blocks to 2.5cm (1in)
Tapestry Needle Size: 24

This winter scene has been stitched using two strands of stranded cotton (floss) for the cross stitch and one strand for the back stitch outlining. It is charted on page 180 of the Motif Library. See Working the Projects page 126.

• You can turn your work and the chart upside down if you prefer to work towards you, but never turn halfway – your stitches will end up facing the wrong way!

• Check your relative position regularly so that you do not belatedly discover mistakes and have lots of stitches to unpick.

• I make a photocopy of a chart from which I am working so that I can lightly colour in the chart as I proceed to avoid looking at the wrong section.

• You may find a metal board with magnetic strips helpful. It keeps the chart in position and marks your place.

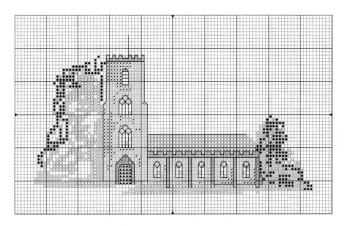

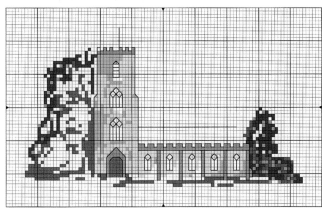

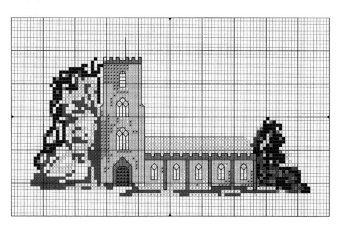

Equipment

The equipment needed for cross stitch couldn't be simpler – essentially just a selection of tapestry needles, some scissors and perhaps a hoop or frame will get you going. You will need other items for making up projects, for example, sewing thread, double-sided adhesive tape, frames, mounts and so on but these will be given under the relevant finishing instructions at the back of the book.

Needles

• When working counted cross stitch you will need blunt tapestry needles of various sizes depending on your fabric selection. A blunt needle is required because you should be *parting* the threads of the fabric rather than piercing the material. You want to avoid splitting the fibres as you stitch.

• The most commonly used tapestry needles for cross stitch are sizes 24 and 26, although needles are available in sizes 20, 22, 24, 26 and 28.

• When using needle sizes 26 and 28, avoid using too many strands of stranded cotton (floss) because the eye is very delicate and will break. Adjust the needle size to match the project. If you are not sure what size of needle to choose, check in the following way: when the needle is pushed through the fabric it should pass through without enlarging the hole, but also without falling through too easily.

• Avoid leaving your needle in the fabric when it is put away as it may leave a mark (unless you are working with gold-plated needles).

• The nickel plating on needles varies and some stitchers find they are allergic to the nickel and therefore prefer gold-plated needles.

• When the use of beads is suggested in a project they may be attached using a special beading needle. A blunt beading needle size 26 has been specially developed for cross stitchers (see Suppliers).

Scissors

• Keep a small, sharp pair of pointed scissors exclusively for your embroidery.

• Use dressmaker's shears for cutting fabric.

Frames and Hoops

• Frames or hoops are not essential for cross stitchers and I have worked without either for many years. I prefer to work my cross stitch in my hand as this allows a sewing action (see Forming a Cross Stitch page 20) but this is a matter of personal preference.

• If you must use a hoop, please use one large enough to hold the complete design – moving a hoop across your beautifully formed stitches is criminal!

• Frames and hoops are useful when you are working in miniature and also when adding beads or combining cross stitch with silk ribbon.

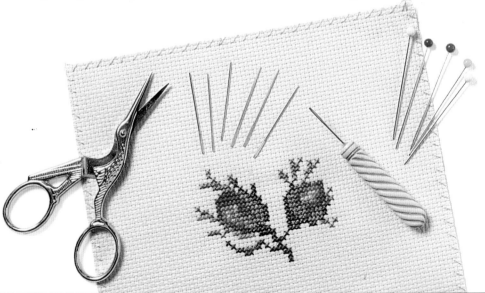

Choosing and Managing Threads

The most commonly used thread for counted embroidery is stranded cotton (floss) but you will see Flower Threads, perlé cottons, assorted metallics and spaced-dyed specialist threads used within the Creative Options section (colour-coded yellow). The following guidelines apply to stranded cotton (floss) as information about other yarns will be found in the relevant sections.

• All the motifs in the Motif Library were stitched using DMC stranded cotton (floss) unless stated otherwise. Anchor alternatives are given in brackets. If you do change to an alternative Anchor number bear in mind that an exact colour match is not always possible.

• Where two shade numbers are quoted for one stitch this is known as tweeding. This straight-forward practice is a simple way to increase the numbers of colours in your palate without buying more thread. To tweed, combine more than one coloured thread in the needle at the same time and work as one. You can apply tweeding to working French knots and bullion bars to great effect.

• When selecting threads, always have the fabric you are intending to use close at hand, because the colour of your background fabric will affect your choice of thread colours. When in a shop, check the colour of the thread in daylight as electric light can 'kill' some shades.

• It is possible to buy 'daylight' bulbs to use in normal spotlights at home – a great help when shading a design in the evening.

• Cross stitch is generally worked using two strands of stranded cotton when working on 14 and 16-count Aida.

• If you are working on Aida and are not sure how many strands to use, try working a small section, stitching a few complete cross stitches and looking at the stitching in daylight. Some colours may need the number of strands adjusting to suit the project.

• If you are working on evenweave and do not know how many strands of stranded cotton (floss) to use, carefully pull a thread from the edge of the fabric and compare the thread with the strands of cotton. The strands on the needle should be a similar weight.

• When using two strands or more for your

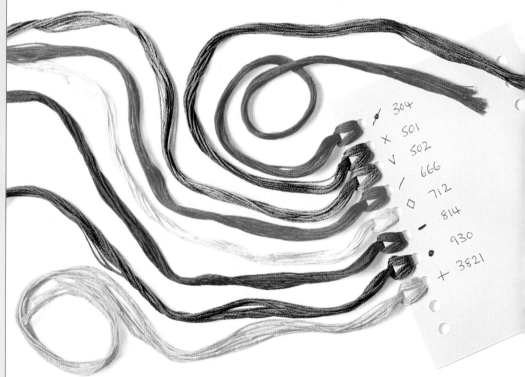

cross stitch, you will need to re-align the strands before starting to stitch. Simply separate the strands and then realign them before threading your needle. When using some fibres it is helpful to pass the threads through a lightly dampened sponge which helps to remove unwanted static from the threads.

• Before laundering or tea-dyeing a piece of work (see page 32) you need to ensure that the threads are colourfast. To do this place the work face down on a clean surface and using a clean, damp white tissue, press the back of the stitches. Any trace of colour on the tissue means the thread colours are not fast, so do not wash or tea-dye. You should have no trouble with reputable brands such as DMC, Anchor and Madeira but take extra care with Christmas reds.

Organising Your Threads

It really does pay to start with good habits if possible and have an organiser system for your threads.

• There are many excellent organiser systems on the market, but I make my own organiser cards as shown in the photograph. The card from inside a packet of tights is excellent, but any stiff card will do.

• Punch holes down each side of the card and take a skein of stranded cotton (floss). Cut the cotton into manageable lengths of about 80cm (30in) double them and thread them through the holes as shown. It is quite simple to remove one length of thread from the card without disturbing the rest.

• If you label the card with the manufacturer's name and shade number, when the project is complete all the threads will be labelled ready for another project.

✳ *Poppy and Daisy Posy* ✳
Stitch Count: 29 x 39
Design Size: 6 x 7.5cm (2¹/₄ x 3in)
Fabric Selection: Zweigart Cashel linen 28 threads to 2.5cm (1in)
Tapestry Needle Size: 24

Two strands of stranded cotton (floss) were used for the cross stitch with one strand of the shade indicated in the chart key to add the optional back stitch outline. It is charted on page 129 of the Motif Library. See Working the Projects page 126.

Starting to Stitch

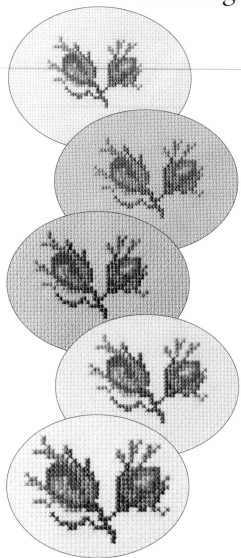

This section of the book is intended to create the background for the later sections, Creative Options and Exploring Choices. Whether you are an expert cross stitcher or just beginning, please read through this section in case there are tips and hints you may not have heard before. You may be able to see the reasons for some of the things you do or perhaps the reasons why you should! When working the projects in the book beginners might find the section called Working the Projects on page 126 useful as it provides a checklist to get your project started.

Fabrics for Cross Stitching

The fabric predominantly used for counted needlework is divided into two main groups: Aida – woven in definite blocks, or evenweave – woven in single threads. (Refer also to page 24 Choosing and Using Fabrics.)

Stitching on Aida

All the fabrics in the Aida family are woven with the threads grouped in bundles to form a square pattern on the fabric which in turn creates obvious holes. The stitches are formed using these holes. Aida is available in many different colours and counts. The rosebud motif on this page (charted on page 128 in two colourways) has been stitched on different coloured fabrics with different thread counts. As you can see the colour changes make it look quite different and using various counts results in different sized motifs. To check the thread count, lay a ruler on top of the material and, using a needle, count the number of threads or blocks to 2.5cm (1in).

Stitching on Evenweave

This is the name given to a range of fabrics where the threads are woven singly rather than in blocks. Evenweaves are available in many colours and counts and working on evenweave is not difficult, just different. The designs opposite are the same size on evenweave as on Aida because each stitch is formed over two threads instead of one block, therefore a 28-count evenweave has the same stitch count as a 14-count Aida (28 threads to 2.5cm = 14 blocks to 2.5cm). Evenweave can be worked over one thread (see page 31) or when very fine detail is required. It is also possible to stitch poems or other text

✳ *Pink Rosebuds* ✳

Stitch Count: 33 x 24
Fabric Selection: Aida in five different thread counts 11, 14, 16, 18 and 20 to 2.5cm (1in)
Tapestry Needle Size: 24–26

A simple rosebud has been stitched on different counts of Aida to show how the size of the design is altered by the fabric count and how different coloured fabrics affect the overall look of the design. The cross stitch has been stitched using two strands for the 11, 14 and 16-count fabrics and one strand for the 18 and 20-count materials. The rosebud chart is on page 128 of the Motif Library. See Working the Projects page 126.

within a small sampler if the border is worked over two threads and the text over one thread.

How Many Strands?

The number of strands of stranded cotton (floss) used depends mainly on the stitch count of the fabric you are using. When in doubt, work a few cross stitches in the fabric margin and decide how many strands you prefer. If the chart you wish to stitch does not indicate how many strands to use, you can check by pulling a thread from the edge of the fabric and comparing it with the strands of cotton. They should be a similar weight to the threads in the fabric.

Calculating Design Size

This is the area that many stitchers avoid if they possibly can, but if you are going to progress from purchased cross stitch kits and move to working from charts or better still, your own designs, you must know how to work out design sizes. It is this calculation which decides how much fabric you will need to stitch your project or whether a particular motif will fit in a card aperture. There is nothing worse than working a project and realising belatedly that the whole design will not fit on the fabric!

All counted designs are made up of squares or parts of squares and the fabrics used for counted cross stitch are produced to have the same number of threads or blocks in each direction so that you will produce nice square stitches. All that determines the size of a cross stitch design is the number stitches up and down and the thread count of the fabric. To calculate the size of a design follow these principles:

• Look at your completed chart and count the number of stitches in each direction.

• Divide this number by the number of stitches to 2.5cm (1in) on the fabric of your choice and this will determine the completed design size. For example, 140 stitches divided by 14-count Aida equals a design size of 10in.

• Always add a margin for stretching, framing or finishing. I always add 13cm (5in) to both dimensions when designing a picture or sampler. This can be reduced to 7.5cm (3in) for smaller projects. Remember when creating a card or trinket pot to allow the margin on the aperture size not the stitch count.

✳ *Yellow Rosebuds* ✳

Stitch Count: 33 x 24
Fabric Selection: Aida in five different thread counts 11, 14, 16, 18 and 20 to 2.5cm (1in)
Tapestry Needle Size: 24–26

Here, the rosebud has been stitched in a yellow colourway, again on different counts of Aida. The cross stitch has been stitched using two strands for the 11, 14 and 16-count fabrics and one strand for the 18 and 20-count materials. The rosebud chart is on page 128 of the Motif Library. See Working the Projects page 126.

Where to Start

Unless indicated otherwise by the designer, start stitching in the middle of a design to ensure an adequate margin for stretching and framing.

- To find the middle of the fabric, fold it in four and press lightly.
- Open out and work a narrow line of tacking (basting) stitches following the threads to mark the fold and the centre. These stitches are removed when the work is completed.
- Rule a line on the chart (if using a copy) to match the tacking (basting) stitches.
- Check you have all the colours you need and mount all the threads on a piece of card alongside its shade number (see page 15).
- Sew a narrow hem or oversew the raw edges to prevent fraying. This can be removed on completion. Avoid sticky tape and any clear glues as they have a habit of creeping and will attract grime to your fabric.
- Work one large cross stitch at the top of your work away from the stitching to remind you which is the top and which way the work is facing.
- If using evenweave, start your stitching to the left of the vertical thread (see Fig 1).

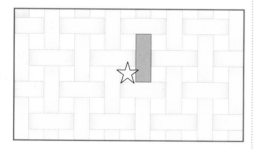

Fig 1 Starting the stitching to the left of a vertical thread

How to Start

It is important to start and finish your stitching neatly, avoiding the use of knots which would create ugly lumps in the finished piece.

Knotless Loop Start

Starting with a knotless loop (fig 2) can be very useful with stranded cotton (floss), but it only works if you are intending to stitch with an *even* number of threads, i.e. 2, 4, or 6.

- Cut the stranded cotton (floss) roughly twice the length you would normally need and carefully separate one strand.
- Double this thread and then thread your needle with the two ends.
- Pierce your fabric from the wrong side where you intend to place your first stitch, leaving the looped end at the rear of the work.
- Return your needle to the wrong side after forming a half cross stitch, and pass the needle through the waiting loop.
- The stitch is now anchored and you may begin to stitch.

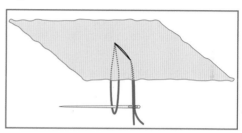

Fig 2 Knotless loop start

Away Waste Knot

Start with an away waste knot (fig 3) if working with an *odd* number of strands or when tweeding threads (where you use one strand each of two or more colours to achieve a mottled, tweedy appearance – see page 14). An away waste knot is situated on the front of the fabric and you work towards it and cut it off when the threads are anchored. Avoid using this method with black thread as it may leave a small shadow on the fabric. (See also Linen Masterclass Stitch Perfect page 22.)

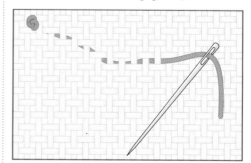

Fig 3 Away waste knot start

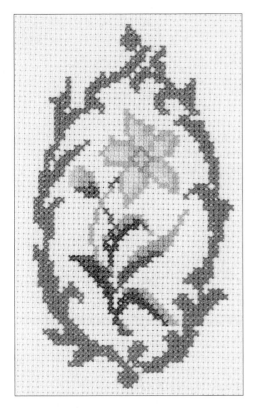

Stitch & Park

When working with a number of different shades you can use a number of needles at a time to avoid stopping and starting over again. Work a few stitches in one shade, bring the needle out to the front of the work and park it above where you are stitching. Introduce another colour, work a few stitches and then park before bringing back the previous colour, working under the back of the stitches. Use a gold-plated needle to avoid any risk of the needle marking the fabric.

Working a Cross Stitch

A cross stitch has two parts and can be worked in one of two ways – a complete stitch can be worked, or a number of half stitches may be stitched in one line, then completed on the return journey. Your cross stitch may face either direction but the one essential rule is that *all* the top stitches should face the same direction to produce the neatest result.

✳ *Victorian Flower Garland* ✳

Stitch Count: 40 x 69
Design Size: 7.5 x 12.5cm (3 x 5in)
Fabric Selection: Cream Aida 14 blocks to 2.5cm (1in)
or pure antique white linen 28 threads to 2.5cm (1in)
Tapestry Needle Size: 24

These two identical designs have been worked using two strands of stranded cotton (floss) for the cross stitch – one on Aida and one on evenweave so you can compare the results. The chart for this design is on page 129 of the Motif Library. See Working the Projects page 126.

To create perfect cross stitches the strands of thread first need to be aligned. Take two strands of stranded cotton (floss), separate the strands completely and then realign them before threading your needle. When using some fibres it is helpful to pass the threads through a lightly dampened sponge which helps remove unwanted static and make stitching easier.

Forming a Single Cross Stitch on Aida or Evenweave

Bring the needle up from the wrong side of the fabric at the bottom left of an Aida block or to the left of a vertical evenweave thread (see fig 1 page 18). Cross one block of Aida or two threads of evenweave and insert the needle into the top right-hand corner (see figs 4 and 5). Push through and come up at the bottom right-hand corner. Complete the stitch in the top left-hand corner. To work an adjacent stitch, bring the needle up at the bottom right-hand corner of the first stitch.

Forming Cross Stitch in Two Journeys

Work the first leg of the cross stitch as above but instead of completing the stitch, work the next half stitch and continue to the end of the row. Complete the cross stitches on the return journey. I recommend this method as it forms neater vertical lines on the back of the work.

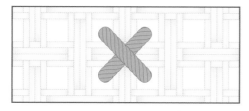

Fig 4 A cross stitch on Aida

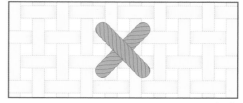

Fig 5 A cross stitch on evenweave

✛ Stitch Perfect ✛

• Use the correct size needle for the fabric and the number of strands of thread required.

• When you start stitching on evenweave fabric, always start to the left of a vertical thread (see fig 1 page 18) as this will help to prevent counting mistakes.

• Start with a knotless loop start or an away waste knot but avoid using a knot on the reverse of the work.

• Work the cross stitch in two journeys (see page 84) forming neat vertical lines on the wrong side of the work. Use a sewing movement, half cross stitch in one direction, covering these original stitches with the second row. This useful and rapid sewing movement is not possible when working with a hoop or frame.

• To prevent the thread twisting when working the cross stitch in two journeys, either turn the work upside down and let the needle spin, or learn to twist the needle as you stitch. Each time you take the needle out of the fabric, give the needle a half turn and the stitches will lie flat.

• The top stitches should all face the same direction.

• Come up through unoccupied holes where possible to help keep your stitches beautifully formed.

• Plan your route around the chart counting over short distances to avoid counting mistakes (see Charts page 10).

• Do not travel across the back of the fabric for more than two stitches as trailing thread will show on the front of the work (see Stitch & Park page 19).

• When finishing off, push the needle under the vertical loops on the back and snip the thread off close to the stitching.

Back Stitch Outlining with Cross Stitch

You will see from the crocus motif right, that additional back stitches are often used to add definition and dimension to a cross stitch project, although this is a matter of personal taste. Try using subtle shades for the back stitch to avoid adding a hard edge to the stitches (see picture page 126). Avoid black for outlining unless needed for wrought iron or similar motifs. (See page 60 for advice on blackwork.)

As a general rule, I use one strand of stranded cotton and a slightly smaller size needle when adding the back stitch outline, using a thread colour that will enhance the design rather than over-power it. Work back stitch over individual blocks on Aida or pairs of threads on evenweave and avoid working long stitches unless it is to illustrate something like cat's whiskers or ships' rigging. The finished effect will be worth it!

How to Change Threads and Finish Off

Changing threads and finishing your work off correctly will pay dividends, creating a neat appearance and a safe piece of stitching that will stand the test of time.

- At the back of the work, pass the needle under several stitches of the same or similar colour and then snip off the loose end close to the stitching (see fig 6). Small loose ends have a nasty habit of pulling through to the right side!
- Finish the stitches in the direction that you are working. To do this, when the thread needs replacing stop stitching and park the needle above the design. Thread a new needle with the replacement thread and form a few stitches. Now un-park the needle and finish the old thread under the new stitches. This will prevent any stitch distortion on the front of the work.

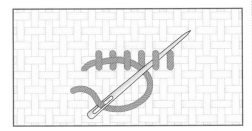

Fig 6 Finishing off a thread

❋ *Purple Crocus* ❋

Stitch Count: 29 x 39
Design Size: 6 x 7.5cm (2$^{1}/_{4}$ x 3in)
Fabric Selection: Cream Jobelan evenweave 27 threads to 2.5cm (1in)
Tapestry Needle Size: 26

This simple but effective crocus motif has been stitched twice, using two techniques but on the same fabric. The top version has been stitched in two strands of stranded cotton (floss) and back stitch outlined in one strand. The outline colour has been taken from the colours used for the cross stitch to ensure a soft, realistic look.

The second version, worked from the same chart (page 152 of the Motif Library), has been stitched using one strand of Flower Thread and the outline has been omitted. You can see that both techniques are effective but give quite a different feel. (See Working the Projects page 126.)

Linen Masterclass

Linen is made from the fibres of the flax plant *Linium usitatissimum*. Unlike other fabrics, linen increases in strength when wet, and it is the perfect choice for cross stitch on table or bed linen and for pulled and drawn thread work.

Linen is an evenweave fabric (see page 16): this means that there are the same number of vertical and horizontal threads to 2.5cm (1in); it does not mean that the threads are all the same thickness or that there will be no slubs or wobbly threads! Unfortunately, these naturally occurring irregularities in the fabric can dissuade some stitchers from using it. Stitching on linen is not difficult, just different: follow my advice and you will discover just how satisfying it is to use.

Railroading

This technique is used to force two strands of stranded cotton (floss) to lie flat and parallel to each other. When pushing the needle through the fabric, pass it in between the two strands of stranded cotton (floss). You can select to railroad both parts of the cross stitch or only the top stitch.

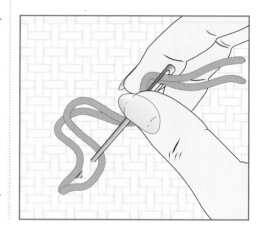

✛ Stitch Perfect ✛

The general instructions for working on evenweave fabrics (see pages 16–21) also apply to linen.

• Use the correct size needle for the fabric (see page 12). To check how many strands of thread you should be stitching with, pull out one thread from the fabric: the thread in your needle should be about the same weight.

• Separate each strand of stranded cotton (floss) and then re-combine ensuring the twist is running in the same direction on each strand.

• To avoid reversing the twist, start stitching with an away waste knot (page 18) rather than the loop method.

• Work cross stitches over two threads in each direction to even out any discrepancies. If more detail is required, stitches can be formed over one thread.

• When stitching over one thread, work the stitches singly rather than in two journeys. This will prevent the stitches sliding under the fabric threads.

• Learn to railroad (see above). Although a time-consuming technique, it does produce effective results. Even simpler, twist the needle as you stitch. As you take the needle out of the fabric, give the needle a half turn: this will keep the thread from twisting and the stitches will lie flat.

• To finish neatly, push the needle under the vertical loops on the back, then snip the thread off close to the stitching.

• When working across the fabric (i.e. on a band sampler), it is good practice to finish the stitches in the direction that you are working. If you run out of thread before the end of the row, see How to Change Threads page 21.

✳ *Lilies* ✳

Stitch Count: 53 x 74

Design Size: 9.5 x 13.25cm ($3^3/_4$ x $5^1/_4$in)

Fabric Selection: Unbleached linen 28 threads to 2.5cm (1in)

Tapestry Needle Size: 24–26

These classic lilies are worked on unbleached pure linen using two strands of DMC stranded cotton (floss). The chart for this design is included in the Motif Library (page 137) and could be stitched on any fabric including Aida if preferred. See Working the Projects page 126.

The design has been highlighted with back stitch in one strand of stranded cotton (floss) and the stamen of each lily added with random long stitches.

Creative Options

T his section is an invaluable closer look at some of the fabric and thread options open to the cross stitcher. You will see how easy and rewarding it is to cross stitch on a variety of materials, including perforated paper, silk, waste canvas, non-evenweave and double canvas. Some of the many threads available are explored, showing how effective cross stitching is with yarns other than stranded cotton (floss), such as Flower Thread, space-dyed thread, rayon, metallics and blending filaments.

✕✕✕✕✕

Choosing and Using Fabrics

When I first started stitching the choice of fabric was simple – cream 14-count Aida or linen, bleached or unbleached! Now there is so much choice, both in thread count and in colour, so the only limit is your imagination and your eyesight! The secret is to select the right fabric for the project, bearing in mind whether it is for decoration or a more functional use, and select a thread count you can manage without the frustration of working on material which strains your eyes. Most charted designs will adapt to suit different fabrics, for example, you can transfer cross stitch patterns onto canvas and vice versa. The sunflower design on page 40 has been stitched on double canvas in wool and again on unbleached linen in stranded cotton (floss).

The teddy, borage flower, topiary garden, rosebud, pansy, poppy and rose shown below have been stitched from the Motif Library on a variety of fabrics using two or three strands of stranded cotton (floss) for the cross stitch. They were stitched over one block of Aida fabrics or over two threads of evenweave fabrics and various needles sizes were used depending on the fabric count. See Working the Projects page 126. Note: Take care with some fabrics as they mark and crease easily, as seen by the embroidery hoop mark still visible on the borage design.

Design	Stitch Count/Design Size	Fabric Selection
Teddy chart on page 158	61 x 70 8 x 10cm (3 x 3$\frac{1}{2}$in)	Acrylic Afghan (stitched over one thread)
Borage Flower chart on page 141	33 x 28 7.5 x 6.5cm (3 x 2$\frac{1}{2}$in)	Damask with Aida panel 11 blocks to 2.5cm (1in) (stitched over one block)
Topiary Garden chart on page 141	48 x 47 9 x 9cm (3$\frac{1}{2}$ x 3$\frac{1}{2}$in)	Antique white linen 28 threads to 2.5cm (1in) (stitched over two threads)
Rosebud chart on page 141	24 x 45 4.5 x 8.5cm (1$\frac{3}{4}$ x 3$\frac{1}{4}$in)	Zweigart pure wool Aida 14 blocks to 2.5cm (1in) (stitched over one block)
Purple Pansy chart on page 151	29 x 24 5 x 4cm (2 x 1$\frac{1}{2}$in)	Pale green Aida 16 blocks to 2.5cm (1in) (stitched over one block)
Victorian Poppy chart on page 127	25 x 26 5 x 5cm (2 x 2in)	Zweigart Cashel unbleached linen 28 threads to 2.5cm (1in) (stitched over two threads)
Cabbage Rose chart on page 127	26 x 25 5 x 5cm (2 x 2in)	Yorkshire Aida 14 blocks to 2.5cm (1in) (stitched over one block)

Embroidery Threads

There is now a vast range of thread types available for cross stitch embroidery. Some of the most common are shown here.

Perlé Cotton reel
Glossy, single-ply pure cotton thread often used for Hardanger embroidery

Flower Thread (German) on card or skein
Unmercerised single-ply pure cotton thread with a matt finish

Stranded Cotton (DMC and Anchor)
Six strand mercerised cotton thread, usually divided before use. Supplied as solid or variegated colours

Variegated stranded cotton (DMC & Anchor)
See above

Perlé Cotton skein
Glossy, single-ply pure cotton thread often used for Hardanger embroidery

Caron Collection Watercolours
Space-dyed (hand-painted), pure cotton 3-ply thread. May be divided before use

Caron Collection Waterlilies
Space-dyed (hand-painted), 12-ply pure silk thread. May be divided before use

Appleton Crewel Wool
Fine embroidery wool which may be used singly or combined to suit the ground fabric

Stranded Rayon Thread
Very shiny non-metallic, 4-ply divisible thread ideal used as a contrast with other yarns

Silk Ribbon
Produced specially by YLI for embroiderers, these ribbons may be used like embroidery thread in a needle or may be added to the surface of the project and stitched in position. Commonly used widths are 2mm, 3mm and 4mm.

Cross Stitch on Stitching Paper

Fabric isn't the only material you can cross stitch on. Stitching paper (also called perforated paper) can be stitched, folded, glued and cut to make pretty cross stitch projects and used to fill scrap books and treasure albums. Stitching paper is based on early Victorian punched paper, also referred to as Bristol Board and made in England as early as 1840. The Victorians used it to work bookmarks, needlecases, pincushions, glove and handkerchief boxes, notebook covers and greeting cards. You will see from the photographs here that the style of cross stitch work on paper can look very different. The cut-out of the small Berlin rose posy has a very different feel to the jolly Christmas-style cut-outs and the wild strawberry card. See page 185 for mounting work into cards.

✚ **Stitch Perfect** ✚

• Although stitching paper is quite strong, it needs to be handled with care.

• There is a right and a wrong side to the paper, the smoother side being the right side.

• Avoid folding the paper unless this is part of the design.

• Find the centre with a ruler and mark with a pencil. Pencil lines can be removed with a soft rubber.

• Use three strands of stranded cotton (floss) for the cross stitch and two strands for back stitch outlining and lettering.

• Complete all the stitching before starting any cutting.

• Draw the cutting lines on the back of the completed stitching using a soft pencil.

• Use small, sharp-pointed scissors or a good craft knife to cut out the design and any decorative elements of the pattern.

• Stick completed sections together using double-sided adhesive tape.

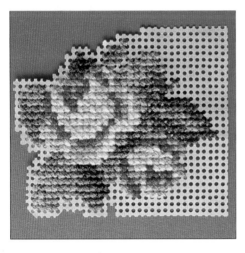

✳ *Berlin Rose Posy* ✳

Stitch Count: 30 x 26
Design Size: 6 x 5cm (2¹/₄ x 2in)
Fabric Selection: *Stitching paper 14 stitches to 2.5cm 1in*
Tapestry Needle Size: *24*

Cutting perforated paper after stitching allows you to create a decorative edging, as shown with this Berlin Rose Posy design, where one line of squares outlines the design. The design could then be mounted on a different coloured stitching paper, with further decorative cutting. The posy was cross stitched using three strands of stranded cotton (floss) and is charted on page 139 of the Motif Library.

✳ *Poinsettia Cracker Trim* ✳

Stitch Count: 52 x 15
Design Size: 10 x 2.5cm (4 x 1in)

✳ *Bells Cracker Trim* ✳

Stitch Count: 41 x 22
Design Size: 7.5 x 4cm (3 x 1¹/₂in)

These cracker trims (charts on page 139 of the Motif Library) have been worked on stitching paper 14 stitches to 2.5cm (1in) with a size 24 tapestry needle. Three strands of stranded cotton (floss) were used for the cross stitch and two for back stitch. The stitched designs were cut out and fixed to crackers with double-sided tape.

❋ *Strawberry Card* ❋

Stitch Count: 43 x 58

Design Size: 8 x 10cm (3 x 4in) completed card size

❋ *Bible and Cross Card* ❋

Stitch Count: 43 x 58

Design Size: 8 x 10cm (3 x 4in) completed card size

These pretty Victorian-style cards are worked on stitching paper 14 stitches to 2.5cm (1in) with a size 24 tapestry needle. Three strands of stranded cotton (floss) were used for the cross stitch and two for the back stitch detail. The stitched designs were cut out, mounted onto layers of different coloured stitching paper and plain card and fixed together with double-sided tape. The decoration can be embellished by use of careful cutting, as shown in the Berlin Rose Posy opposite. The designs are charted on page 140 of the Motif Library.

Stitching in Miniature

The photographs here demonstrate at a glance the effect achieved by changing the fabric count used for a project to create not just a smaller version of the design but a different image. The two flower motifs, a rose and pansy (charted in the Motif Library, pages 127 and 151 respectively) have been stitched in miniature using two different stitches to suit the specific fabric. Both flowers have been stitched twice – once in tent stitch on evenweave and once in cross stitch on silk gauze. Both motifs have also been stitched on 'normal' stitch counts – see pages 24/25.

Cross stitchers generally think stitching on silk gauze 40 stitches to 2.5cm (1in) is out of the question because it sounds so fine but it is much less taxing than first imagined. Silk gauze is constructed in such a way that although the stitch count is high, the holes in the fabric are large and are easier to see than you think! The secret is to have the fabric prepared as described below and work in a good light with the correct size gold-plated needle. I use a size 28 needle and work under a standard lamp which gives a wonderful light but doesn't get too hot!

When working on silk gauze you will need to use a simple mount board frame. Cut two pieces of stiff mount board to the size of your fabric. Now cut two sections out of the centre of each piece of board – the cut-out sections need to be just big enough to work the embroidery. Then, using double-sided adhesive tape, sandwich the silk gauze piece between the two boards. The frame can easily be removed once stitching is completed.

✳ *Cabbage Rose* ✳

Stitch Count: 26 x 25
Design Size: Silk gauze 2 x 2cm (³/₄ x ³/₄in); linen 2.5 x 2.5cm (1 x 1in)
Fabric Selection: Silk gauze 40 threads to 2.5cm (1in)
or pure linen 28 threads to 2.5cm (1in)
Tapestry Needle Size: 26–28

This tiny rose, made up as a pretty brooch and card, is worked in cross stitch over one thread of the silk gauze or in tent stitch over one thread of linen, using one strand of stranded cotton (floss). It is charted on page 127 of the Motif Library. See Working the Projects page 126 and Mounting Work in Cards page 185.

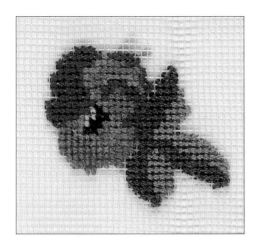 

❋ *Purple Pansy* ❋

Stitch Count: 29 x 24
Design Size: Silk gauze 2 x 2cm ($^3/_4$ x $^3/_4$in);
linen 2.5 x 2.5cm (1 x 1in)
Fabric Selection: Silk gauze 40 threads to 2.5cm (1in)
or pure linen 28 threads to 2.5cm (1in)
Tapestry Needle Size: 26–28

This tiny pansy has been worked in cross stitch over one thread of silk gauze (shown on the left) and again in tent stitch over one thread of linen (on the right), using one strand of stranded cotton. It is charted on page 151 of the Motif Library. See Working the Projects page 126.

✢ Stitch Perfect ✢
Working on Evenweave in Miniature

• If working cross stitch over one thread on evenweave, work each stitch individually rather than in two journeys to stop the underneath stitches sliding under neighbouring fabric threads.

• If working over one thread on linen (or any evenweave) use tent stitch rather than half cross stitch as tent stitch will give better coverage of the fabric and keep the stitches in position. If half cross stitch is used the threads will slide under neighbouring fabric threads.

• Select fabric with care, with the minimum of slubs and imperfections which are less easily disguised working over one thread.

✢ Stitch Perfect ✢
Working on Silk Gauze in Miniature

• Silk gauze should be worked in a small mount board frame to prevent the fabric distorting (see page 30).

• Silk gauze is constructed in a similar way to interlock canvas, to ensure that the threads will not slide.

• Half cross stitch or full cross stitch may be used successfully.

• Try stitching a small section to check your tension because you may find that half cross stitch is adequate.

• Avoid carrying threads across the back of work because it will show from the front – as you can see!

Stitching on Non-Evenweave

So far we have seen how cross stitching looks on evenweave fabrics but non-evenweave or un-evenweave linen was used to create samplers and counted masterpieces long before the concept of evenweave had been invented, and it is exciting to attempt to recreate a design on non-evenweave material. The traditional Acorn and Flower Sampler shown here has been stitched on linen scrim, a non-evenweave but pure linen fabric which usually ends up as tea-towels or dish-cloths and is not intended for embroidery.

The term 'evenweave' refers to the method used to manufacture the fabrics we use for cross stitch and does not mean that the material will have no lumps and bumps! This misunderstood term means that when the fabric is woven, the number of warp and weft threads (along the length and across the width) are the same. This is why when you work a cross stitch on evenweave fabric, the stitch appears square rather than squashed, shortened or elongated. However, cross stitches worked on non-evenweave fabric *will* be affected by the uneven weave, becoming slightly shortened or elongated, therefore you will need to experiment with the characteristics of the fabric to achieve the best results.

Ageing Linen

It is easy to add the appearance of age to a piece of linen by dipping it in black tea. The fabric to be aged in this way must be a pure, natural fabric such as pure cotton or pure linen. Tea-dyeing can be done on the fabric alone before you start stitching or to the whole piece when the embroidery is completed, though you need to make sure that the threads used are colour-fast (see page 15). After dipping the fabric or needlework in the tea, allow it to dry naturally and then press as normal.

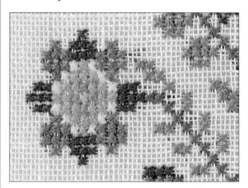

✳ *Acorn and Flower Sampler* ✳
Stitch Count: 81 x 101
Design Size: 17.5 x 21.5cm (7 x 8$^{1}/_{2}$in)
Fabric Selection: Non-evenweave linen 24 threads to 2.5cm (1in)
Tapestry Needle Size: 22

This example of a traditional child's-style sampler was stitched using three strands of stranded cottons (floss) for the cross stitch. The design assumes a slightly different shape as the fabric is not evenweave. The design is charted on page 130/131 of the Motif Library. Use the alphabet charted on page 142 to stitch your own initials (or use any suitable alphabet from the Motif Library). See Working the Projects page 126.

✜ Stitch Perfect ✜

• To know non-evenweave fabric and its foibles, work a square of twenty tacking stitches counting over two threads, and you will see the way in which the fabric creates a landscape (long) or portrait (tall) shape.

• Work a small test piece on the fabric and check you have the effect you require.

• If you are planning a traditional sampler, it is important to select motifs which are of the right style and weight and which will benefit from the effect produced by non-evenweave fabric ie, a rabbit when stitched may look more like a hare!

• Don't be afraid to experiment with different motifs which will alter depending on the fabric direction. Trial and error is the way you will achieve the most successful results.

• You may need to use a loose tension to avoid the threads distorting and giving a pulled thread appearance to the design.

Using Waste Canvas

Waste canvas is a really useful material which enables the cross stitcher to transfer charted designs on to fabrics which were not intended for that purpose and therefore do not have an even, countable weave. Today, the most commonly used application for this technique is to add designs to sweat shirts, T-shirts and baby clothes.

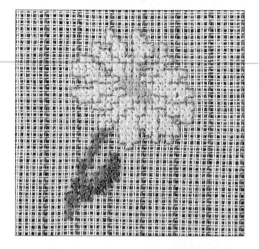

Waste canvas is a comparatively new product although the technique has been used for many years but with linen as the 'waste' fabric. Waste canvas is a double canvas treated with a water-soluble starch product which makes it simple to remove the threads after stitching, but is quite unsuitable for any other type of use. It is easily distinguished by the blue line running through the fabric. The waste material is applied to the garment or fabric and the grid is used to count whilst the design is stitched and then the threads of the canvas are removed. As you can see by the photographs here, the technique is worked in three stages and is described fully in Stitch Perfect.

1 Tack the waste fabric in position.
2 Stitch the design from the chart.
3 Remove the waste threads.

Once all the waste threads have been removed, check for any missed stitches and add any additional back stitch outlining that might be needed to complete the design. Press the finished piece of stitching from the wrong side on soft towels (see page 182).

❋ *Single Daisy* ❋
Stitch Count: 19 x 30
Design Size: 4 x 5cm (1^1/$_2$ x 2^1/$_4$in)
Fabric Selection: Waste canvas 14 blocks to 2.5cm (1in)
on to a piece of blue denim
Tapestry Needle Size: 24

These pictures show the three stages for stitching with waste canvas. The daisy was stitched using two strands of stranded cotton (floss) working each stitch individually through the grid of the waste canvas and the ground fabric. The first stage shows the design stitched on the waste canvas. The second stage shows the waste canvas threads being removed and the third stage reveals the daisy on the denim. The design is charted on page 156 of the Motif Library. See Working the Projects page 126.

❋ *Ox-eye Daisy* ❋ *and Poppy Spray*

Stitch Count: 39 x 57
Design Size: 7.5 x 10cm (3 x 4in)
Fabric Selection: Waste canvas 14 blocks to 2.5cm (1in) on to a piece of blue denim
Tapestry Needle Size: 24

This design was stitched using two strands of stranded cotton (floss) working each stitch individually through the grid of the waste canvas and the ground fabric. The design is charted on page 157 of the Motif Library. See Working the Projects page 126.

✦ Stitch Perfect ✦

• Select the correct stitch count waste fabric for the design and if unsure, work a small test piece confirming the number of strands of stranded cotton (floss) required.

• Use the best quality thread (e.g. DMC, Anchor or Madeira) to avoid colour runs.

• Cut waste canvas at least 5cm (2in) larger than the completed design size.

• Tack the waste fabric in position care-fully, as it must stay put whilst you work, using horizontal and vertical tacking lines.

• Work the cross stitch design from a chart, working each stitch individually though the grid of the canvas and the ground fabric.

• When working on a large count waste material, work through the small holes on the canvas as this will keep the stitches firmly in position and prevents variable tension.

• When the stitching is complete, trim away any excess waste canvas and lightly spray with cold water. This releases the starch and makes removing the threads easier, but rather sticky, so wash your hands regularly or better still use tweezers.

• Pull out the threads one at a time, varying the direction from which you are working to avoid any distortion.

• When all the waste canvas has been removed check for missed stitches which may be added carefully with a sharp needle.

• If using this technique on clothing (like the denim in the photographs) wash on the normal wash cycle for the garment but press the stitched section on the wrong side where possible.

Three-Dimensional Cross Stitch

Working counted cross stitch is very satisfying although it is sometimes described as working in a single dimension and critics of the craft think that the finished work is rather flat! We believe that this is ill-informed but what better way of proving this than asking Meg Evershed of the Nutmeg Company to design a three-dimensional piece for this book. Meg is a UK designer, well known for her three-dimensional embroidery. She uses traditional cross stitch fabrics like Aida and evenweave but also uses plastic canvas in ready-cut shapes as templates to support her designs. The plastic canvas is not used for the stitching. Her beautiful Carousel Trinket Box illustrated here is a perfect demonstration of the versatility of cross stitch. The measurements for making the box are given in metric only for accuracy.

There are three stages in making a three-dimensional cross stitch piece:

Stitching – working the cross stitch design on the fabric from a cross stitch chart.

Mounting – attaching the fabric to plastic canvas pieces cut to a given size and shape.

Assembly – stitching the pieces together to form the finished design.

×××××

❋ *The Carousel Trinket Box* ❋

Stitch Count: see charts on pages 132/133 of the Motif Library
Fabric Selection: Antique white Aida 18 blocks to 2.5cm (1in)
Tapestry Needle Size: 24

You Will Need
39 x 11cm 18-count Aida in antique white
30 x 23cm 28-count evenweave in ivory
7.5cm diameter circle of wadding (batting)
Two 7.5cm diameter plastic canvas circles
25 x 9cm 7-mesh plastic canvas
DMC stranded cotton as listed in the chart key on pages 132/133
Matching sewing thread
Size 26 tapestry needle and a sewing needle
Embroidery frame if required

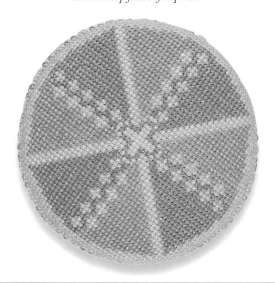

✛ Stitch Perfect ✛

• Before you begin to cross stitch the carousel trinket box, cut the side, inner edge and lid rim from the plastic canvas. Roll them up together and place a rubber band around them to encourage them to assume a circular shape.

• Be careful when stitching the top of the box. It's very easy to lose your sense of direction working a circular design so that the top strokes of the stitches end up

lying in different directions. It will help if you mark the top edge of the design.

• The 'stitch & park' technique (see page 19) is very useful for all the different shaded colours on the ponies.

• Make sure you have completed all the cross stitch before you begin the back stitch, referring to the chart on pages 132/133 for shade numbers.

Stitching

1 Work the top, rim and sides for the trinket box on 18-count Aida from the design given in the Motif Library on pages 132/133. Note that the charts for the rim and sides must be repeated twice to give the full length.

Box Top

Rim

Side

Fig 1

2 Position the designs on the fabric with a margin of at least 1cm around them on all sides. Mark the areas to be stitched on the fabric using tacking (basting) stitches (remembering that the rim and sides are worked twice).

3 Work all the cross stitch, back stitch and the French knots for the ponies' noses using one strand of thread only. Complete all the cross stitch before you begin the back stitch. This is worked only on the ponies and their poles, and all the back stitching on the poles is worked using DMC stranded cotton (floss) 413.

For all the ponies, back stitch the eyes and mouths using DMC 413. Work French knots for the nostrils with one strand of thread, keeping them as small as possible.

On the blue ponies, outline their heads using DMC 341. Work the back stitch outlining the chests and legs using DMC 340, and all the remaining back stitch using DMC 3746.

On the pink ponies, back stitch around the heads using DMC 3609. Work the outlining for the chests and legs using DMC 3608, and all the remaining back stitch on these ponies using DMC 3607. Remove the outlining tacking stitches when you have completed the embroidery.

Mounting

1 From a sheet of 7-mesh plastic canvas, cut the plastic pieces for the box side, inner edge and lid rim. The rim should measure 24 x 1.7cm (on 7-mesh canvas this will be 63 holes x 3 holes); the sides should measure 24 x 2.8cm (63 holes x 7 holes) and the inner edge should measure 22.6 x 3.2cm (58 holes x 8 holes). The sides of the box are mounted on these cut pieces, and the lid and base are each mounted on a plastic canvas circle.

2 For the top of the trinket box, cover one of the plastic circles with wadding (batting), over-sewing around the outside edge. Carefully cut the cross stitched top from the Aida fabric, leaving a margin of at least 1cm all round the embroidery. Run a gathering thread around the outside edge of the Aida and lay the wadding-covered circle on the wrong side of the embroidery, with the wadding (batting) against the stitching. Pull up the gathering thread so that the cross stitched design fits over the plastic circle. Fasten off, and work lacing stitches across the back of the circle to ensure that the Aida is firmly attached to the plastic (see fig 2). Cut a circle of evenweave 7.5cm in diameter and sew or stick it to the underside of the box top.

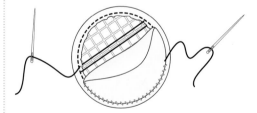

Fig 2

3 For the base of the box, cover the remaining plastic circle with evenweave in the same way as for the top but omit the wadding (batting). Sew or stick another circle of evenweave to the inside of the base.

4 Separate the cross stitched side and lid rim, leaving a margin of at least 1cm around each piece on all sides. Lay the plastic canvas pieces on the wrong side of the stitching, turn in the fabric margins and lace the fabric to the plastic canvas with sewing thread.

5 For the rim, cut a piece of evenweave 25.5

x 3cm and press a narrow seam allowance on all sides with an iron. Sew this to the inside of the rim, so the lacing stitches are covered (fig 3).

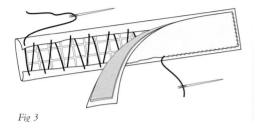

Fig 3

6 For the inner edge, cut a piece of evenweave 24.5 x 8.5cm and press a narrow seam allowance on all sides. Fold the fabric in half, wrong sides facing and long edges together, and press again. Enclose the plastic strip for the inner edge in the fabric, oversewing the edges together (fig 4).

Fig 4

Assembly

1 Join the short edges of the rim, sides and inner edge to produce three circles. Stitch the top edge of the rim around the prepared box top to complete the lid.

2 Put the sides over the inner edge, making sure the joins are at different points. Slip stitch them together keeping the bottom of the inner edge about 2mm above the bottom of the sides. Now stitch the sides to the prepared base (see fig 5). This completes the box. Fit the lid over the inner edge, matching the ponies' poles to give the appearance of a carousel.

Fig 5

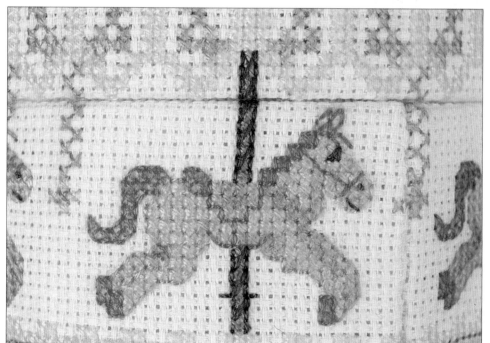

Comparing Double Canvas and Evenweave

Cross stitch charts may be used to work designs on canvas and vice versa, as you can see demonstrated in the photographs below. The sunflower design has been stitched once on linen in stranded cotton (floss) and once on double canvas in Appleton crewel wool. The pansy design has also been stitched twice – once made up into a scissors keeper and worked in beads and stranded cottons on double canvas, with Appleton crewel wool for the background in a colour of your choice. The design was stitched again, this time on linen using stranded cotton (floss) and beads with a simple border worked in a single strand of cotton using four-sided stitch.

The choice of fabric will depend on the stitches used, your eyesight and whether the project is decorative or functional (eg, cushions, chair seats etc.). Canvas is most commonly available in four mesh sizes – 10, 12, 14 and 18-count (threads to 2.5cm/1in). Any gauge of canvas can be used with any chart. Canvas is available in two main types: double-thread (duo) canvas and single-thread (mono) canvas. Refer also to page 42 for working on single canvas.

Double-thread/Duo/Penelope Canvas

This type of canvas is the same as mono canvas except that the threads are grouped in twos in each direction and are usually finer. As with an evenweave fabric, stitches are worked over the

✲ Sunflower ✲

Stitch Count: 54 x 72
Design Size: Linen 10 x 13cm (4 x 5$^{1}/_{4}$in);
canvas 11.5 x 15cm (4$^{1}/_{2}$ x 6in)
Fabric Selection: Zweigart Cashel unbleached linen 28 threads to 2.5cm (1in) or double canvas 12 blocks to 2.5cm (1in)
Tapestry Needle Size: 24–22

This sunflower has been cross stitched once on linen worked over two threads using two strands of stranded cotton (floss) and adding back stitch in one strand. The second version uses Appleton crewel wool on double canvas over two threads, with the centre worked over one thread for more detail. The chart is on page 144 of the Motif Library. The bee motif may be omitted if you prefer. See Working the Projects page 126.

✳ *Beaded Pansy Scissors Keeper* ✳
& Beaded Pansy Picture

Stitch Count: 27 x 25 (pansy only)
Design Size: Linen 5 x 5cm (2 x 2in);
canvas 6 x 6cm (2¹/₄ x 2¹/₄in)
Fabric Selection: Picture on ivory linen 28 threads to
2.5cm (1in) and the scissors keeper on double canvas
12 blocks to 2.5cm (1in)
Tapestry Needle Size: 24–22

double threads but if you want to put more detail into part of a design, you can make four times as many stitches by using every canvas thread (see the centre of the canvaswork sunflower opposite). Half cross stitch, full cross stitch and tent stitch may be worked on double canvas.

Designed by Sue Hawkins, Technical Director of the Cross Stitch Guild, both of these pieces are stitched in stranded cotton with the background in Appleton crewel wool. The pansy is charted on page 153 of the Motif Library. The beads used were from Beadesign (see Suppliers). See Working the Projects page 126.

✛ Stitch Perfect ✛

• Before stitching, use a thick tapestry needle to push apart the double threads. This is known as pricking out the canvas and will make stitching easier if you intend to combine working one and two threads.

• When adding beads to a design, using double canvas creates the most satisfactory results as the beads stay in position, not wobbling as they do on single canvas.

• When counting canvas, always count the threads and not the holes, because your stitches are made over threads and not in holes. This is a common stumbling block but you will always get it right if you remember that holes cannot be counted because they are empty and therefore do not exist!

• It is a good idea to bind the edge of your canvas with masking tape before you begin to stitch as this will protect your hands and prevent the yarn repeatedly catching on the cut edge. Ideally this masking tape edge is cut off before you stretch the finished piece.

• A frame is not essential when working on double canvas but is useful if you are using tent stitch.

Working on Single Canvas

I enjoy the contrast of working cross stitch designs on single canvas for a change of effect and I have designed projects commercially using canvas as an alternative to Aida or evenweave. Stitchers are sometimes nervous of transferring designs on to canvas when they were designed for fabric but the principles are the same. Early French samplers were generally stitched on canvas with the background left unstitched with great effect, so have a go. Just remember to count the thread of the canvas and not the holes!

The Knot Garden Pincushion shown here was inspired by the talented UK embroiderer and teacher, Mary Jenkins and has been stitched on single canvas using space-dyed threads and DMC stranded cotton (floss). The knot garden uses double cross stitch, long-legged cross stitch, tent stitch, large cross stitch, queen stitch and French knots – all to great effect. This type of cross stitch design is great fun to work because the framework of the pattern (the dark green hedges and border) is counted but then you can fill sections without looking at the chart all the time! (See page 50 for tips on working with space-dyed threads.)

Single-thread/Mono Canvas

This canvas is constructed of a simple, even weave and is also available in a deluxe quality where the threads are polished before the canvas is woven and so the yarn passes smoothly through the canvas as you stitch. Deluxe is always worth the extra expense to prevent snarling the yarn. This type of canvas is suitable for any piece of work but especially upholstery, such as seat covers where the embroidery will be stretched unevenly when the seat is sat on. The canvas threads are free to move a little on each other and so adjust to the stress rather than tearing. You will find both ordinary and deluxe canvas in white or brown (the latter is known as antique) and you should choose according to the colours of yarn that you will be using.

Interlock Canvas

Single/Mono canvas is also available as interlock canvas. In this type of canvas the threads along the length are in fact double threads, twisted together to hold the cross threads firmly in place. This produces a more stable canvas, ideal for designs which include long stitches, which might otherwise pull loose canvas threads together and so make holes in your work. The disadvantage of interlock canvas is that it is only available in white so you must take care not to stitch too tightly or the white will show through the work. Interlock is very easy to make up once the embroidery is finished because it does not fray at all, unlike mono deluxe canvas which will very quickly fray right to the edge of the stitching unless great care is taken.

✢ Stitch Perfect ✢

• When stitching on mono canvas (ie, single), half cross stitch is not suitable. Refer to the tent stitch photographs on page 95 of the Stitch Library to see the different effects created by half cross stitch and tent stitch.

• If you use half cross stitch on single canvas some of them may actually slip under the weave of the canvas and then they will be very uneven. On single canvas it is best to use continental or diagonal tent stitch (see Stitching in Miniature for working over one thread on linen page 31).

• A word of warning: some commercial kits tell you to work half cross stitch on single canvas. A much better result can be obtained by using tent stitch, but you will probably run out of wool as tent stitch uses about half as much yarn again as half cross stitch. You have to decide whether to purchase more wool or settle for a rather thin-looking finished piece with inferior wearing qualities.

This little sampler is worked in tent stitch with stranded cottons (floss) and a background of Appleton wools, and uses elements from the Motif Library. You can see why canvas projects need to be finished as described on page 183, to remove the distortion that can occur during tent stitching

✳ Knot Garden Pincushion ✳

Stitch Count: 63 x 62
Design Size: 11.5 x 11.5cm (4^1/$_2$ x 4^1/$_2$in)
Fabric Selection: Single canvas 14 threads to 2.5cm (1in)
Tapestry Needle Size: 22

This design has been worked using a combination of counted stitches with stranded cotton (floss) and space-dyed Caron Watercolours thread. The simplest way to work this project is to create the circular hedges as shown on the chart on page 150 of the Motif Library and then fill with colours and stitches suggested on the chart, or stitches of your own choice. See Working the Projects page 126.

Combining Flower Thread and Stranded Cotton

One of the joys of working cross stitch is that the stitch stays the same throughout the project but the effect can be changed by clever use of different fibres. The effect achieved can be demonstrated by looking at the two violet designs illustrated below. These delicate little flowers have been stitched using two different yarns – stranded cotton (floss) and German Flower Thread.

Stranded cotton is mercerised when manufactured to add a silk-like sheen and is supplied in divisible lengths, whereas Flower Thread is not mercerised and is single-ply, with a matt finish. The soft effect created by this thread is ideal for small flower motifs, and you might try it on the crocus or daisy designs in the Motif Library on pages 152 and 156.

The contrast of thread types can also be clearly illustrated by looking at the Antique Flower Scissors Keeper and Pincushion shown opposite, where the threads used include Flower Thread, stranded cotton (floss) and rayon threads. The pincushion has been cleverly joined together using counted chain stitch which I have whipped using one strand of rayon so that you can see the join! The scissors keeper is also illustrated un-made up so that you can see how it has been constructed.

✦ Stitch Perfect ✦

• Experiment with the thread thickness of Flower Thread as it varies slightly.

• Use the correct number of strands for the fabric in question.

• Avoid using Flower Thread for back stitch as it never looks as good as when stitched in one strand of stranded cotton (floss).

• Use shorter lengths of Flower Thread as it becomes rather fluffy if pulled through the fabric too many times.

❋ *Wild Violets* ❋

Stitch Count: 24 x 31
Design Size: 4.5 x 6cm (1³/₄ x 2¹/₄in)
Fabric Selection: Zweigart Cashel cream linen
28 threads to 2.5cm (1in)
Tapestry Needle Size: 24

These delicate little flowers have been stitched over two threads of linen, using two different yarns: the top version in two strands of stranded cotton (floss) and the bottom one in one strand of Flower Thread. The back stitch outline was added using one strand of stranded cotton (floss) on both flowers. The chart is on page 128 of the Motif Library. See Working the Projects page 126.

✳ *Antique Flower* ✳ *Scissors Keeper*

Stitch Count: 22 x 22 (front section only)
Design Size: 4.5 x 4.5cm ($1^3/_4$ x $1^3/_4$in)
Fabric Selection: Unbleached linen 28 threads to 2.5cm (1in)
Tapestry Needle Size: 24–26

This antique flower design made up as a scissors keeper has been worked over two threads of linen in a mixture of Flower Thread, stranded cotton (floss) and rayon, using one strand of Flower Thread and two strands of cotton and rayon. The scissors keeper is also illustrated un-made up (below) to show the two sections worked with a line of counted chain stitch stitched in preparation for joining at the sides. The chart is on page 163 of the Motif Library. See Working the Projects page 126.

✳ *Antique Flower Pincushion* ✳

Stitch Count: 33 x 33
Design Size: 6.5 x 6.5cm ($2^1/_2$ x $2^1/_2$in)
Fabric Selection: Unbleached linen 28 threads to 2.5cm (1in)
Tapestry Needle Size: 24–26

The pincushion (above) has been worked over two threads of linen using a mixture of Flower Thread, stranded cotton (floss) and rayon, using one strand of Flower Thread and two strands of cotton and rayon. The completed project was made up using counted chain stitch whipped together. I have used non-matching thread so that you can see the detail on the sides. Normally this thread would match and not be visible. The chart is on page 163 of the Motif Library. See Working the Projects page 126.

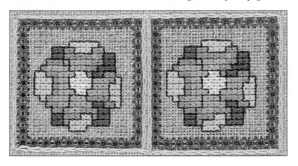

Using Metallic Threads and Blending Filaments

There are now dozens of wonderful vibrant metallic, sparkly and glow-in-the-dark threads available to the cross stitcher. The Christmas tree (right) has been stitched using some rayon thread combined with some of the exciting stranded metallic threads now available. Although metallic threads have been generally regarded as the most difficult to use, the tips included here are from Kreinik who produce the largest range of metallic and blending filaments – so they should help!

I think the secret of using metallic threads is to find the style and thickness needed for the project by looking at the threads when you make your selection. Some fine yarns are referred to as 'braids' but look like normal thread so it is much easier to select by eye unless you have a specific requirement list from the designer. Some yarns are stitched using a needle and some are added to the surface of the design and then stitched in place, so be prepared to experiment. (Silk ribbon and fine lace may also be treated in this way.) When using very glossy metallic gold or silver threads, it is vital that you work with short lengths and a needle large enough help the threads through the fabric. If you work with long lengths you will find that the gold or silver flakes away from the core thread as you work and you lose the metallic effect.

✛ Stitch Perfect ✛

• When using metallic threads and blending filaments stitch more slowly and more attentively, and use a needle large enough to 'open' the hole in the fabric sufficiently to allow the thread to go through easily.

• Use short lengths of thread 46cm (18in) or less to avoid excessive abrasion when pulling the thread through the fabric.

• Let your needle hang frequently (after one or two stitches) so that the thread can untwist.

• Stitch using the 'stab' method rather than the 'hand sewing' method, working your stitches in two movements – up vertically, then down vertically through the fabric.

• To vary the amount of shine, change the number of strands of metallic thread – more strands give a greater sheen, and vice versa.

❋ *Christmas Tree* ❋

Stitch Count: 39 x 53
Design Size: 7.5 x 10cm (3 x 4in)
Fabric Selection: Cream Aida 14 blocks to 2.5cm (1in)
Tapestry Needle Size: 24

This decorative Christmas card has been worked using a variety of stranded metallic threads combined with stranded cotton (floss). The chart is on page 151 of the Motif Library. See Working the Projects page 126.

There are many metallics available and an assortment is shown here.

Blending Filaments

Blending Filaments are light, delicate threads intended to be combined with other fibres, usually with stranded cotton (floss) to add a glisten or sparkle. For example, pearl blending filament is ideal combined with white stranded cotton to create snow effects, as you can see in this pretty snow scene that has been made up into a card.

When combining Blending Filament with stranded cotton (floss) in one needle, you must first knot the metallic thread onto the needle as follows. Loop the thread and pass the loop through the eye of the needle, leaving a short tail. Pull the loop over the point of the needle and tighten the loop at the end of the eye by pulling the two ends of the thread. Gently stroke the knotted thread to 'lock' it in place. Add the stranded cotton by threading onto the needle in the usual way, and you are ready to start stitching.

✳ *Snow Scene* ✳

Stitch Count: 117 x 57
Design Size: 21.25 x 10.25cm (8¼ x 4in)
Fabric Selection: Unbleached Zweigart linen 28 threads to 2.5cm (1in)
Tapestry Needle Size: 24

This chilly winter scene above has been given that extra something by adding pearl blending filament to the snow. The design has been stitched in stranded cottons (floss) but with the blending filament added to all the white used in the project. The chart is on page 178/179 of the Motif Library. See Working the Projects page 126.

✳ *Celebrations* ✳

Stitch Count: 54 x 41
Design Size: 10 x 7.5cm (4 x 3in)
Fabric Selection: Pure linen 28 threads to 2.5cm (1in)
Tapestry Needle Size: 24

This card design, right, which includes three celebration motifs, has been stitched twice, once in stranded cotton (floss) and once using the same stranded colours but with added blending filament. As you can see, the design was pretty when stitched in the normal way but extraordinary with the sparkle added. The chart is on page 181 of the Motif Library. See Working the Projects page 126.

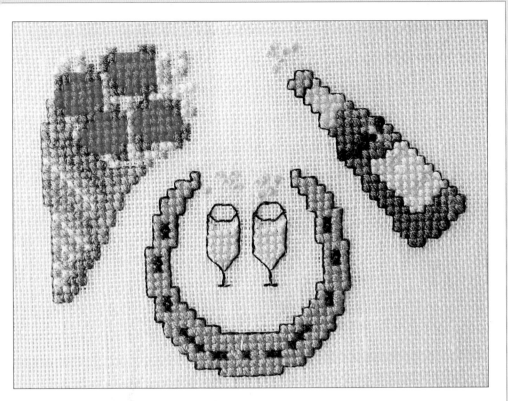

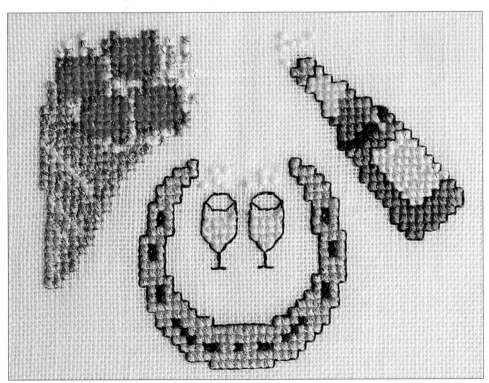

Using Space-Dyed Threads

This section of the book shows you how to create a piece of stitching following a chart in the usual way but with an end result that looks quite different from any one else's version. It is a type of designing without the angst! There are dozens of manufacturers of specialist space-dyed fibres so feel free to experiment. If you cannot find the exact version used in my stitched piece try something else. Space-dyed threads are not random dyed but have shades and patterns of colour making it possible for you to decide where you want a particular shade. Follow the basic guidelines for using space-dyed threads and the effects will surprise you.

You can see from the photograph opposite that the hemmed bookmark has been stitched using stranded cottons (floss) effectively but it has also been stitched using   Caron Collection

Waterlilies to produce a very different look. It is a very relaxing way to stitch as the whole project is worked from the same skein. The knot garden pincushion shown on page 43 and the autumn panel below (and which also features some Hardanger work), have been stitched using a single strand of space-dyed thread (Caron Watercolours). The Hardanger flower chatelaine shown on pages 2 and 75 also uses some space-dyed threads.

You may like to use variegated threads to introduce a different look to your work. Variegated threads are completely randomly dyed so choosing different sections of colour and predicting how they will change as the thread is used is not possible as it is with space-dyed threads but variegated threads can be useful for working greenery, brick walls and so on.

❋ *Autumn Jewel Panel* ❋
Stitch Count: 60 x 60
Design Size: 12.5 x 12.5cm (5 x 5in)
Fabric Selection: Zweigart Dublin linen 25 threads to
2.5cm (1in)
Tapestry Needle Size: 24–22

This pretty tile is worked in two strands of stranded cottons and one strand of Caron Watercolours thread 062 and includes a little simple Hardanger, Queen stitch, Rhodes stitch, half Rhodes stitch and Algerian eye. The chart is on page 165 of the Motif Library. See Working the Projects page 126. Refer also to the Stitch Library starting on page 83 and Hardanger Embroidery page 70.

✤ Stitch Perfect ✤

• When combining stranded cottons (floss) with space-dyed threads, compare the colours carefully along the length of the thread to check that the shades tone successfully.

• Look at the skein and cut the thread so you can see where colours start and finish.

• Irrespective of the number of strands used for the project, always start with an away waste knot and not the loop start, as the colour order will be disrupted.

• When threading the needle, check the colour you intend to use is near the away waste knot.

• When working cross stitches always complete each cross as you go and do not form cross stitches in two journeys.

• Use a length of thread *only* whilst the colours suit the project. Do not attempt to use the whole length of thread if the colour of that section is not appropriate.

✳ *Hemmed Bookmarks* ✳

Stitch Count: *32 x 79*
Design Size: *6.5 x 14.5cm (2¹/₂ x 5³/₄in)*
Fabric Selection: *Pure linen 28 threads to 2.5cm (1in)*
Tapestry Needle Size: *26*

The design for these delicate self-hemmed bookmarks has been stitched twice – once in stranded cotton (floss) (left) and then in Caron Collection Waterlilies thread (093) (right). You can see how effective the Caron thread is at producing a multi-coloured design from a single skein. Both bookmarks have been finished with four-sided stitch and single or double hem stitching. The narrow ends have been frayed and the design cut out to the hem stitching. The chart is on page 148 of the Motif Library. See Working the Projects page 126.

Exploring Choices

T̶his section features a range of exciting designs showing how easy it is to combine cross stitch with many other counted embroidery techniques. You will discover how much fun it is to bring a whole new dimension to your embroidery with the addition of buttons, charms, beads and ribbon, and how simple it is to enhance your cross stitch with other techniques such as pulled work, drawn thread work, Hardanger, blackwork and hem stitching. There is also invaluable advice on adapting kits and designing your own work.

Using Charms, Buttons and Embellishments

Charms, buttons and other embellishments may be added to a completed piece of stitching to great effect, although there are pitfalls to avoid. You will need to ensure that the charm size is correct for the project, for example, the animal buttons on the Ark pictured right are the correct scale for the border, just as the bee is the perfect size for the beehive design on page 55.

When selecting metal charms for a completed piece of stitching, avoid cheap, stamped versions as your work deserves the best. Brass charms are manufactured using strong processes and there will be chemical residues left on a charm if it has not been 'finished'. A process of 'dip, tub and roll' is the scouring method used to clean charms for use on embroidery, which prevents potential damage. If a completed piece of stitching is exposed to a damp atmosphere, a chemical reaction may be set up and the fabric could become discoloured. It is possible for blue fabric to have an orange patch where the charm has been in contact with the fabric.

❋ *The Ark and its Creatures* ❋

Stitch Count: 80 x 80
Design Size: 14.5 x 14.5cm (5³/₄ x 5³/₄in)
Fabric Selection: Zweigart Yorkshire Aida 14 blocks to 2.5cm (1in)
Tapestry Needle Size: 24

This charming quilt-style sampler was stitched using two strands of stranded cotton (floss) for the cross stitch over one block of Aida and one strand for the back stitch outline. The decorative porcelain buttons were added with two strands of matching thread. The chart is on page 155 of the Motif Library. See Working the Projects page 126.

✳ *Birdhouse* ✳

Stitch Count: 58 x 39
Design Size: 11 x 7.5cm (4¹/₄ x 3in)
Fabric Selection: Half-bleached linen 28 threads to 2.5cm (1in)
Tapestry Needle Size: 24–26

This nostalgic little picture was stitched over two threads using two strands of stranded cotton (floss) for the cross stitch and one strand for the back stitch. French knots were added in 2mm silk ribbon made by YLI (see Suppliers) and/or one strand of stranded cotton (floss). A brass butterfly charm (see Suppliers) was attached with matching thread. The chart is on page 145 of the Motif Library. See Working the Projects page 126.

There is an increasing array of buttons available, in the craft shops and through mail order. Both decorative buttons (as used on The Ark and its Creatures) and simple mother-of-pearl or shell buttons may be added to cross stitch to great effect and may also be combined with charms and beads. When adding buttons use a strong thread that matches the button rather than the ground fabric so that the decorative effect is not spoiled.

Other embellishments may be added to your cross stitch designs and include using ribbon roses, tiny artificial flowers and even doll's house miniatures. Why not try adding tiny items of cutlery to a kitchen sampler with buttons for the plates on the dresser and flower-pot charms to the fireplace.

✻ *Beehive* ✻

Stitch Count: 43 x 30
Design Size: 7.5 x 6cm (3 x 2¼in)
Fabric Selection: Half-bleached linen 28 threads to 2.5cm (1in)
Tapestry Needle Size: 24

This pretty little design was stitched using two strands of stranded cottons (floss) for the cross stitch over two threads of linen. French knots were added after the cross stitch was complete using one and two strands of stranded cotton (floss). Finally the brass honey bee charm (see Suppliers) was attached with matching thread. The chart is on page 145 of the Motif Library. See Working the Projects page 126.

✛ Stitch Perfect ✛

• Clean a metal charm thoroughly with a paper towel before applying it to your stitching and if concerned, coat the back of the charm with clear nail polish.

• The size and scale of charms and buttons should match the scale of the cross stitch design.

• Attach charms and buttons using a thread which matches the fabric.

• Starting with a loop start, position the charm (or button) and pass the needle through the hole in the charm from the right side thus marking the position. Slip the charm off the eye of the needle and pass the needle in and out of the fabric and through the loop on the right side. Stitch the charm in position, ensuring that the threads on the needle stay taut and do not form an unsightly loop in the hole of the charm.

• If additional stitches are to be added in direct relationship to the charm or button, stitch the charm in position first and then carefully stitch as shown (see the freehand leaf motif by the dove on the Ark project).

Beads and Cross Stitch

Now that you have learnt the basic skills needed to work counted cross stitch, this section of the book will encourage you to try other exciting options whilst staying with the counted thread concept. Substituting beads for stranded cottons (floss) on parts of a charted design as in the violet design opposite is a wonderful way to begin to explore your creative powers. Working with beads in this way is easier than you can imagine. As all the beads are stitched on using only one colour thread you can work across the pattern row by row instead of working blocks of colour as you would for cross stitch.

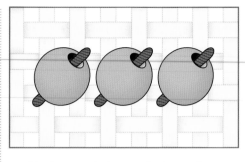

Seed beads are attached using a beading needle or very fine 'sharp' needle and a half cross stitch

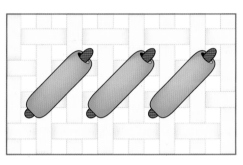

Although bugle beads can be included in a cross stitch pattern, generally they are added to the design after the cross stitch is completed. For example, bugle beads added to the end of the lily stamens on page 23 would add dimension to the project

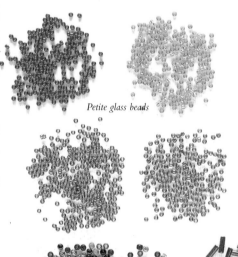

Petite glass beads

Bugle beads

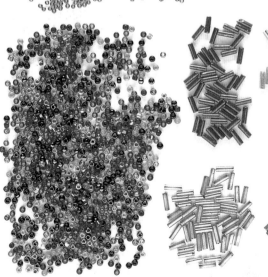

Glass seed beads

There are dozens of different shapes and sizes of bead available to the stitcher, although, unless you are adding beads at random, you will need to choose beads that are the correct size for the fabric

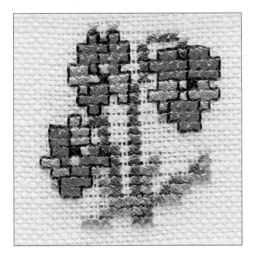

✳ *Violets* ✳

Stitch Count: 18 x 20
Design Size: 3 x 4cm (1¼ x 1½in)
Fabric Selection: Ivory or antique white linen 28 threads to 2.5cm (1in)
Needle size: Tapestry No. 26 and beading needle

This exquisite little design is worked on 28-count ivory linen over two threads, first in cross stitch using DMC stranded cottons (floss), and second replacing the flower colours with seed beads (from Beadesign, see Suppliers). In both cases the stems and leaves are worked in cross stitch over two threads using two strands of stranded cotton (floss). The chart for this design is included in the Motif Library (page 128).

✝ Stitch Perfect ✝

- To substitute beads for stranded cottons (floss) on a chart design, gather together the stranded cottons and match the beads to the threads. Choosing beads in isolation is very difficult.

- Treat bright yellow and orange beads with caution as they can outshine other more subtle colours.

- Apply beads using ordinary sewing thread matched to the fabric colour. To make sure you cannot see the thread through the beads, stitch a few on to the corner of the fabric.

- Remember polyester mixture threads are stronger than pure cotton.

- Choose your fabric carefully. Beads will sit better on evenweave rather than Aida, and on double canvas rather than on single weave.

- Choose beads that are suitable for your fabric count. If the beads are too large the design will distort and the beads will crowd on top of each other. Most seed beads, for example, are perfect for 14 count fabric or canvas (i.e. 14 blocks or 28 threads to 2.5cm (1in)).

- Consider using a frame or a hoop when working with beads. This will keep the fabric taut, and you can pull the thread firmly as you work to keep the beads in position.

Silk Ribbon and Cross Stitch

Adding silk ribbon embroidery to cross stitch can introduce a wonderful new dimension and variety to a piece of stitching, creating a fresh, three-dimensional feel. The Silk Ribbon Sampler illustrated opposite demonstrates the dramatic effect achieved by adding lazy daisy stitches in silk ribbon to the decorative border as well as adding some ribbon French knots to the house. The sampler could be stitched with a cross stitch border if you prefer. The delightful little birdhouse on page 54 also features some ribbon work.

You may wish to try other stitches using silk ribbon such as tent stitch, satin stitch or even bullion stitches and if you are keen to develop the use of silk ribbon in your work it is worth investing in a good ribbon embroidery book (see Bibliography).

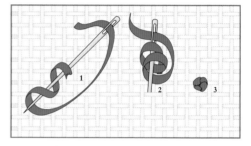

Lazy daisy stitch worked in silk ribbon is very effective when combined with cross stitch. Work the stitch as shown in the diagram, keeping the ribbon untwisted as you form the stitch and don't pull the stitch too tightly

Work the French knot in the same way as described in the Stitch Library (page 116) but use a large gold-plated needle and do not pull the ribbon stitch too tight. You may need to experiment on a spare piece of fabric to perfect your technique

✚ Stitch Perfect ✚

• The use of an embroidery hoop is recommended for silk ribbon embroidery.

• Use a large chenille needle (size 20) for ribbon embroidery, and size 24 tapestry needle when using stranded cotton (floss).

• Work over two threads of the fabric or as stated on the chart.

• Use pure silk ribbon, readily available in 2mm, 3mm or 4mm widths.

• Work with 30cm (12in) lengths of ribbon, cutting the ends at an angle to prevent fraying and make needle threading easier.

• To begin, make a knot at one end of the ribbon and come up through the fabric from the back. Remove any twists in the ribbon before stitching.

• Work with a loose tension to give the required effect – the eye of the size 20 needle should pass under the ribbon with ease.

• When finishing off silk ribbon embroidery, take the ribbon through to the back of the fabric, and using sewing thread, back stitch the end of the ribbon to the nearest stitch of ribbon and then cut off close to the fabric.

• When framing ribbon embroidery, ensure that it does not get squashed by the underside of the glass. Insert very narrow strips of board (spacers) into the edges of the frame, between the glass and the mounted embroidery to hold them apart, before you assemble the frame.

❋ *Silk Ribbon Sampler* ❋

Stitch Count: 100 x 92

Design Size: 18.5 x 17cm (7^1/$_4$ x 6^3/$_4$in)

Fabric Selection: Zweigart Cashel antique white linen 28 threads to 2.5cm (1in)

Tapestry Needle Size: 24

The sampler is stitched over two threads of linen using two strands of stranded cotton for the cross stitch and one for back stitch, and 2mm silk ribbon from YLI. You can change the initials by using the alphabet in the sampler. The design is charted on page 160/161 of the Motif Library.

See Working the Projects page 126.

Blackwork Embroidery

When designing a sampler, I often like to include sections of blackwork as a contrast to the areas of cross stitch included in a pattern. The name blackwork tends to mislead but the lovely lacy effect achieved can enhance a pure cross stitch pattern.

Blackwork is an embroidery technique consisting of geometric patterns built up using double running (Holbein) stitch (see diagram) and was traditionally worked in black thread against a contrasting (usually white) background with gold metallic highlights added for extra impact. During Elizabethan times blackwork embroidery was used to decorate clothing to imitate the appearance of lace. The name is rather misleading as this type of counted embroidery can be stitched in any colour you choose. Many different effects can be achieved by varying the thickness of the thread, and careful selection of patterns with dark, medium and light tones. You will see from the page of blackwork designs overleaf that you can select different patterns to create the dark and light effects.

Modern blackwork makes good use of different colours and as you can see from the photographs can create amazing effects. The prancing deer is worked in traditional style using black and gold but the holly and berry motif are worked using red and green stranded cotton (floss). As you can see from the illustration, any cross stitch chart can be adapted to suit black-work treatment. I have taken the outline of the black cat on page 76 and worked a blackwork pattern with great success.

✛ Stitch Perfect ✛

• Blackwork is traditionally worked using double running stitch or Holbein stitch, rather than back stitch.

• Holbein stitch will give a smoother effect and the back of your work will look almost as good as the front, so it is particularly useful for table linen.

• Before starting to stitch you will need to plan the direction you are working so that you can return to fill the gaps without ending up a blind alley!

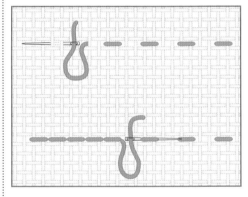

To work double running or Holbein stitch, begin by working a running stitch under and over two threads of evenweave or one block of Aida. Then stitch the return journey, filling in the gaps

✳ Holly and Berries ✳

Stitch Count: 32 x 25
Design Size: 6.5 x 5cm ($2^{1}/_{2}$ x 2in)
Fabric Selection: Antique white linen 28 threads to 2.5cm (1in)
Tapestry Needle Size: 24

The outline of this design was worked in two strands of green stranded cotton (floss) over two threads of linen with the repeating patterns worked in green and red stranded cotton (floss). The chart for this design is included in the Motif Library (page 136) although there are examples of blackwork patterns overleaf on page 62. See Working the Projects page 126.

❊ *Prancing Deer* ❊

Stitch Count: 37 x 37
Design Size: 7.5 x 7.5cm (3 x 3in)
Fabric Selection: Antique white
linen 28 threads to 2.5cm (1in)
Tapestry Needle Size: 26

This blackwork design shows how the outline shape of a motif is worked and then filled with traditional blackwork stitches. The outline was worked in two strands of black stranded cotton (floss) over two threads of the linen with the repeating patterns worked in gold metallic thread and a single strand of black stranded cotton (floss). The chart for this design is in the Motif Library (page 136) although there are further examples of blackwork patterns overleaf on page 62. See Working the Projects page 126.

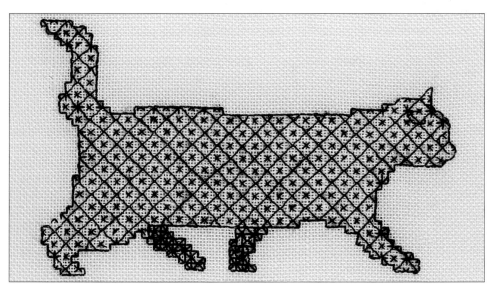

❊ *Black Cat* ❊

Stitch Count: 66 x 41
Design Size: 12 x 7.5cm (4³/₄ x 3in)
Fabric Selection: Ivory linen 28 threads to 2.5cm (1in)
Tapestry Needle Size: 24

This design uses the chart for the Cat on a Wall, shown on page 76 and charted in the Motif Library on page 138. The outline of the design was worked in two strands of black stranded cotton (floss) over two threads of linen with the repeating pattern worked in one strand of black. See Working the Projects page 126.

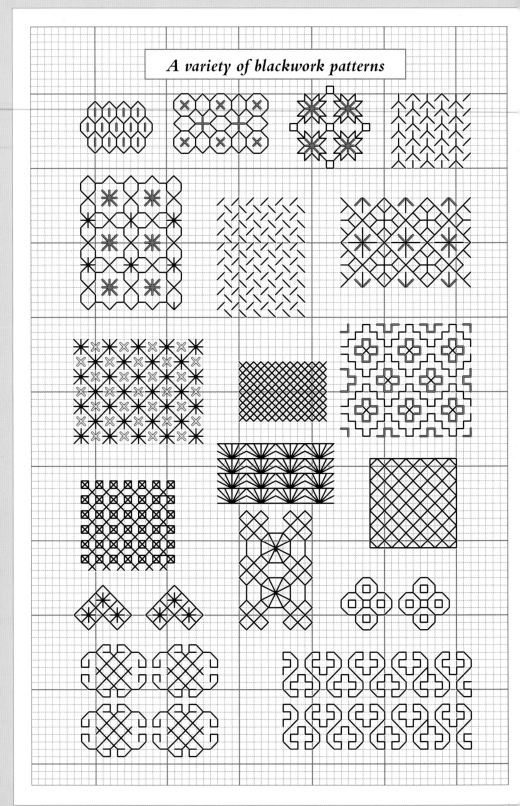

A variety of blackwork patterns

Assisi Embroidery

This style of cross stitch, named after the town in Italy, can be described as pure cross stitch although in reverse. The design is transferred to the fabric by working a back stitch outline first, then the background of the design is stitched leaving the motif shown as blank fabric.

The example in the colour picture below illustrates the versatility of a cross stitch chart because the outline used for the yellow rose on Lurex fabric has been used as the framework for the Assisi rose embroidery using a delicate Caron Waterlilies thread (code 098). You could choose almost any design from the Motif Library and work it in the same way.

✛ Stitch Perfect ✛

• Work the outline in back stitch or Holbein stitch (see page 60), carefully counting from the chart.

• Experiment with the number of strands needed to create the effect required.

• Work the cross stitch in two journeys to keep a neat tension throughout and perfect vertical lines on the reverse. If using a brighter coloured Caron thread with more distinctive colour changes it would be best to work the cross stitches individually.

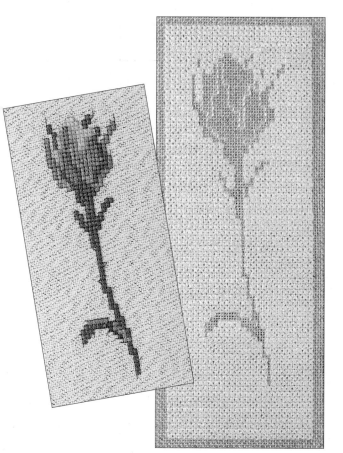

✳ *Assisi Rose* ✳

Stitch Count: 18 x 65
Design Size: 4 x 12cm
(1^1/$_2$ x 4^3/$_4$in)
Fabric Selection: Unbleached linen
28 threads to 2.5cm (1in)
Tapestry Needle Size: 26

This lovely rose design has been stitched in reverse therefore the stitch count refers to the actual design rather than the completed picture. The flower has been stitched from the chart for the yellow rose on page 146, originally stitched on gold Lurex fabric. Using the back stitch outline only, the design has been left bare whilst the background has been cross stitched in one strand of Caron Waterlilies thread (098). Outlines from other motifs in the Motif Library could be treated in the same way. See Working the Projects page 126.

Counted but Free

It is quite possible to take an original cross stitch chart and to work it in quite a different way to create a textured, almost three-dimensional effect to your stitching. This is achieved by replacing blocks of cross stitch with other counted stitches specially chosen to give the effect of a particular material, for example long stitch can be used to create a thatching effect. These substituted stitches are worked in the same colour stranded cottons (floss) as the original chart, but the end result will be very different. Many cross stitchers are very nervous of any type of free embroidery, but as this technique uses only counted stitches they no longer need to be.

To practise the 'counted but free' approach, simply outline the areas on the original chart that you wish to fill with textured stitches and transfer on to a blank piece of graph paper: you might be able to use the highlighting back stitch lines on the original chart as a start point as I have for the re-worked rose cottage design. Now, using the Stitch Library, choose suitable stitches to recreate the textured effects you are hoping to achieve. Using a different colour for each selected stitch, colour in each block of your outline as a guide, and then get stitching.

Here are some ideas of how to achieve some textures, but have fun experimenting with some of your own.

Bricks	Vertical, diagonal and horizontal satin stitch
Corn Sheaves	Half Rhodes stitch
Flower Heads	Algerian eye
Roses	Bullion bars
Flower Stems	Counted chain stitch

On those occasions that you want to stitch almost at random, in a garden area for instance, select the coloured threads used in the original cross stitch pattern, work a back stitch border around the section, and then add the stitches freely using the colours in a less rigid way. In this way a flower bed could be completely filled with French knots randomly stitched but following the colour guidance of the original design.

✤ Stitch Perfect ✤

• You can use Aida for limited effect when trying the 'counted but free' technique, but to explore the idea fully work on evenweave fabric.

• As the back stitch outline on the fabric will be covered by your 'free' stitches, the shade of thread used for this is unimportant.

• Add further back stitch for definition after some of the free embroidered sections are completed.

• If you are intending to work long stitches or a large amount of satin stitch, a frame or hoop may be useful.

• Try using different thickness of threads when stitching, or silk ribbon or fine wool for an interesting textural effect.

• Choose alternative stitches to match the type of effect you want.

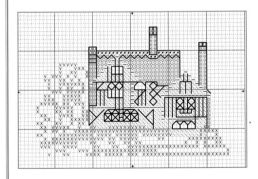

Transfer the back stitch lines from this original cross stitch chart on to graph paper and use these to plan which additional stitches to work within these lines.

✳ *Rose Gable Cottage* ✳

Stitch Count: 51 x 33
Design Size: 9 x 6cm ($3^1/_2$ x $2^1/_2$in)
Fabric Selection: Ivory linen 28 threads to 2.5cm (1in)
Tapestry Needle Size: 24

Both the cross stitch and 'counted but free' version of this design have been worked in two strands of stranded cotton over two threads of linen. The textured version of the cottage has been worked using the original cross stitch chart as a guide. I outlined the building carefully counting from the chart, but added straw-coloured long stitch for the thatched roof, cream long stitch for the front gables and double cross stitch for the chimneys. After the remainder of the design was completed I added random French knots in greens and pinks on top of the stitching to indicate roses. The original cross stitch design can be found in the Motif Library on page 159.

Pulled Thread and Drawn Thread Work

These two techniques work extremely well with cross stitch, particularly for band samplers, as you can see in the four seasonal samplers shown in the Stitch Library. These beautiful pieces demonstrate the exciting variety of counted stitches and how techniques can be combined. This section is intended to be used in conjunction with the Stitch Library, particularly queen stitch, Algerian eye and hem stitch variations.

There is sometimes confusion between pulled thread work and drawn thread work and a clear explanation of the difference between the two techniques is needed before the stitching can be tackled successfully.

Pulled Thread Work

This refers to a type of embroidery where patterns of holes are created in fabric, usually linen, by *pulling* threads together with various stitches. The holes produced by the pulled-work stitches form patterns that are, perhaps confusingly, referred to as fillings. *No threads are cut or removed in pulled thread work.* Pulled stitches, such as four-sided stitch, Algerian eye, hem stitch and Queen stitch, can be worked alone or with cross stitch to form borders, to create abstract or geometric motifs or as patterns for filling spaces in a design, for example in the four seasonal samplers. A detail from the Summer Sampler shown below illustrates the use of pulled stitches. (See also the following section on Hem Stitching.)

Linen is used for this type of embroidery because the fibres are very strong and even stronger when wet. Linen has a tendency to crease easily, so excess folding and crumpling of the fabric should be avoided but this makes it ideal for pulled-work projects because, when the threads are pulled together, they bend or crease and stay in place, producing the lacy effects of pulled work. Linen is so hardwearing, it is the best choice for projects that require many hours of work, or items that will be used and laundered often.

A detail from the Summer Sampler (page 98) showing some pulled stitches – Queen stitch and Algerian eye

---

✛ Stitch Perfect ✛
Pulled Thread Work

- Use linen for pulled thread work, particularly for tableware, samplers and pillow covers.

- Pull the stitches so that the threads of the fabric are drawn together to form holes.

- With some stitches in pulled work, e.g. Algerian eye, the central hole is formed by pulling the thread firmly. This takes a little practice in order to produce even holes and tension, and cross stitchers often find this odd at first as they do not distort the fabric normally.

- Examples of pulled stitches are described in the Stitch Library (see page 83 for index) and include Algerian eye, several other eyelet variations, four-sided stitch, queen stitch, hem stitch and variations of hem stitch.

Drawn Thread Work

Drawn thread work may superficially look like pulled work but their methods are quite different because in drawn thread work, *threads are cut and drawn out* from the ground fabric. The technique is often used after hem stitch or four-sided stitch have been worked. (See also the following section on Hem Stitching.) With reference to figs 1–3, you will see that the drawn fabric threads can be treated in one of two ways: they can be cut off after satin stitching or woven into the edge of the fabric to form a selvedge.

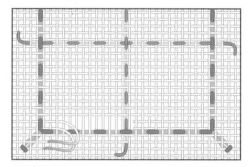

Fig 1 This shows the fabric with two horizontal threads cut, beginning to be unwoven

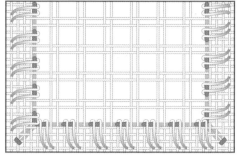

Fig 2 This shows the cut threads withdrawn to the edge of the fabric

Fig 3 (left) This shows the cut threads removed and the loose ends woven into the fabric edges

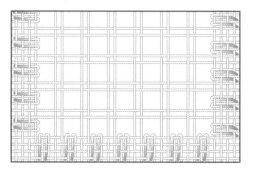

A detail from the Spring Sampler (page 90) showing some drawn thread work

---

✣ Stitch Perfect ✣
Drawn Thread Work

• If a square of hem stitch or four-sided stitch is worked as in the detail from the Spring Sampler above, alternate pairs of vertical and horizontal linen threads can be cut and pulled back to the hem stitching leaving a two-thread margin.

• Drawn threads are taken to the back of the stitching and tacked out of the way.

• A row of satin stitch is then worked inside the hem stitch square anchoring the threads which are then trimmed away.

• The remaining groups of threads can be decorated with simple wrapping as illustrated or with dove's eye stitch if preferred.

• When bands of hem stitching are worked as shown in this sampler detail, only the horizontal threads are snipped.

• The drawn threads are taken back to the edge of the section and woven in to the body of the fabric leaving vertical threads to be embellished as shown.

Hem Stitching

This section is intended to be used in conjunction with the Stitch Library, particularly pages 111-114. Included within the Stitch Library you will see four samplers, Spring, Summer, Autumn and Winter (pages 90, 98, 108 and 124 respectively), all of which are stitched on linen and include not just cross stitch and a variety of other exciting counted stitches but also the chance to try decorative hem stitching. Hem stitching and other decorative edgings are sometimes referred to as 'finishing'. The hem stitch is a wonderfully versatile stitch allowing you to hem a raw edge, form a folded hem or remove horizontal threads from the fabric leaving the vertical threads to

be decorated. Hem stitching can therefore be purely decorative or functional and works well with pulled work and drawn thread work (see page 66).

You can see from the stitched examples that the art of decorative hem stitching is not difficult but must be worked in stages. The bookmarks on page 51 illustrate the effect of cutting the threads after hem stitching has been worked to form a safe edge. The samples stitched and illustrated here show the folded hem method allowing you to form a neat hem on the wrong side of the fabric showing a delicate pattern of pulled holes on the right side.

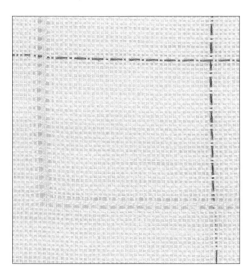

Two rows of hem stitch worked without the withdrawal of any threads but with tacking stitches in place

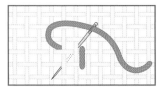

Hem stitch worked, with alternate threads cut, withdrawn to the hem stitch and tacked out of the way, leaving threads remaining for decoration

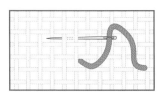

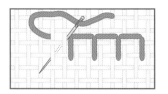

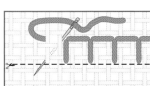

These four diagrams show the stages of working hem stitch, in this case over two threads in each direction. Work a straight stitch over two threads, turning the needle horizontally to create a stitch at right angles. Turn the needle diagonally and repeat the straight and horizontal stitches along the row, counting carefully. After hem stitching, thread withdrawal may take place

✛ Stitch Perfect ✛

- To form a perfect fold when stitching a hem try scoring the fabric. Place the fabric on a clean, flat surface (not French polished) and place the needle in a line of threads which will form the fold. Carefully pull the fabric not the needle which will create a score mark on the fabric making turning the material simple.

- Count the site very carefully and if nervous work a line of tacking threads over and under two threads of the linen prior to thread withdrawal.

- The next step is to cut the thread. Count to the centre of area to be hemmed and snip one horizontal thread once. Then carefully unravel the cut thread from the middle to the edge.

- Weave the linen thread into the side of the fabric as shown below to form a selvedge.

- Using two strands of stranded cotton (floss), work the hem stitch as indicated on a chart taking care to count two threads carefully.

- Start and finish at the end of each section. Do not begin a new thread in the middle of a row.

Stitching a Folded Hem

The most common method is to withdraw a thread across and down the fabric which will, when stitched, form the decorative pattern on the front of the folded hem (see picture right). The withdrawn thread is woven into the fabric at the edge of the hemmed area to form a selvedge. Once the fabric is prepared the raw edge can be folded and the hem stitch worked from the wrong side. When working hem stitch as part of a sampler and for decorative purposes, I prefer to work two rows of hem stitches and then withdraw the threads. Either way is acceptable and depends on the project.

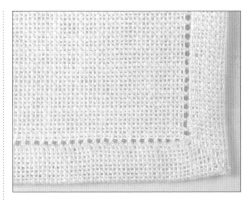

This shows the front view of a hem-stitched corner

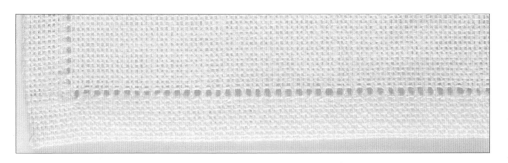

This shows the back or wrong side of a hem-stitched corner, showing the fold

Hardanger Embroidery

Hardanger embroidery or cut work is easy to do and is extremely effective when combined with cross stitch but it seems to strike terror in the hearts of all cross stitchers, possibly because they have snipped a fabric thread in error whilst unpicking!

Hardanger, a town in Norway, gave its name to this type of counted embroidery, where cut work was a feature of the local dress. This section of the book is intended to give you a taste of Hardanger embroidery and if you find that you want to experiment further there is an excellent guide listed in the Bibliography.

This section is intended to be used in conjunction with the Stitch Library, particularly pages 120 to 123.

At its simplest, Hardanger work basically consists of three stages which are described over the next few pages:

1 Stitching Kloster blocks.
2 Cutting threads.
3 Decorating the remaining threads and spaces.

The secret of successful cut work embroidery is working Kloster blocks (the framework needed for the decorative filling stitches) and to count the Kloster blocks correctly. If they are in the right place the threads may be cut out and the stitching will not fall to pieces!

Hardanger embroidery may be worked on evenweave fabric of any thread count or on Hardanger fabric which is supplied with 22 blocks to 2.5cm (1in). If working on Hardanger fabric, treat each block as one thread.

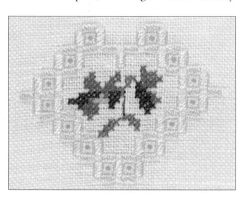

✳ *Hardanger Violet Coaster* ✳

Stitch Count: 38 x 30
Design Size: 7 x 5cm ($2^3/4$ x 2in) excluding
buttonhole stitched edge
Fabric Selection: Ivory linen 28 threads to 2.5cm (1in)
Tapestry Needle Size: 24 and 22

The heart shape in this coaster has been created with Kloster blocks worked in cotton perlé, with the eyelet stitches worked in two strands of stranded cotton (floss), creating decorative holes without any cutting of threads (see Pulled Thread Work on page 66). The violet cross stitch motif has been stitched using two strands of stranded cotton (floss) from a chart on page 153 of the Motif Library. This project could be completed with the buttonhole edging and cut out as illustrated on page 73.

✢ Stitch Perfect ✢
Kloster Blocks

• To form Kloster blocks, work the stitches side by side so that they look the same on the wrong side of the fabric.

• The vertical and horizontal blocks must meet at the corners, sharing the corner hole.

• Check that you have counted correctly as you stitch and check that each block is in the correct position.

• Check that vertical Kloster blocks are opposite one another and horizontal blocks are opposite horizontal ones.

• Work all the Kloster blocks in a pattern, checking that the blocks meet where they should.

• Never start cutting until the Kloster blocks are completed and match everywhere.

• Do not travel between blocks at the back unless under existing Kloster blocks.

Stitching Kloster Blocks

Kloster blocks form the framework for the cut areas in Hardanger embroidery. They are worked in patterns, formed with 5 vertical or 5 horizontal straight stitches, each of them over 4 threads on evenweave or 4 blocks if working on Hardanger fabric. The stitches are worked side by side, following the grain of the fabric (see fig 1). Do not let thread cross over open space on the back of the fabric (see fig 2).

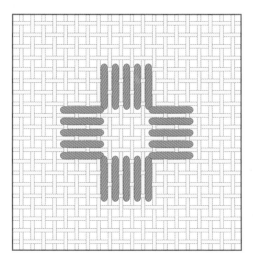

Fig 1 Kloster blocks worked but left without threads cut and removed (shows the right side)

Fig 2 Kloster blocks from the wrong side - the red route is to be avoided

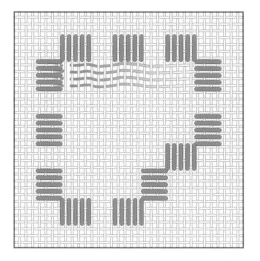

Fig 3 Kloster blocks stitched, with some threads cut awaiting withdrawal

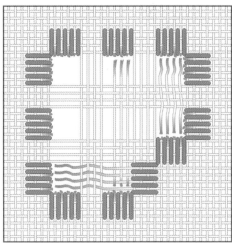

Fig 4 Kloster blocks stitched with some threads cut and some withdrawn

Cutting Threads

When the Kloster blocks have been stitched, the threads between them are cut and drawn out. The secret to successful cutting is to work all the Kloster blocks, checking that you have counted correctly and that all the blocks are exactly opposite each other. Looking at the photographs of the Hardanger heart opposite you can see that the Kloster blocks are formed in vertical and horizontal lines. The threads should be cut, in pairs, with very sharp, pointed scissors at the end of the Kloster blocks, as shown in fig 3 (page 71), not at the side. Remember to cut where the needle has pierced the fabric. Withdraw the cut threads carefully (see fig 4) and when all the cut threads are removed the work should look like fig 5 (and the second stage of the Hardanger Heart coaster opposite).

If you do make a mistake and cut a thread unintentionally it is easy to correct this. Just remove the fabric thread you've cut by mistake, then take a strand of stranded cotton (floss) the same colour as your fabric and darn it in and out so that it replaces the accidentally cut thread leaving a long thread hanging on the wrong side. Needleweave or wrap this section next to anchor the threads, then the loose thread can be trimmed.

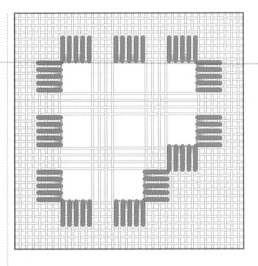

Fig 5 Kloster blocks stitched and with all the correct threads cut and withdrawn ready for decorating. After cutting, do not worry if you can see some small whiskers at the cut sites. Leave these until the piece is finished. Many will withdraw as the work is handled, but if necessary they can be carefully trimmed when the piece is complete

---

✛ Stitch Perfect ✛
Cutting Threads

- Work slowly, in a good light and with small, pointed, sharp scissors.

- The cutting side is where the long straight stitches enter the fabric. *Never* cut alongside the long edges of the stitches.

- Cut the threads at the end of each Kloster block, working from a corner outwards. You will be cutting four threads, but cut them in twos.

- Pass the point of the scissors into the corner-shared hole and lift the threads.

- Check that you can see both points of the scissors and that you are only cutting two threads, then lean slightly towards the Kloster block and cut.

- It is easier to cut all the relevant threads in one direction first then turn the fabric to cut in another direction.

- Pull out the loose threads using tweezers if necessary. The stitching should look like the second photograph (opposite) with groups of four threads vertically and horizontally left to decorate.

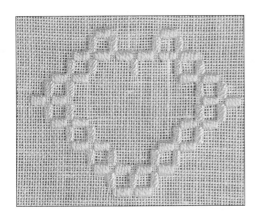

This first stage shows the Kloster blocks completed

This shows the back of the stitching to show that the Kloster blocks should look similar back and front

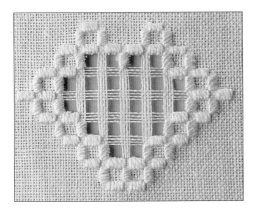

This second stage shows the fabric threads cut and withdrawn, ready to be decorated

✳ *Hardanger Heart Coaster* ✳

Stitch Count: 42 x 38
Design Size: 7.5 x 7cm (3 x 2³/₄in)
Fabric Selection: Ivory linen 28 threads to 2.5cm (1in)
Tapestry Needle Size: 22

This exquisite Hardanger Heart Coaster has been stitched using one strand of perlé cotton No.5 in ecru for the Kloster blocks and the buttonhole edging. After the Kloster blocks were completed, the fabric threads were cut and withdrawn. The needleweaving and dove's eyes were then worked using one strand of ecru perlé cotton No.8. The chart is on page 153 of the Motif Library.

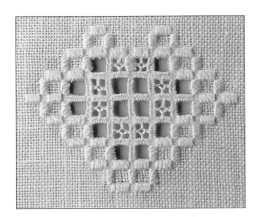

The third stage showing base threads and void areas completed with needleweaving and dove's eyes

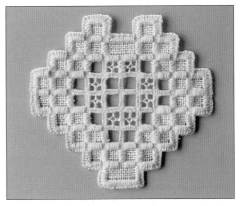

The Hardanger Heart Coaster with a buttonhole edging completed and excess fabric cut away

Decorating Threads and Voids

When Kloster blocks are completed and the threads are cut and removed, you are left with groups of threads and spaces, void areas, to strengthen and decorate (see fig 5 page 72). There are many ways to do this but there is only room to give you a taste of Hardanger embroidery here and in the Stitch Library so only the basic principles will be covered.

Needleweaving (see Stitch Library page 122 for full instructions) is one of the most commonly used methods of embellishing threads left after cutting, especially over larger areas, and creates covered bars (see fig 6) which can be worked alone or combined with filling stitches such as dove's eye and picots. When needleweaving use a slightly finer thread than for stitching Kloster blocks.

Wrapped bars (see Stitch Library page 120 for full instructions) are also used to embellish threads left after cutting (see fig 7). They may be worked alone or as part of other decorative stitches such as spider's webs.

Filling stitches (see Stitch Library pages 121 and 123 for full instructions) are used to decorate the voids left by cutting threads. Some of the basic ones you might like to try include dove's eye stitch, spider's web stitch and picots.

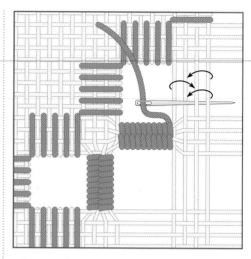

Fig 6 Needleweaving – full instructions page 122

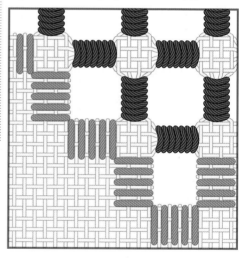

Fig 7 Wrapped bars – full instructions page 120

✣ Stitch Perfect ✣
Needleweaving

• When needleweaving use a slightly finer thread than for stitching the Kloster blocks.

• To weave a bar, bring the needle up in a void area and work over and under pairs of threads.

• After completing one bar, weave the next one at right angles to it, working around the design, taking care not to run threads across the back of the cut areas.

• Needleweaving shouldn't alter the shape of the bar, which should stay flat and straight.

✳ *Hardanger Flower Chatelaine,* ✳
Scissors Keeper and Needlecase

Stitch Count: see small designs in Motif Library page 162
Fabric Selection: Ivory linen band 6cm (2¹/₂in) wide and ivory linen 28 threads to 2.5cm (1in)
Tapestry Needle Size: 24 and 22

These items were worked over two linen threads, using stranded cotton (floss) (two strands), perlé cotton (one strand) and Caron Watercolours (093 or 171) thread (one strand). The scissors keeper and needlecase are charted on page 162. The chatelaine uses motifs from pages 162 and 136. You could work them as shown here or rearrange the elements in a design of your own.

Adapting Chart Designs

There can be no better introduction to cross stitch than working one of the many small kits available. However, there is no reason why the more experienced embroiderer should not enjoy these too. They are still the cheapest way to collect the essentials to complete a picture, and they can provide the perfect opportunity to develop simple designing techniques using the chart from the kit as a starting point. It is possible, with just a little imagination, to create many new designs from the original provided, and the photograph opposite shows what a difference can be made by adapting just a few basic elements.

✕✕✕✕✕

❋ *Cat on a Wall* ❋

Stitch Count: 99 x 56
Design Size: 18 x 11cm (7 x 4¹/₄in)
Fabric Selection:
Above: 16-count Aida
Below: Ivory linen 28 threads to 2.5cm (1in)
Tapestry Needle Size: 24

The small cross stitch kit can offer the perfect opportunity for the stitcher to begin to develop their design skills as they adapt the chart to their own preferences. The picture opposite shows one of my bestselling cross stitch kits. Above, the stitching has been completed on 16-count Aida exactly matching the picture on the kit front. Below, the design has been stitched again, this time on ivory linen, but with some distinctive changes. The black and white cat remains the same, but the wall has changed from brick to old stone and is now decorated with random French knot roses. I photocopied the original cross stitch chart, slightly enlarged it and wrote notes to myself directly onto it to remind me of what I intended to do. I exchanged the red brick for Cotswold stone shades and added extra greenery to square off the end of the design. The French knots were added at random after the cross stitch was complete. The chart for my new version can be found in the Motif Library on page 138.

✢ First Steps to Design ✢

People buy ready-made cross stitch kits partly for convenience and partly to avoid making design decisions. This section will start you thinking of ways to change and personalise kits — the beginning of designing for yourself.

● Consider adding names and dates to the finished piece to make it unique.

● To add wording, draw the letters on to a clean sheet of graph paper, mark the centre, then stitch in position.

● Look at the picture of the kit design and try a simple change of colour. You may prefer a blue and gold border rather than pink and gold, for example.

● Always make a copy of the original chart, and write yourself notes on to this. Keep the notes simple, e.g. 'French knots here' — the colours and detail can come as you stitch.

● Keep records of what colour was used for each change so that you can ensure that both sides of the design match if this is crucial.

● Avoid adding too many different colours to a pattern: instead use different shades of the same colour.

● When you have tried these simple tips to experiment with altering purchased kits, consider: is it time to try designing for yourself?

Designing a Sampler

There are whole books devoted to embroidery design so this section can only give you some basic tips on how to start designing your own work. If you wish to begin with a simple project, such as the sampler shown here, then it might be useful to remember that a sampler usually contains the following elements:

- A border round the design.
- A selection of motifs or patterns within the border, which may be single or mirror image and may reflect a specific theme.
- An alphabet and perhaps a set of numbers.
- Some initials or a name and date.

There are many borders in the Motif Library that you could use for your own sampler or piece of work. Of course you could design your own border, either a simple one as I did here and for the Traditional Cross Stitch Sampler on page 82, or a more complicated border, perhaps to reflect the theme you have chosen for your sampler (e.g., the Acorn and Flower Sampler on page 33).

You can make borders turn corners by placing a small mirror at a 45 degree angle to a border and moving it along until a satisfactory corner is reflected in the mirror. This corner can then be copied onto graph paper. Alternatively you could leave the corners open, stopping the border just short.

Your choice of motifs or patterns to use in a sampler needs to take into account various things - who the embroidery is for, whether the motifs should reflect a particular theme, and your own personal preferences as to style and colour. There are hundreds and hundreds of charted motifs available commercially which you can use in your designs and adapt in various ways (see Adapting Chart designs page 77). If you wish to chart your own drawing of an image simply copy it onto tracing graph paper and then square off the design and colour it in. If the image is the wrong size to begin with you could enlarge or reduce it on a photocopier before you start to square it off.

As with motifs and patterns, there are many books available with all sorts of charted alphabets and number styles for you to use in your embroidery. If composing a line of text or verse, use graph paper to initially plan out the letters to ensure the spacing looks pleasing. Initials used could be your own or the recipients.

Basic Design Decisions

When designing for the first time the idea may seem daunting but try dealing with it in small, bite-sized pieces. You will need to make fairly basic decisions before you start work.

- What size do you want your piece of work to be? A sampler can be any size or shape, generally determined by how much time you have to stitch and if you have a special deadline.
- Are you planning to work the design entirely in cross stitch or use additional stitches as well?
- What is the end use of your piece of stitching? A sampler does not have to be made into a picture – a small design might look well in a card or even as a pincushion.
- Are you designing a traditional piece or one with a more modern feel? This will affect what motifs you choose and how you combine them, particularly for a traditional sampler, where it is important to select motifs which are of the right style and weight. An extreme example would be adding a Ferrari car to a traditional border and stylised trees and flowers!
- When selecting a house motif, relate the size and style of the house to any figures included and adjust the choices of flowers and trees to suit the overall plan.
- A balance needs to be achieved between the motifs you select and the size of the overall design. A large heavy alphabet may be better on its own rather than part of a mixed sampler.
- When designing a large sampler project consider selecting a deep, strong border rather than a narrow, rather mean style. Use the simple narrow border designs around smaller projects.
- Is the design intended to be read like a verse or a prayer? If so the style of the letters must be kept simple or they may be difficult to read. (Look through the Motif Library for ideas.)
- Check dates and the spelling of names when including them in your stitching. We have all made mistakes!
- If you are selecting a motif for a card or trinket pot, make sure that the design will fit the aperture.

Selecting Fabric

The next stage in the process could be to select the fabric type you wish to work on, considering the following:

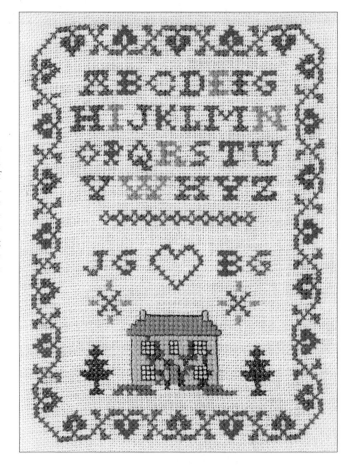

❋ *Simple Sampler* ❋

Stitch Count: 61 x 83
Design Size: 11.5 x 15cm
(4¹/₂ x 6in)
Fabric Selection: Pure linen
28 threads to 2.5cm (1in)
Tapestry Needle Size: 24

This tiny traditional sampler was worked in two strands of stranded cotton (floss) over two threads of the linen fabric. The initials added are taken from the alphabet on the sampler so you can replace these with initials of your choice. (See page 80 for ways of personalising your work.) The chart is on page 149 of the Motif Library. See Working the Projects page 126.

- Whether the design is very traditional and would suit an evenweave rather than an Aida fabric.
- Your eyesight and the amount of time you have to complete the stitching.
- The overall size of the chart you have created and the need for a high stitch count ie 18-count Aida.
- Whether your chart includes a large number of three-quarter cross stitches (which are easier to stitch on evenweave than on Aida).

Design Content

Now you are ready to decide on the actual content of your design so you will need to consider the following:

- Before you start planning a sampler you need to consider doing a little research. Is the design for a family member or special friend and is it a secret?
- Consider referring to older or more distant relatives for family details. Draw out the family tree to include the receiver.
- If planning a local design to include maps or plans, use libraries to collect information about the local area.
- Make lists of the receiver's hobbies and favourite pastimes.
- Don't be afraid to experiment with using different motifs. Trial and error will achieve the most successful results. You could have a master chart on which you can temporarily stick motifs to judge the overall effect.

Having read all the above don't be disheartened by the work involved because the pleasure and pride you will feel when your own design is stitched and framed will be overwhelming! Whether the sampler is for yourself, a family member or a friend, the feeling of achievement will outweigh the anguish of designing and stitching it!

Personalising Your Work

Many cross stitch charts and purchased kits, particularly samplers, include somewhere to add the name of the stitcher and possibly the date completed or the date of the special occasion for which it was stitched. This is a very important part of our responsibility when a piece of work is completed, to leave some information about the piece of work. Designs worked on linen will certainly be here when we are gone and it would be so helpful, not to mention interesting, to a descendant if some information was available.

✢ Stitch Perfect ✢

- If you do not wish to include your full name on a project, you could add your initials and the date, out of sight but inside the frame.

- You may wish to include a simple trade mark. I know one designer who adds a tiny flower head amongst the design!

- When framing a completed piece, why not write a paragraph about the design, its date and how it came to be. Add your own details and pop it inside the back of the frame.

- Why not draw a simple label ready to stick on the back of completed framed pieces along these lines:

  Designed and stitched by …
  Completed and presented on…
  On the occasion of …

  You could also add notes on why you wanted to design the project and how you collected the information.

- Take a photograph of work you are giving away so that you can keep a record.

Designing Monograms

This technique, an excellent way of constructing your own trade mark, is very simple to do and can be stitched quickly, ideal for the emergency present or card. The monograms stitched opposite are worked from the alphabets in the Motif Library pages 134–135 and any letters in any colour and thread type may be combined to great effect. (These were inspired by monograms designed by Brenda Keyes of the Sampler Company, a UK designer and author.)

✢ Stitch Perfect ✢

- You can use letters from different alphabets but check that they are of similar style and size.

- Copy the letters you require on to two pieces of squared paper.

- Tape one letter to the window and add the second sheet so that you can see both letters at the same time. Rearrange the letters until you are happy with them.

- Copy the letter on the bottom sheet on to the top sheet using a different colour pen.

- As you can see from the stitched examples on page 81, the letters look more effective if some of the curves in the letters intertwine.

❊ *Monograms* ❊

Stitch Count: depends on letters selected
Fabric Selection: Linen 28 threads to 2.5cm (1in)
Tapestry Needle Size: 24

These are some simple monogram designs stitched on linen from the two alphabets included in the Motif Library (see pages 134-135).

Computer-Aided Design

Since I started using a computer, people (not stitchers) have asked me what I do with the spare time! Having a computer has changed my working life but perhaps not in the way people think. I do not use a scanner to produce my cross stitch patterns (purely because I can always tell when a design is scanned) so I use a computer to take the drudgery out of designing. When designing a lovely complicated border I can spend time perfecting the pattern repeat rather than spending time copying or tracing mirror images. The computer replaces the pen, paper, scissors, Tipp-ex and eraser but does not 'produce' designs by magic.

If you have access to a computer and wish to try designing for yourself there are a number of dedicated cross stitch programmes from which to select. The various stitching and embroidery magazines available are a good place to start looking for information and advertisements.

Before choosing the correct programme ask yourself the following questions:
- What type of computer do I need?
- How much money am I prepared to spend on the programme?
- How much computer memory is necessary for the programme of my choice?
- Are the designs I produce going to be used professionally or for my own enjoyment?
- Am I going to convert designs into charts using a scanner?
- Do I want to create designs including stitches other than cross stitch?
- Will I need to send my designs to other people, magazines or publishers?
- Will the programme allow me to send charts via e-mail?
- Will the programme allow me to print in colour and black and white.
- Can the programme of my choice be upgraded as technology improves?

❋ *Traditional Cross Stitch Sampler* ❋

Stitch Count: 78 x 98
Design Size: 14.5 x 17.5cm (5³/₄ x 7in)
Fabric Selection: Antique white linen 28 threads to 2.5cm (1in)
Tapestry Needle Size: 24

This is an example of how to combine two different stitches from the cross stitch family. The cross stitch was worked over two threads and the double cross stitch over four threads of the fabric, all worked using two strands of stranded cotton (floss). The chart is on page 142/143 of the Motif Library. See Working the Projects page 126.

Stitch Library

This personal selection of stitches has been developed and selected over a number of years as I have continued to be an avid cross stitcher but one who enjoys adding and or embellishing her work with other counted stitches and even a little cut work and drawn thread embroidery. In most cases the stitches included in the Stitch Library may be stitched on Aida, evenweave or canvas unless otherwise stated, although some pulled stitches are not as effective when worked on Aida fabric. Some of the stitches illustrated show the stitch worked over two or four fabric threads. Remember that when working the stitch, the construction will stay the same but the size and number of fabric threads used may alter. Always refer to the chart for the correct number of fabric threads involved.

Each stitch in the Stitch Library is first shown enlarged, so you can see exactly what the stitch looks like. There are other photographs showing the stitch in a piece of work featured in the book, plus clear diagrams showing exactly how to work the stitch. Some of the captions to the diagrams are numbered to indicate that there are several steps to working the stitch.

To help you find the stitch you want within the Library, the stitches have been grouped in families and an index is also included here.

XXXXX

Index of Stitches

Cross Stitch

This simple little stitch, the most important and most commonly used stitch in this book, is the key to counted embroidery. A cross stitch, though very simple, can look exquisite or rather untidy and the following guidelines are to ensure that your stitches are just perfect! Even if you have stitched for years see what you think of the following tips.

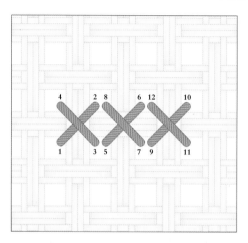

To work a complete cross stitch, follow the numbered sequence, bringing the needle up through the Aida fabric at the bottom left corner of the stitch, cross one block of the fabric and insert the needle at the top right corner. Push the needle through, then bring it up at the bottom right-hand corner, ready to complete the stitch in the top left-hand corner. To work the adjacent stitch, bring the needle up at the bottom right-hand corner of the first stitch.

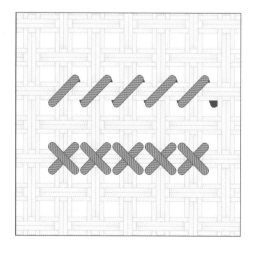

Cross Stitch on Aida Fabric

Cross stitch on Aida fabric is normally worked over one block. The cross stitches can be worked singly or in two journeys. It doesn't matter which method you use but make sure that all the top stitches face the same direction.

To work cross stitches in two journeys, work the first leg of the cross stitch as above but instead of completing the stitch, work the adjacent half stitch and continue on to the end of the row. Complete all the crosses by working the other diagonals on the return journey.

Cross Stitch on Evenweave Fabric

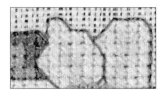

Stitching on evenweave fabric, such as linen, is no more difficult than stitching on Aida fabric – you only need to be able to count to two! To work a cross stitch on evenweave, follow the instructions given for Aida but work across *two* threads of evenweave fabric instead of one block of Aida, only counting the threads, not the holes.

✕✕✕✕✕

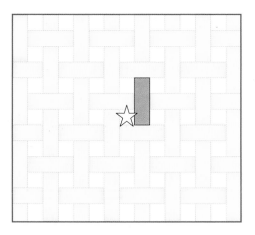

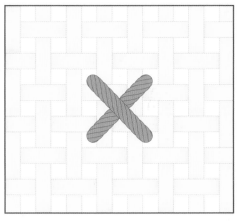

When working on a single weave fabric (an evenweave such as linen), start stitching to the left of a vertical thread. This makes it easier to see when you have made a mistake in counting, because every stitch will start in the same position relevant to adjacent threads of the fabric, making mistakes easy to spot.

As with Aida you can work complete cross stitches on evenweave one at a time.

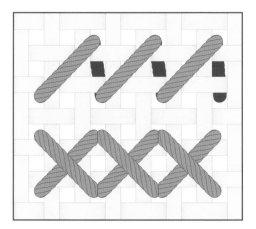

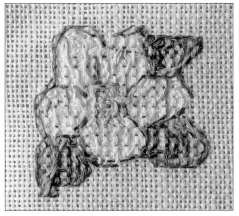

Cross stitches can also be worked on evenweave as rows in two journeys. This is a quicker method and creates a neater appearance on the wrong side, as the photograph (right) shows.

This shows the wrong side of the Christmas rose motif included in the Winter Sampler on page 124. The cross stitch has been worked in two journeys, thus forming neat vertical lines on the reverse.

Three-Quarter Cross Stitch

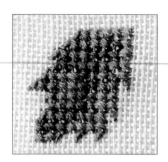

Three-quarter cross stitch is a fractional stitch which helps to produce the illusion of curves when working cross stitch designs. This stitch, a modern addition to the cross stitcher's repertoire, can completely alter the style of your stitching. It is not always popular with stitchers, generally because it is attempted on Aida fabric and it is really intended for even-weave. The stitch can be formed on either material but if you are planning a project that includes many three-quarter cross stitches, do try evenweave, as the formation of the cross stitch leaves a vacant hole for the fractional stitch.

✕✕✕✕✕

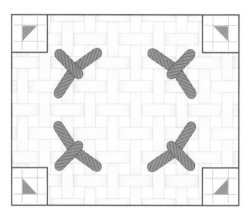

To work a three-quarter cross stitch, work the first half of the cross stitch as usual, sloping the stitch in the direction shown on the chart you are using. Always work the second 'quarter' stitch over the top and down into the central hole to anchor the first half of the stitch. If using Aida, you will need to push the needle through the centre of a block of the fabric.

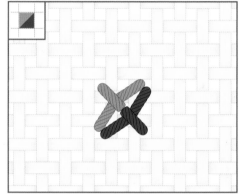

Where two three-quarter stitches lie back-to-back in the space of one full cross stitch, work both of the respective 'quarter' stitches into the central hole.

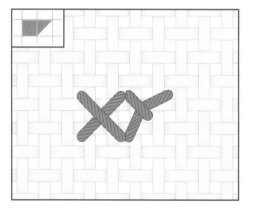

Working a three-quarter cross stitch alongside a full cross stitch.

These pretty pointed leaves could not have been achieved without the use of three-quarter cross stitches. They would have needed to be much larger and much less delicate looking.

Reversible Cross Stitch

There are a number of versions of this stitch but although they are often described as reversible they may not have cross stitch on both sides but create four-sided stitches or a braid-like effect on the back. This stitch is truly reversible, although it has the addition of a vertical line at the end of a row which cannot be avoided. The stitch is quite time consuming as each row is worked four times but it is very useful for book-marks and table linen. The vertical line created at the end of rows can appear as the back stitch outline if you plan your route carefully.

✕✕✕✕✕

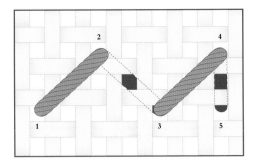

1 *The first journey across two threads on the front of the fabric, working diagonally across the back of the next two threads, missing the stitch on the front.*

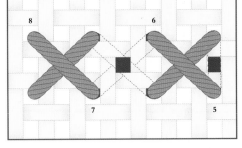

2 *The return journey shows covering the first diagonal threads on the front and back of the work.*

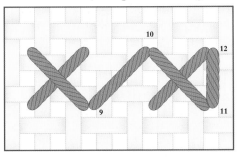

3 *The third journey filling missed stitches back and front.*

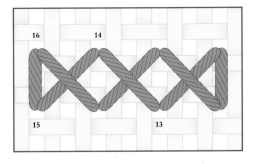

4 *The final journey completing the row.*

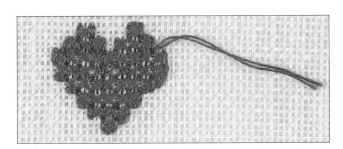

This picture shows the back of the little red heart shown at the top of the page. Reversible cross stitch takes a little time but looks very effective if both sides are to be seen.

Double Cross Stitch

Also known as Smyrna or Leviathan stitch

Double cross stitch may be worked over two or four threads of an evenweave fabric or over two blocks of Aida, to create a series of bold crosses or 'stars'. Tiny double cross stitches may be formed over two threads of evenweave but they are difficult to work on one block of Aida. To keep all double cross stitches uniform make sure that the direction of the stitches within them is the same.

✕✕✕✕✕

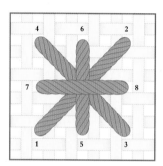

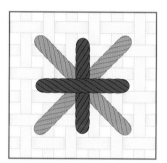

To work a double cross stitch, start to the left of a vertical thread and following the numbered sequence, work a diagonal cross stitch and then add a vertical cross on top.

The second vertical cross may be worked in a different colour to add interest if you prefer, in which case work the stitch in two stages – all lower crosses first, followed by the top crosses.

Tiny double cross stitches may be formed over two threads of evenweave in a single colour. Their small size makes them unsuitable for Aida fabric.

Vertical Double Cross Stitch

Vertical double cross stitch may be worked in two colours in the same way as described for the diagonal version above.

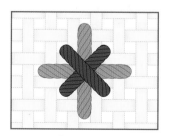

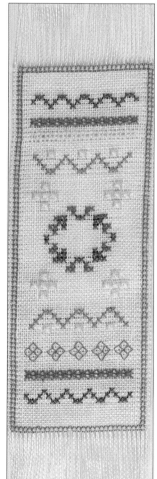

This is one of two bookmarks worked on pure linen (see page 51). This one is stitched in stranded cotton and includes double cross stitch as one of the decorative bands.

Long-Legged Cross Stitch
Also known as long-armed Slav stitch and Portuguese stitch

Long-legged cross stitch seems very uninteresting when first seen but looks wonderful when worked in rows because it forms a plaited braid effect which is ideal for borders, or for the outside edges of pieces to be made up as a pincushion or a scissors keeper. Long-legged cross stitch can also be worked on Aida across two blocks and upwards over one. The stitch may be used to join sections, as shown below.

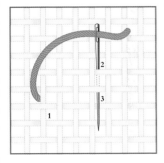

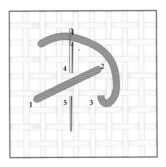

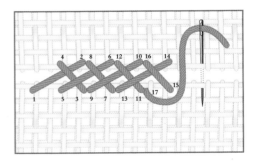

This detail illustrates the lovely braid effect produced by long-legged cross stitch, in this case using six strands of stranded cotton (floss) to form the stitches.

1 *To work long-legged cross stitch on evenweave, begin to the left of a vertical thread. Following the numbered sequence, insert the needle four threads forwards and two threads upwards in a long diagonal 'leg'.*

2 *Insert the needle two threads upwards and two threads backwards diagonally to make the short leg.*

3 *To work a row of long-legged cross stitch, follow the numbered sequence shown in the diagram below.*

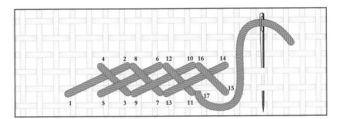

Long-legged Cross Stitch as a Joining Stitch

Long-legged cross stitch is invaluable as it can be used to join two pieces of work as shown in the diagram here. It is easy to do when working on canvas but can also be stitched on Aida or linen effectively.

To join two pieces of work using long-legged cross stitch, the sections to be joined need to be folded along a row of threads and then stitched, picking up threads from either side of the gap as illustrated.

✳ *The Spring Sampler* ✳

Stitch Count: 88 x 159
Design Size: 16.5 x 29cm (6½ x 11½in)
Fabric Selection: Zweigart Cashel linen 28 threads to 2.5cm (1in)
Tapestry Needle Size: 24–22

This is the first of four seasonal samplers included in this section of the book. It is worked as a band sampler and the stitches needed are described on the chart on pages 166-168 and include cross stitch, back stitch and a number of more unusual counted stitches, pulled thread work and Hardanger embroidery. All the stitches in this sampler are included in the Stitch Library but I recommend that you also read Pulled and Drawn Thread Work and Hardanger Embroidery (pages 66 and 70) before starting to stitch.

The chart is over three pages with no overlapping. You might find it easiest to photocopy the parts and tape them together.

Using stranded cottons (floss) unless otherwise stated, work the cross stitch first, followed by the other counted stitches and then the Hardanger and other pulled or drawn stitches. Refer to the Stitch Library for the stitch diagrams and relevant instructions as you need them.

Work the Bands as follows:
- Use two strands of stranded cotton (floss) for the full and three-quarter cross stitches, double cross stitch, Algerian eye, French knots, palestrina knots, stem stitch, hem stitch and Queen stitch.
- Use three strands of stranded cotton for the satin stitch.
- Add back stitch outline where required, using one strand of the colour indicated on the chart.
- Where rice stitch is worked in two colours, work the large cross over *four* threads in two strands of stranded cotton (floss) and add the small stitches in *one* strand of gold metallic.
- Add the random French knots in stranded cotton to the blossom trees after completing the cross stitch on the tree.

- Work the cut work section by working two rows of hem stitch around the rectangle as shown on the chart. Referring to the Pulled and Drawn Thread Work page 66, snip alternate pairs of threads vertically and horizontally and carefully un-do the threads back to the edge of the square leaving a two-thread margin. Tack these loose threads out of the way (as illustrated on page 68).
- Using one strand of perlé cotton No. 8 in ecru, and working either across or down the square, needleweave the remaining threads, adding picots and dove's eyes where marked.
- Work the somersault stitch section by working two rows of hem stitch following the chart. Working from the centre of the hem-stitched box, carefully snip each horizontal linen thread *down the centre line* once and using a needle, un-pick the linen threads back to the two outside edges and carefully weave the threads into the fabric thus forming a selvedge. You should be left with vertical threads only.
- Referring to the diagrams on page 113 work two rows of somersault stitch in the same shade as the hem stitch as indicated. Take care to keep the central lines straight and avoid excessive handling to prevent distortion (as seen here).

Work the Hardanger as follows:
- Work the Kloster blocks using one strand of perlé cotton No. 5, counting over four threads of the linen. Keep checking that the blocks are directly opposite each other, referring to the diagrams as necessary.
- When all the Kloster blocks are complete, use very sharp, pointed scissors to cut across the ends of the blocks as shown. Take this section slowly, counting and cutting two threads each time.
- Needleweave the remaining linen threads using one strand of perlé cotton No. 8, adding dove's eyes and picots as indicated.

Rhodes Stitch

Rhodes stitch gives a solid, slightly raised, three-dimensional effect, almost like a series of 'studs' on the fabric. It is particularly successful when worked in thread which has a sheen, to emphasise areas of light and shade. The diagrams illustrate one version but the size of the stitch can be altered to suit your purposes depending how many threads are included. This stitch does not work well on Aida. Check the chart to see how many threads are in each stitch.

✕✕✕✕✕

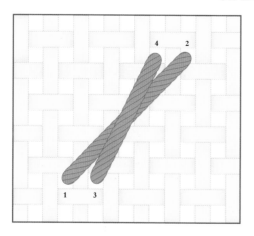

1 *To work a Rhodes stitch begin to the left of a vertical thread, working each stitch over squares of two, four or more threads of evenweave fabric. (Rhodes stitch does not work well on Aida fabric.)*

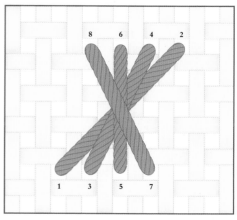

2 *Build the stitch up, working in an anticlockwise direction around the square.*

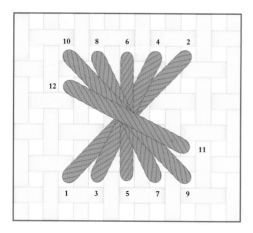

3 *As the numbered sequence is followed, the centre of the stitch becomes raised.*

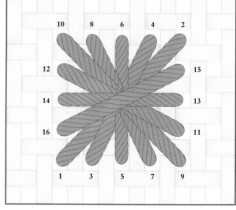

4 *A completed Rhodes stitch. Maintain the same sequence for every stitch for a uniform effect.*

Half Rhodes Stitch with Bar

This is an adaptation of Rhodes stitch, producing a decorative stitch shaped rather like an old-fashioned sheaf of corn, with a straight bar across the centre to tie the threads together. Buttonhole stitching could be added to the bar.

✕✕✕✕✕

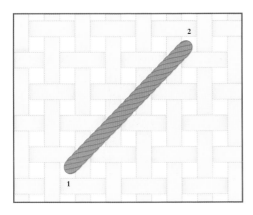

1 *Half Rhodes stitch is worked over squares of two, four, six or eight threads of evenweave fabric, in an anticlockwise direction, slanting as for Rhodes stitch.*

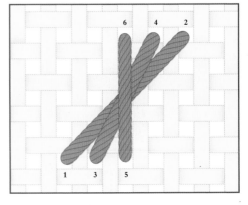

2 *Follow the numbered sequence shown but only working the vertical stages.*

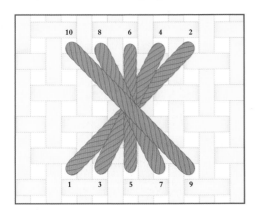

3 *Complete the half Rhodes stitch and maintain the same sequence for every stitch to achieve a uniform effect.*

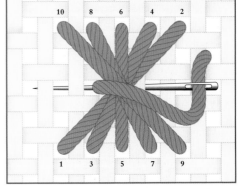

4 *To finish a half Rhodes stitch with a bar, add a single straight stitch across the centre, holding the threads firmly. Add the optional buttonhole stitch (see page 115) across the bar as shown, taking care not to include any of the main stitch as you work. The bar and buttonhole stitching could be worked in a different colour from the half Rhodes stitch to create an interesting alternative.*

Rice Stitch

Rice stitch is a cross stitch with an additional stitch worked over each 'leg' or corner of the cross. It can be worked in two stages: a row of normal cross stitches, followed by the additional stitches as a second row. This makes it ideal for working in two colours, which can create very pretty effects. When using two colours, work all large crosses first, followed by the additional stitches in the second colour. Rice stitch is worked over an even number of threads, usually over four threads of an evenweave fabric but it can also be worked to occupy the space of four blocks of Aida. Do not pull the stitch and form holes around the edge.

××××

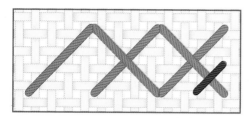

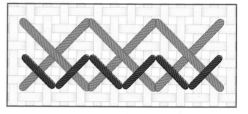

1 *Rice stitch is formed by starting to the left of a vertical thread, working a half cross stitch across four evenweave threads, returning to complete the cross. By the third stage of Fig 1 additional stitches have been added in a second colour.*

2 *The additional stitches across the legs are traditionally worked as a back stitch into the central side hole in each case.*

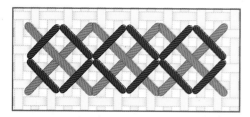

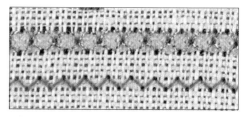

3 *Three completed rice stitches. To ensure uniformity across a project, remember in which direction you stitched, and do all the additional stitches in the same way.*

In this section of the Spring Sampler, rice stitch has been stitched in a single colour with metallic gold added as a second colour.

Diagonal Rice Stitch

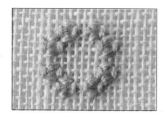

For an interesting variation rice stitch can be worked diagonally, in which case the stitch appears vertically.

Diagonal rice stitch is very effective worked in two colours.

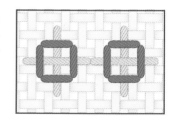

Tent Stitch

Also known as continental tent stitch

Tent stitch is best known as a canvaswork stitch. It has long slanting stitches on the back and even, full stitches on the front. It is the long slanting stitches on the back which cause the distortion of the canvas which is characteristic of this stitch. Tent stitch is sometimes mistaken for half cross stitch but it uses a third more wool than half cross stitch and creates a much thicker and harder-wearing stitch, which makes it ideal for furnishings.

✗✗✗✗✗

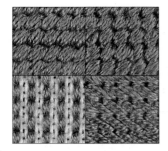

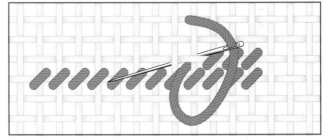

Top left: half cross stitch.
Bottom left: the back of half cross stitch.
Top right: tent stitch.
Bottom right: the back of tent stitch.

Tent stitch is a diagonal stitch formed by the needle being taken under the stitches from right to left thus supporting the stitches, using more thread and so forming a fuller stitch. Ensure that you don't use tent stitch in one direction and half cross stitch in the other. This gives the work the appearance of a furrowed field and is very disappointing.

Diagonal Tent Stitch

The alternative name for diagonal tent stitch is basketweave stitch because of the woven effect produced on the reverse.

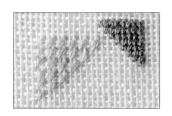

Diagonal tent stitch worked over one thread (right) and two threads (left).

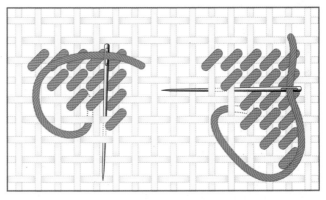

The stitches used in diagonal tent stitch are worked diagonally across the canvas threads so they distort the canvas less than ordinary tent stitch. This method produces a full, even stitch and is pleasing to work. It is a good idea to use straight lines of tent stitch for working a design and then complete the background in diagonal tent stitch.

Gobelin Stitch

Gobelin stitch is a straight stitch often used as a filling stitch as it can mimic the appearance of a woven tapestry. The stitch can be worked to form regular shapes or be worked in encroaching rows to create softer shapes. It can also be worked as long stitches in zigzag rows to form the Florentine pattern. When worked as Florentine or flame stitch, the work created is often known as bargello and is used as a hard-wearing stitch for upholstery.

Gobelin stitch can be worked in stranded cotton or in crewel or tapestry wool and should not be pulled too tight.

✖✖✖✖✖

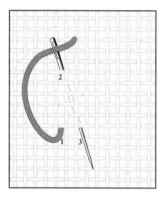

1 *Work a long, straight stitch over the number of threads indicated on the chart following the numbered sequence in the diagram. The stitch should lie flat and not pull or distort the fabric.*

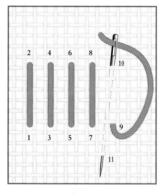

2 *Leaving a space for the second row, work along the row positioning the needle to return to fill the gaps.*

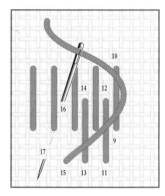

3 *Continuing to follow the numbered sequence in the diagram, work the second row of stitches which should encroach on the first row.*

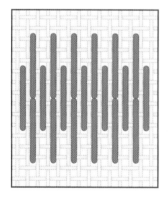

4 *This diagram shows the way a third row of straight stitches fits the space.*

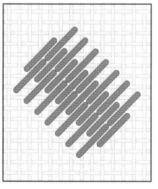

The same stitching principles apply when working a slanted version of gobelin stitch.

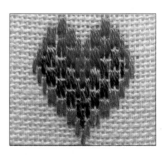

The two heart motifs on this page show the effect that may be created when different colours are used for gobelin stitch. The top version of the heart is worked in one colour while the same motif stitched below illustrates a Florentine pattern as used in bargello.

Satin Stitch

Also known as damask stitch

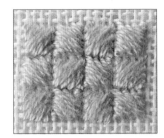

This is a long, smooth stitch which covers the fabric and is often used to fill in shapes. When worked in a glossy thread like stranded cotton (floss), the stitch should have a velvety sheen and can look very effective when worked in blocks facing in different directions. Avoid using very long lengths of thread as this will suffer by being pulled through the fabric too many times. You may like to experiment with the number of strands of thread used, to vary the effect – many strands can give an almost padded look.

✕✕✕✕✕

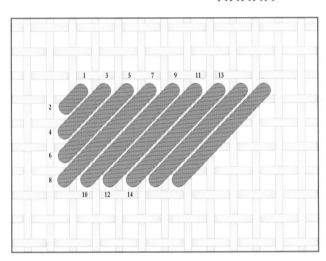

To work satin stitch, start a thread with an away waste knot (see page 18) rather than the loop method which reverses the twist on the thread. Beginning to the left of a vertical thread, follow the numbered sequence in the diagram, laying flat stitches side by side. Always come up the same side and down the other side, so that the back of the fabric is covered. In this way, the stitches will lie closely and neatly beside each other. Take care not to pull satin stitch too tight; it is not intended to distort the fabric. It can be worked diagonally as shown, horizontally or vertically.

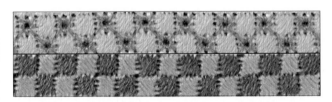

Satin stitch can be worked in the same direction or in a checkerboard style. The shaded effect created by changing direction gives the illusion that two colours have been used.

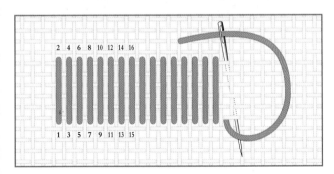

Satin stitch worked vertically.

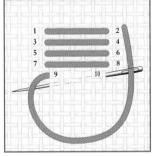

Satin stitch worked horizontally.

✳ The Summer Sampler ✳

Stitch Count: 90 x 169

Design Size: 16.5 x 31cm (6½ x 12¼in)

Fabric Selection: Ivory or antique white linen 28 threads to 2.5cm (1in)

Tapestry Needle Size: 26 and 22

This is the second seasonal sampler. It is worked as a band sampler and the stitches needed are described on the chart on pages 169-171 and include cross stitch, back stitch and a number of more unusual counted stitches, pulled thread work and Hardanger embroidery. All the stitches in this sampler are included in the Stitch Library but I recommend that you also read Pulled and Drawn Thread Work and Hardanger Embroidery (pages 66 and 70) before starting to stitch.

The chart is over three pages with no overlapping. You might find it easiest to photocopy the parts and tape them together.

Using stranded cottons (floss) unless otherwise stated, work the cross stitch first, followed by the additional counted stitches and then the Hardanger and other pulled or drawn stitches. Refer to the Stitch Library for the stitch diagrams and relevant instructions as you need them.

Work the Bands as follows:

- Use two strands of stranded cotton for the full and three-quarter cross stitches, double cross stitch, Algerian eye, French knots, queen stitch and Rhodes stitch.
- Use three strands of stranded cotton (floss) for the satin stitch.

- Add back stitch outline where required, using one strand of the colour indicated on the chart.
- Add the random French knots in dark pink stranded cotton (floss) to the large individual strawberries after completing the cross stitch.
- When working the Algerian eyes, remember to keep the working thread away from the small hole in the centre of the stitch. *Always* form the stitch by passing the needle *down* the centre hole each time.
- Use one strand of gold metallic thread where indicated on the chart (see page 46 for tips and hints on using metallics).

Work the Hardanger as follows:

- Work the Kloster blocks using one strand of ecru perlé cotton No. 5, counting over four threads of the linen. Keep checking that the blocks are directly opposite each other, referring to the diagrams on page 71 as necessary.
- When all the Kloster blocks are complete, use very sharp, pointed scissors to cut across the ends of the blocks. Take this section slowly, counting and cutting four threads each time.
- Needleweave the remaining linen threads using one strand of ecru perlé cotton No. 8, adding the dove's eye stitches as you needleweave, as indicated on the chart.

Back Stitch

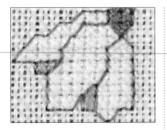

Back stitch is used for creating an outline around a design or part of a design, to add detail or emphasis. The addition of a back stitch outline to a counted cross stitch pattern is a modern idea and in some cases excessive outlining is used to disguise rather poor design so it should be treated with caution. It is not always necessary and is often a matter of taste. On a chart, back stitch is usually indicated by solid lines surrounding the symbols with the suggested shade indicated on the chart or in the key. It is added after the cross stitch has been completed, to prevent the back stitch line being broken by the cross stitches. Try to use a shade of thread for the back stitch that defines the cross stitch but avoid black unless it is specifically required (e.g. for wrought iron railings).

Another important use of back stitch is for lettering and numerals, allowing you to stitch verses, messages, dates and so on and thus personalise your work. You may like to experiment with different back stitch alphabets, thread colours and the number of strands of cotton (floss) used. Refer to page 21 for tips on working back stitch outlining.

❌❌❌❌❌

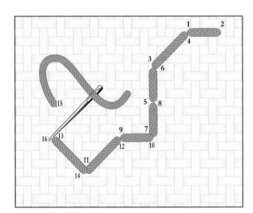

To work back stitches, follow the numbered sequence shown in the diagram, working the stitches over one block of Aida or over two threads of evenweave, unless stated otherwise on the chart. Long loose stitches may be used for ship rigging, cat's whiskers and so on.

This simple but effective crocus motif has been stitched using two techniques but on the same fabric. The top version has been stitched in two strands of stranded cotton (floss) and back stitch outlined in one strand. The outline colour has been taken from the colours used for the cross stitch to ensure a soft, realistic look. The second version, worked from the same chart, has been stitched using one strand of German Flower Thread and the back stitch outline has been omitted. You can see that both techniques are effective but create quite a different feel.

Double Running Stitch
Also known as Holbein stitch

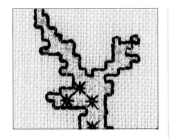

This ancient deer pattern has been embellished with black and metallic gold double running stitch.

Double running or Holbein stitch is the traditional stitch for creating blackwork patterns because the stitch should look the same on the back and front of the work. If back stitch is used instead of double running stitch it creates a rather padded and untidy reverse. The stitch should be created in two journeys, working alternate stitches and then returning to fill the gaps created. The photograph below shows a modern holly and berry motif worked in double running stitch, using green and red stranded cotton (floss). When working blackwork patterns using double running stitch, you need to plan your stitching route so that you can complete all the stitches on the return journey. See page 60 for further advice on blackwork.

XXXXX

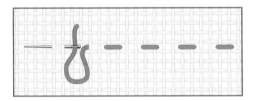

1 To work double running stitch, first work a running stitch, counting to ensure that you work under and over two threads of evenweave or one block of Aida in each case.

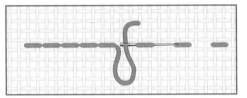

2 Follow the second part of the diagram to fill in the gaps on the return journey, making the stitch truly reversible.

Double running stitch can be worked in two colours by simply changing colour before completing the gaps on the return journey.

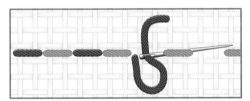

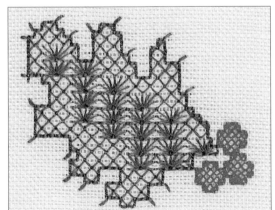

A simple but decorative holly motif created by working the outline first and then filling in with blackwork patterns.

Montenegrin Stitch

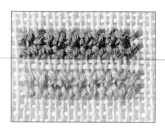

This unusual stitch looks similar to long-legged cross stitch but is constructed in a different way and includes an extra vertical leg which gives it a richer and fuller appearance. The stitch, although not truly reversible, is neat and consistent on the back. It can also be worked on Aida fabric by moving two blocks forward and one block up.

This stitch forms an embossed braid on the front of the stitching and makes a fine, raised edge for folding.

✗✗✗✗✗

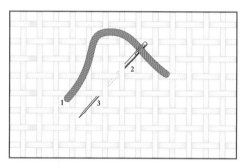

1 *To work Montenegrin stitch on evenweave fabric start to the left of a vertical thread. Following the numbered sequence, work a long diagonal 'leg' by moving four threads forwards and two threads up. Bring the needle two threads back and two threads down to emerge at 3.*

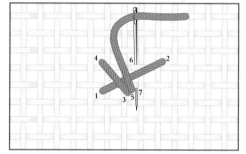

2 *Insert the needle two threads backwards diagonally to make the short leg at 4. Bring the needle back up at 5 and down at 6 to form the final vertical leg.*

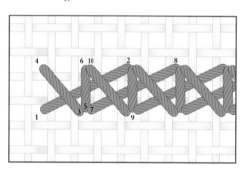

This diagram shows the pattern created by repeating Montenegrin stitch.

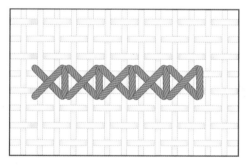

How the back of the work should look after several Montenegrin stitches.

This detail from the Autumn Sampler on page 108 illustrates two rows of Montenegrin stitch in two colours forming a frame for the hem stitched area.

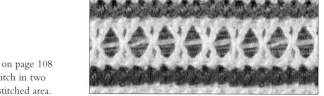

Counted Chain Stitch

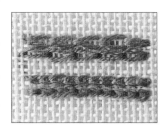

Counted chain stitch is very versatile as it may be used on Aida or evenweave fabric as part of a pattern or to join sections of stitching together. It can be used as an outline stitch or worked in close rows when filling in a pattern.

If using counted chain stitch to join sections of stitching you normally use the same colour thread for the join or you could use a contrasting colour, shown in the photograph below (this clearly illustrates the join).

✕✕✕✕✕

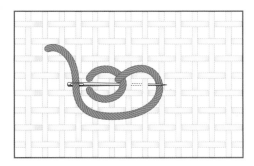

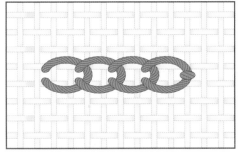

1 *To work chain stitch, start to the left of a vertical thread, bring the needle through the fabric and back down the same hole forming a loop on the surface. Pass the point of the needle under two threads and up to the surface forming another loop. Each new stitch thus anchors the previous stitch and so on.*

2 *If chain stitch is worked as a border the last stitch will anchor the first one. If not, the last and first stitch may be anchored over one thread as shown here.*

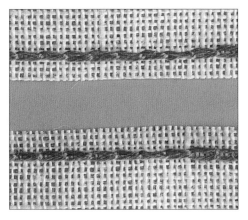

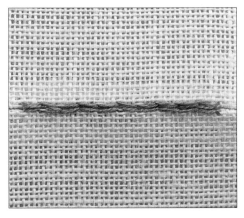

1 *To join two pieces of work, stitch a row of counted chain stitch along the edges of the two pieces. Fold in raw edges and work chain stitch lines side by side.*

2 *Using the same or contrasting thread, weave in and out of the chain stitch to form a pretty join.*

Stem Stitch

Stem stitch is another surface embroidery stitch I have borrowed with success. The secret is to form the stitch in the same manner for the whole project, carefully counting the threads each time. Using spare fabric, experiment with turning gentle corners to perfect your technique. The stitch is most effective on evenweave fabric.

✕✕✕✕✕

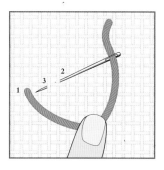

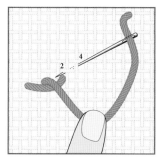

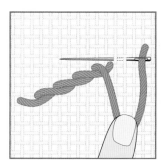

1 *To work stem stitch, follow the numbered sequence in the diagram, working a straight stitch across four threads on evenweave, passing the needle back two threads.*

2 *Make the next stitch by holding the thread over and below the previous stitch and working across four threads again.*

3 *Repeat the stitching sequence so each stitch is formed in the same manner, checking that each new stitch is on the same side to create the rope-like effect required.*

Herringbone Stitch

Also known as plaited stitch, catch stitch, fishnet stitch and witch stitch

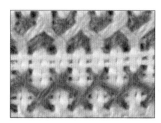

This simple and decorative stitch is often used on band samplers, making it a fine companion to cross stitch and it looks particularly pretty when combined with stitches like long-legged cross stitch. It can also be whipped with a second colour. It is shown here worked over four evenweave threads diagonally and under two horizontally. It can be worked over two and under one to make it smaller, or over and under more threads to make it larger.

✕✕✕✕✕

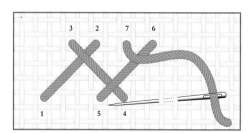

Herringbone stitch is formed starting to the left of a vertical thread, across the number of threads indicated on the chart, following the numbered sequence shown in the diagram.

Algerian Eye

This pretty star-shaped stitch is a pulled stitch which means that when formed correctly holes are pulled in the fabric. It usually occupies the space taken by four cross stitches. It is an ideal stitch to combine with cross stitch as it can add a delicate lacy appearance without the anxiety of cutting threads. Algerian eye can be worked over two or four threads of evenweave as shown and is more successful worked on evenweave than Aida. (See also eyelet variations overleaf.)

✕✕✕✕✕

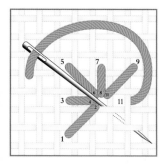

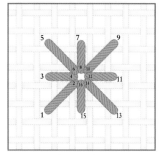

1 *To work an Algerian eye, start to the left of a vertical thread and work from left to right around each stitch in an anticlockwise direction (or vice versa but keeping each stitch the same).*

2 *Always work the stitch by passing the needle down through the central hole, as shown in the diagram, pulling quite firmly so that a small hole is formed in the centre. Take care that trailing threads do not cover this hole as you progress to the next stitch.*

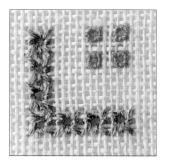

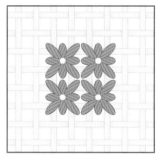

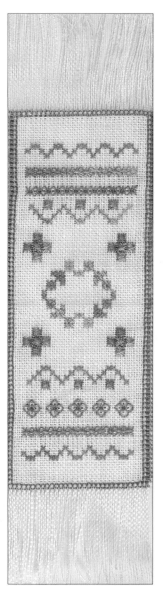

This shows that Algerian eye may be stitched over one or two threads very effectively.

Algerian eye worked over only two evenweave threads.

A bookmark stitched with space-dyed threads (see page 51) showing the use of Algerian eyes.

Eyelet Variations

There are a number of eyelet stitch variations, some of which are shown in the diagrams and photograph here. You can choose the shape you like and work it over more or less threads to create larger or smaller eyelets.

The rules are the same for all eyelets. As with the Algerian eye you need to work the stitch in the correct order and in one direction to ensure that the hole created is uniform and as round as possible. When following the numbered sequence on the diagrams always work the stitch by passing the needle down through the central hole each time, and take care that trailing threads do not cover this hole as you progress to the next stitch.

Why not try inventing eyelet stitches of your own? Work the stitch in the correct sequence and always pass the needle down the central hole, and see what effects you can create.

✕✕✕✕✕

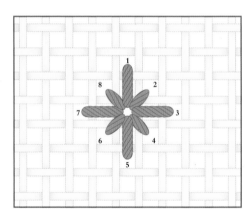

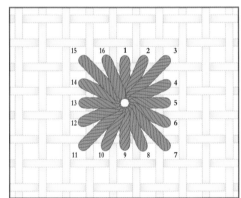

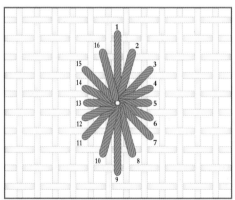

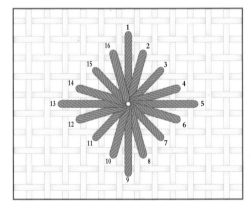

Queen Stitch

Also known as Rococo stitch

This is an ancient pulled stitch made of four parts and forming little dimples in the embroidery by pulling small holes in the fabric. Although this stitch looks fairly unexciting on its own it is gorgeous when worked as a group. As it is a fairly labour-intensive stitch it is best used in small areas like the strawberry detail, left, from the Summer Band Sampler shown on page 98.

Following the instructions and diagrams, work the stitch over a square of four threads in four stages. This stitch is traditionally worked from right to left, but if you find this difficult to count, try working the two middle parts first followed by the outer ones.

✕✕✕✕✕

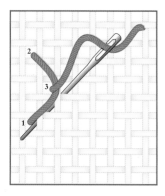

1 Work one long stitch over four threads of the fabric which is then moved two threads to the right by the needle coming up at 3 and a small stitch worked across one thread.

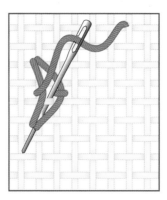

2 Repeat the long stitch from the same position as in fig 1, but this time bending the stitch over one thread only.

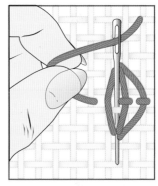

3 Repeat the long stitch from the same position as in fig 1, but this time the long stitch is bent to the left and the needle re-enters the fabric in the centre position.

4 The last stage of the stitch is completed forming a lantern shape on the fabric. Note how the top and bottom hole is shared by each stage of the stitch so forming the holes or little dimples that make this stitch distinctive.

5 You can work Queen stitch individually or in groups. Notice how the stitches are 'joined' together - they may be outlined with back stitch if preferred.

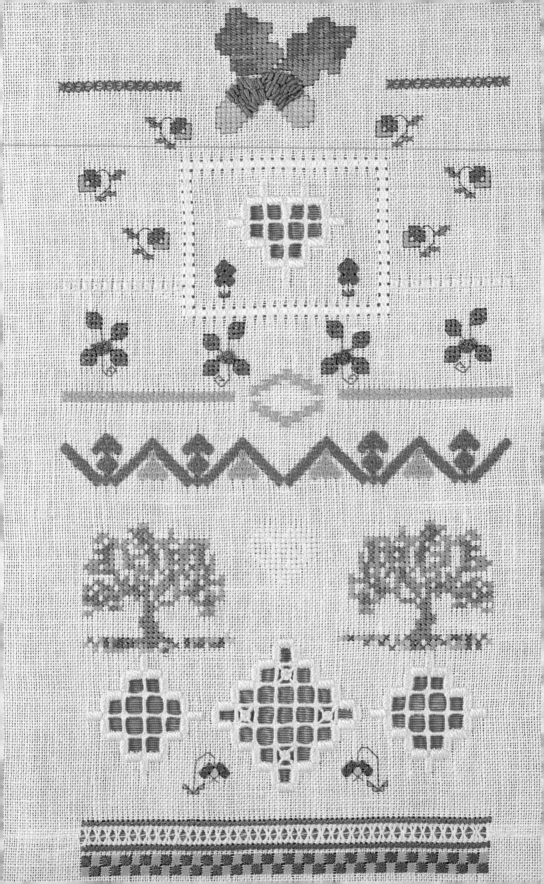

✳ The Autumn Sampler ✳

Stitch Count: 83 x 166
Design Size: 15 x 30cm (6 x 12in)
Fabric Selection: Zweigart Cashel linen 28 threads to 2.5cm (1in)
Tapestry Needle Size: 24–22

This is the third seasonal sampler. It is worked as a band sampler and the stitches needed are described on the chart on pages 172-174 and include cross stitch, back stitch and a number of more unusual counted stitches, pulled thread work and Hardanger embroidery. All the stitches in this sampler are included in the Stitch Library but I recommend that you also read Pulled and Drawn Thread Work and Hardanger Embroidery (pages 66 and 70) before starting to stitch.

The chart is over three pages with no overlapping. You might find it easiest to photocopy the parts and tape them together.

Using stranded cottons (floss) unless otherwise stated, work the cross stitch first, followed by the additional counted stitches and then the Hardanger and other pulled or drawn stitches. Refer to the Stitch Library for the stitch diagrams and relevant instructions as you need them.

Work the Bands as follows:

- Use two strands of stranded cotton for the cross stitch, double cross stitch, rice stitch, French knots, half Rhodes stitch with bar, queen stitch, Montenegrin stitch, four-sided stitch and bullion knots.
- Add back stitch outline where required, using one strand of the colour indicated on the chart.
- Use three strands of stranded cotton (floss) for the satin stitch.
- When working the bullion bars, use a size 22 needle to create full but straight stitches. This is a good opportunity for tweeding, using a mixture

of autumn colours such as 940, 920 and 976.

- For the French knot clusters, tweed the threads to mix the colours (see page 14) and work the stitches at random piling them in groups as shown.
- Where the rice stitch is worked in two colours, work the large cross over *four* threads in two strands of stranded cotton (floss) and add the small stitches in *one* strand of gold metallic.
- Work one row of four-sided stitch around the square as shown on the chart, but work over *four* threads instead of two.
- For the tied hem stitch, work two rows of hem stitch following the chart. Working from the centre of the hem-stitched box, carefully snip each horizontal linen thread down the centre line once and using a needle, un-pick the linen threads back to the two outside edges and carefully weave the threads into the fabric thus forming a selvedge. You should be left with vertical threads only. Referring to the diagrams on page 114, work one row of tied hem stitch.

Work the Hardanger as follows:

- Work the Kloster blocks using one strand of perlé cotton No. 5 counting over four threads of the linen. Keep checking that the blocks are directly opposite each other, referring to the diagrams as necessary.
- When all the Kloster blocks are complete, use very sharp, pointed scissors to cut across the ends of the blocks. Take this section slowly, counting and cutting two threads each time.
- Needleweave the remaining linen threads using one strand of perlé cotton No. 8, adding spider's web filling stitch as indicated.

Four-Sided Stitch

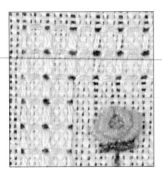

Four-sided stitch is traditionally worked as a pulled stitch to create a lacy effect without the removal of threads from the fabric. It can also be used as a hem stitch when threads are to be cut or removed.

The secret of creating four-sided stitch correctly is to make sure that your needle travels in the correct direction on the back of the stitch. The stitches on the front of your work should be vertical or horizontal whilst on the back they should be diagonal. It is this tension which forms the small holes as the stitch is worked. It is possible to work four-sided stitch on Aida fabric but is not recommended.

✕✕✕✕✕

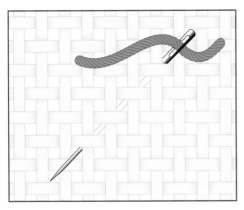

1 *To work four-sided stitch, begin to the left of a vertical thread and work a horizontal straight stitch across four threads (or the number indicated on the chart), passing the needle diagonally across four threads at the back of the work.*

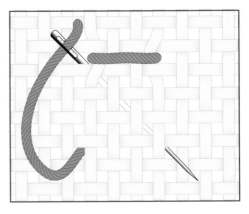

2 *Bring the needle up and form a vertical straight stitch, again passing the needle diagonally across four threads at the back of the work.*

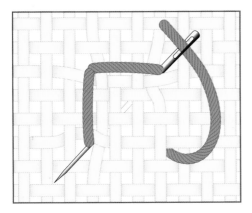

3 *Bring the needle up and form another vertical straight stitch, again passing the needle diagonally across four threads at the back.*

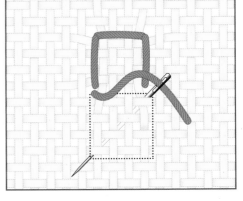

4 *Work a horizontal straight stitch to form the last side of the square but this time pass the needle across diagonally to begin the next stitch.*

Hem Stitch

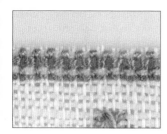

When working hem stitches for the first time it is simple to work them without removing any threads, eliminating the anxiety of cutting too many! When you have perfected the stitch you can experiment with thread removal. As you can see from the diagrams the stitch is made up of parts, two straight stitches and one diagonal on the back. It is this combination which forms the safe barrier if threads are to be cut or removed. If you are intending to cut to the edge, you may prefer to use double hem stitch as described overleaf. Hem stitch can look very effective worked in rows without any threads removed. This stitch is not suitable for Aida.

✗✗✗✗✗

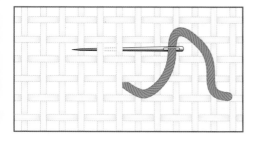

1 *This shows hem stitching over two threads in each direction. Work a straight stitch across two threads, turning the needle to face horizontally.*

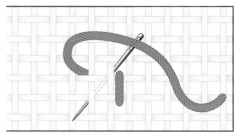

2 *Make another straight stitch across two threads, at right angles to the first stitch, then pass the needle down diagonally under two threads.*

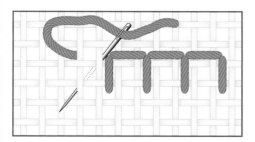

3 *Repeat the straight stitches along the row, counting carefully.*

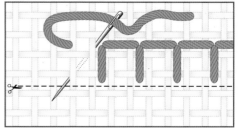

4 *After the hem stitching is complete, the threads indicated may be cut away.*

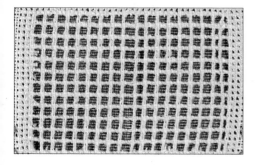

This detail from the Spring Sampler on page 90 illustrates two rows of hem stitching.

Double Hem Stitch

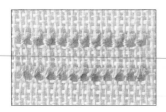

This stitch is formed in the same manner as single hem stitch but worked twice. If you intend to cut to the edge of the stitching and are nervous about it, work the stitches first, pull one thread out adjacent to the stitches and then cut away any excess. The needle should be straight on the front of the work, diagonal on the back. Both single and double hem stitch are usually worked in the same shade as the fabric.

✕✕✕✕✕

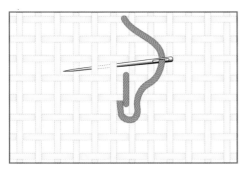

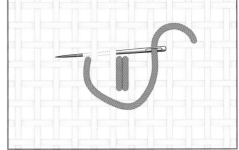

1 *This diagram shows double hem stitching over two threads in each direction. Work two vertical stitches across two threads, turning the needle to face horizontally.*

2 *Work across two threads passing the needle across horizontally under the two threads. Work this stitch twice and note the stitches share entry and exit points.*

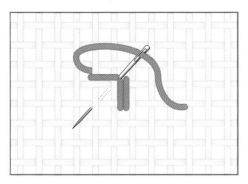

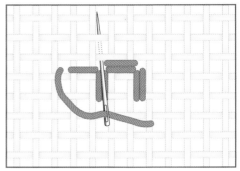

3 *Pass the needle diagonally across the two threads prior to repeating the stitch. Repeat the straight and diagonal stitches along the row counting carefully and checking that the needle travels diagonally at the back of the work.*

4 *This diagram shows how to turn a corner neatly whilst hem stitching.*

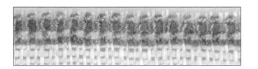

The edge of the space-dyed bookmark (see page 51) showing double hem stitch.

Hem Stitch Variations

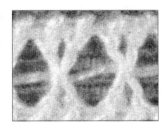

This exquisite group of decorative filling stitches are formed on the remaining vertical threads after hem stitching and thread withdrawal. When working the stitches described here, it is important to refer also to the descriptions of Pulled and Drawn Thread (page 66) and Hem Stitching (page 68). With dozens of filling styles used for decorating and strengthening the remaining threads after thread withdrawal, I can only show a few examples here.

✕✕✕✕✕

Somersault Stitch

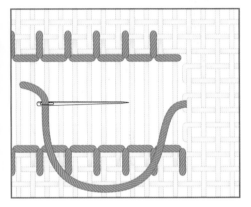

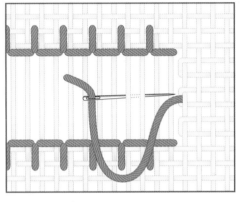

1 *To work a row of somersault stitches on groups of two threads within a hem-stitched frame, first remove the number of fabric threads indicated on the chart you are following. Start with a waste knot and bring the needle up where indicated.*

2 *Count four fabric threads and insert the needle under two threads amd up between the two pairs, so the needle is positioned over the second pair of threads. Don't pull the needle through the work yet.*

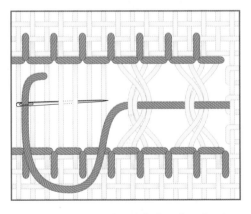

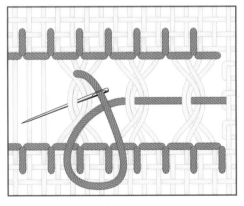

3 *Without removing the needle from these threads, twist the needle until it faces the other way. The threads will twist automatically as you do this.*

4 *Pinch your fingers together over this stitch and gently pull the needle through, keeping the thread horizontal and taut. Repeat this process down the row, fastening off into the fabric edge.*

Double Somersault Stitch

Double somersault stitch is worked in exactly the same way as normal somersault stitch, creating a wonderfully decorative look. It may be worked across large areas of withdrawn threads although it is difficult to keep the lines neat when more than one row is worked.

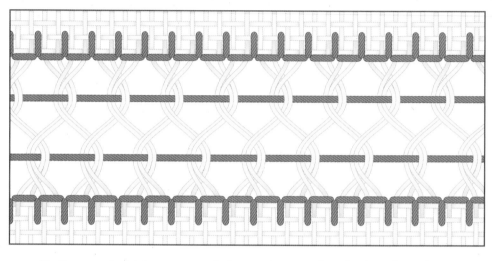

Double somersault stitch has two rows worked on opposite groups of two threads. Perfect stitches should be evenly worked and the lines between the stitches should be as straight as possible.

Tied Hem Stitch

This pretty but very simple hem stitch variation is created by hem stitching two rows, withdrawing the intervening threads and then simply using the needle to tie groups of threads together as shown in the diagrams. Keep the knotted lines as straight as you can.

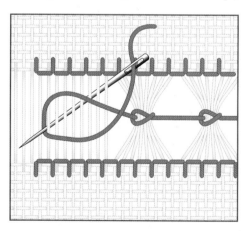

1 *Begin in the same way as somersault stitch, then take the needle and thread over a group of four threads, knotting them around as shown.*

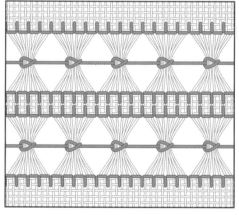

2 *The secret of perfection is to ensure that the tying thread is as straight as possible.*

Buttonhole Stitch

The buttonhole stitches illustrated here are included to allow you to produce projects like the Hardanger coaster heart (shown right and described on page 73). The cross stitch and Hardanger embroidery is completed, then buttonhole stitches are worked around the perimeter so the shape can be cut out without fear of the design falling to pieces!

×××××

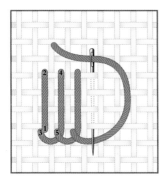

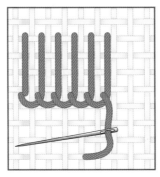

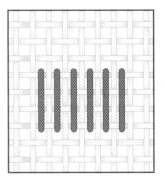

To work buttonhole stitch, start with an away waste knot (see page 18) and work long stitches over four threads (similar to Kloster blocks).

Keep the stitches flat against the fabric and as consistent as possible.

This shows what the stitching should look like at the back.

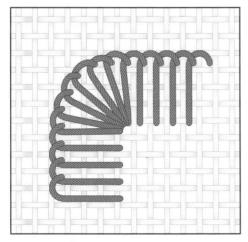

When you turn outer corners in buttonhole stitch, note that the corner hole holds seven threads.

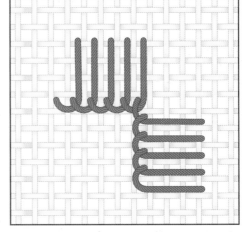

When turning internal corners, note the way the corner stitches are connected.

French Knot

French knots are small but very important stitches but probably cause more distress than any other stitch as they can disappear to the back of the work or worse still, end up as a row of tiny knots on the thread in the needle. They are often crucial to a design as probably their most common use is adding tiny eyes to cross stitched faces.

✕✕✕✕✕

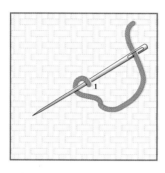

1 *To work a French knot, bring the needle through to the front of the fabric and wind the thread around the needle twice.*

2 *Begin to 'post' the needle partly through to the back, one thread or part of a block away from the entry point. (This will stop the stitch being pulled to the wrong side.)*

3 *Gently pull the thread you have wound so that it sits snugly at the point where the needle enters the fabric. Pull the needle through to the back and you should have a perfect knot in position. If you want bigger knots, add more thread to the needle as this gives a better result than winding more times round the needle.*

Palestrina Knot

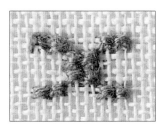

A palestrina knot (see the detail left and the photograph of the decorative thistle on page 116) is a truly counted stitch and is ideal when a uniform and carefully centred stitch is needed. With the best will in the world, French knots do have a habit of wandering on the surface of the fabric whereas a palestrina knot is centred on the square. It can be formed on Aida or even-weave. It takes a little practice so try it on a spare piece of fabric.

✕✕✕✕✕

✳ *Decorative Thistle* ✳

Stitch Count: 56 x 86
Design Size: 10 x 16cm
(4 x 6¹/₄in)
Fabric Selection: Grey Jobelan
27/28 threads to 2.5cm (1in)
Tapestry Needle Size: 24

This gorgeous thistle design (left) was stitched using stranded cotton (floss) and stranded metallic gold thread. The flower head was outlined in back stitch worked from the chart on page 147 and then completely filled in using random French knots and tiny glass beads (from Beadesign – see Suppliers). The stem and leaves are worked in cross stitch with a little back stitch outline. The corner border motifs are worked in a combination of palestrina knots and cross stitch. See Working the Projects page 126.

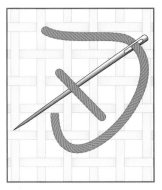

1 *A palestrina knot is formed on the surface of the fabric and occupies the same space as one cross stitch. Start to the left of a vertical thread and form a half cross stitch. Instead of completing the cross stitch, pass the needle under the diagonal stitch to form a loop, keeping the leading thread fairly taut.*

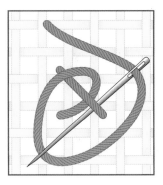

2 *Pass the needle under the diagonal stitch, again forming a second loop and pulling the knot formed firmly.*

3 *Pass the needle down through the fabric in the place indicated in the diagram to complete the square.*

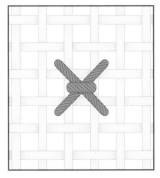

4 *When the stitch is complete, a palestrina knot should look rather like a cross stitch with a full bar across it.*

Bullion Stitch

This unusual stitch is not a counted stitch but can add a three-dimensional texture to a design. It can be formed in straight lines, adapted to make a raised bar, and can also be made to curve for petal shapes and for building up roses (see below). Bullion bars are easier to form using a gold-plated needle! Don't panic when you reach fig 4 – careful teasing with a needle will rescue the apparent disaster.

✕✕✕✕✕

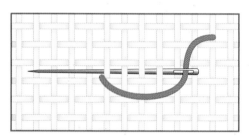

1 To work a straight bullion stitch or bar, start with a back stitch the same length and in the same position as you want the finished bar to be. Do not complete the back stitch but leave the needle in the fabric. It is vital that the point of the needle exits from the hole where it started.

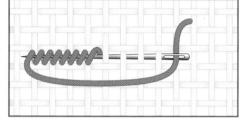

2 Wind the thread round the needle as many times as necessary to make the coil the intended length of the finished bar.

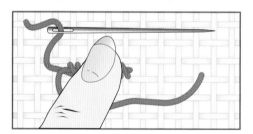

3 Hold the needle and its coil of thread firmly against the fabric with your thumb, then gently but firmly pull the needle through the coil and the fabric.

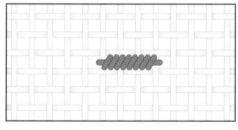

4 Turn the coil back on itself and push the needle through the fabric at the rear of the back stitch. If necessary, hold the thread firmly at the back of the fabric and tease the bullion stitch into shape.

To work bullion bars for the roses in the Bow Band Sampler on page 6, start in the same way as described above in Figs 1 and 2 but wind the thread around the needle more times; these added threads will force the stitch to curl when complete. Roses may be formed by working different lengths of curved bullion bars and by using a number of colours. As can be seen in the photograph, the rose was formed by working three French knots and then placing bullion bars around them, anchoring them into position if necessary.

❊ Framed Canvas Stitch Sampler and ❊ Canvas Stitch Scissors Keeper

Stitch Count: 31 x 31
Design Size: 6 x 6cm (2¼ x 2¼in)
Fabric Selection: Grey Jobelan 27/28 threads to 2.5cm (1in)
Tapestry Needle Size: 22

These two designs are by Sue Hawkins, author, designer and Technical Director of the Cross Stitch Guild. Both are stitched on 14-count single canvas using three strands of Appleton crewel wool over one thread of canvas. The sampler includes Rhodes stitch, tent stitch, satin stitch and long-legged cross stitch and is charted on page 152. To work the sampler, complete the four textured squares as on the chart, then work around the edge with long-legged cross stitch. Add one or two rows of tent stitch as necessary to fill the aperture of your frame so no unstitched canvas shows.

The scissors keeper is not charted but shows what can be achieved by mixing stitches. It includes queen stitch, long-legged cross stitch, tent stitch, French knots, rice stitch and vertical double cross stitch. It has been made up with a twisted cord and a tassel (see page 186).

Wrapped Bars and Spider's Webs

When working the stitches described here, it is important to refer back to the Hardanger Embroidery section (page 70), where all the principles and techniques are described in more detail. The description of these stitches is merely an introduction to the fun that can be had combining them with cross stitch.

After Kloster blocks have been formed (see page 70/71) and the threads have been cut and removed (see page 72) the four remaining threads are reinforced in a decorative fashion using wrapping or needleweaving. Additional decorative elements may be added whilst this is being stitched, such as spider's web stitch with wrapped bars and picots with needleweaving (see page 122).

Needleweaving or wrapping is traditionally done with a finer perlé cotton than that used for stitching the Kloster blocks. Needleweaving (see page 74) involves the thread being woven over and under the threads that remain after cutting. Wrapping bars simply means that the thread is wound around and around two or four threads after cutting. To work these stitches, follow the sequence in the diagrams, ensuring that you work each section in the same manner, counting the wraps or weaves.

✕✕✕✕✕

Wrapped Bars

Wrapped bars may be worked alone to decorate the threads that remain after cutting, or as part of other decorative stitches, such as spider's webs shown opposite. As you wrap each bar you will need to hold the threads you are wrapping quite firmly to prevent them from unravelling as you work. It does take a little practise before your wrapped bars look perfect.

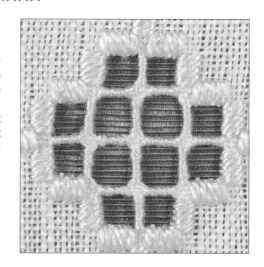

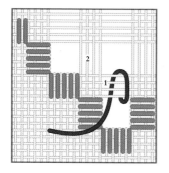

1 *Start by anchoring the thread under adjacent Kloster blocks and begin wrapping from a cut area.*

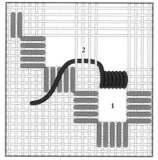

2 *Wind the thread around and around the four threads as shown, then travel to the next group of threads.*

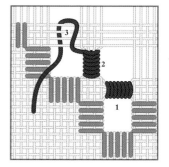

3 *Continue wrapping the bars around as shown, keeping a check on how many times each set is wrapped and keeping all the stitches consistent.*

Spider's Web Stitch

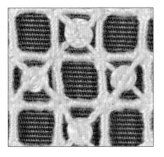

Spider's web is a traditional filling stitch used to decorate the voids left by cutting threads and it is often used with wrapped bars. As with all these stitches although they are not counted it is a good idea to keep notes of numbers of winds and weaves to ensure the stitches are uniform.

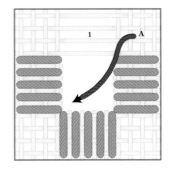

1 *Work three sides in Kloster blocks, wrapped bars or a combination of both as seen here, bringing the needle out at A.*

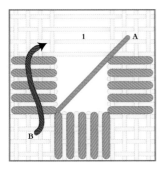

2 *Cross the square, bringing the needle out at B.*

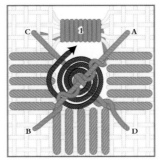

3 *Return to A, winding the thread around the diagonal just formed, ready to complete the final side, shown as a wrapped bar in fig 4.*

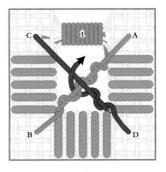

4 *Bring the needle up at C and pass diagonally to D, then wind the thread around the diagonal to the centre (as shown in step 3).*

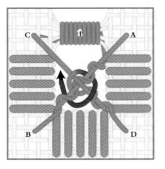

5 *Start weaving the spider's web around the diagonals as shown.*

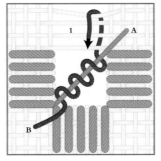

6 *After three winds you may need to tighten and adjust the position of the winds to ensure they are even and in the centre of the square.*

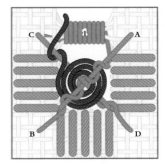

7 *When the web is complete, leave the stitch by winding around the diagonal as before.*

Needleweaving, Picots and Dove's Eyes

Needleweaving

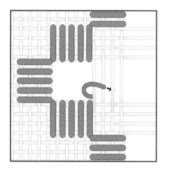

Needleweaving is used on the loose threads that are left when stitched Kloster blocks have been cut, especially over large areas. The needleweaving creates covered bars, and the spaces between the bars can be filled with decorative stitches such as dove's eye (see opposite). The bars themselves can also be decorated with stitches such as picots (see opposite). When working the stitches described here, it is important to refer back to the section on Hardanger (page 70).

✕✕✕✕✕

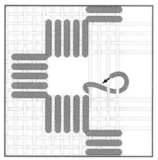

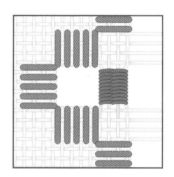

1 *To needleweave, start by anchoring the thread under adjacent Kloster blocks on the reverse of the work.*

2 *Beginning from a cut area, bring the needle up through a void area.*

3 *Weave the needle under and over pairs of threads to form a plaited effect. These stitches should not distort or bend the threads.*

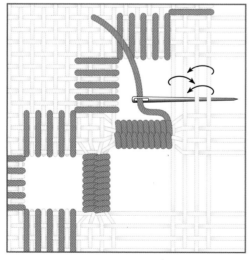

4 *After completing one bar, weave the next one at right angles to it, working around the design and taking care not to run threads across the back of the cut area.*

This shows a detail of some of the needleweaving in the Hardanger Flower Needlecase shown on page 75.

Picots

These pretty, decorative elements are worked as you wrap or needleweave the remaining threads after cutting, taking care to work each section in a uniform style. It will take a little practise to perfect these stitches but when worked they are very effective.

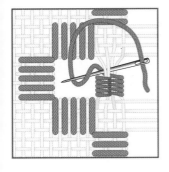

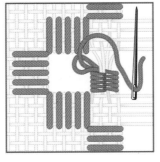

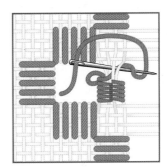

1 *After cutting the threads, needleweave halfway along a set of four threads as described in needleweaving on page 122. Bring the needle out at the side to form the picot. Pass the needle under two threads on the same side and wrap the thread around the needle as shown.*

2 *Pull the needle through carefully, holding the wrapped thread in position. Do not pull too tightly. Pass the needle through the centre of the four fabric threads, ready to make another picot along the other edge in the same way.*

3 *Once both picots have been formed the needleweaving can be completed. Keep a record of how many weaves you make either side of the picots with the aim of keeping all the stitches consistent.*

Dove's Eye Stitch

Dove's eye stitch is a traditional Hardanger stitch which is constructed whilst needleweaving. It is possible to add it as an afterthought but this is not recommended. The stitch should be with the diamond-shaped hole forming in the centre of the void left by cutting. This may take practice and need a 'little pinching and pulling' to achieve perfect results. Refer also to the Hardanger section starting on page 70.

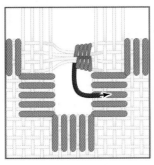

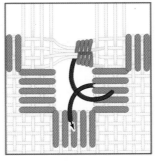

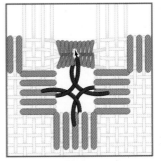

1 *Whilst working the last side of a square, needleweave to the centre of the bar, bringing the needle out through the void area.*

2 *Pierce the neighbouring Kloster block or needlewoven bar halfway along its length, bringing the needle up through the void and through the loop formed by the thread.*

3 *Continue around the square following the sequence in the diagram, but before resuming the needleweaving, loop the needle under the first stitch to form the final twist in the dove's eye.*

✳ *The Winter Sampler* ✳

Stitch Count: 88 x 162
Design Size: 16.5 x 29.5cm (6½ x 11¾in)
Fabric Selection: Zweigart Cashel linen 28 threads to 2.5cm (1in)
Tapestry Needle Size: 24

This is the last of the four seasonal samplers. It is worked as a band sampler and the stitches needed are described on the chart on pages 175–177 and include cross stitch, back stitch and a number of more unusual counted stitches, pulled thread work and Hardanger embroidery. All the stitches in this sampler are included in the Stitch Library but I recommend that you also read Pulled and Drawn Thread Work and Hardanger Embroidery (pages 66 and 70) before starting to stitch.

The chart is over three pages with no overlapping. You might find it easiest to photocopy the parts and tape them together.

Using stranded cottons (floss) unless otherwise stated, work the cross stitch first, followed by the additional counted stitches and then the Hardanger and other pulled or drawn stitches. Refer to the Stitch Library for the stitch diagrams and relevant instructions as you need them.

Work the Bands as follows:
• Use two strands of stranded cotton for the full and three-quarter cross stitches, eyelet stitches, herringbone, double cross stitch, Algerian eye, French knots, hem stitch, bullion knots and queen stitch.
• Use three strands of stranded cotton for the satin stitch.
• Add back stitch outline where required, using one strand of the colour indicated on the chart
• Work the vertical rice stitch in two colours, the large cross over *four* threads in two strands of stranded cotton and add the small stitches in one strand of gold metallic.
• When working the Algerian eye and double cross stitch, check on the chart whether they are worked over two or four threads.
• For the French knots in the centre of the Christmas roses, work the stitches at random,

piling them in groups as shown.
• To form the yellow roses in the top section, work three small French knots in pale green stranded cotton (floss) 368 and then work the bullion bars, filling the needle full to force the stitch to curl slightly.
• Work one row of four-sided stitch around the square as shown on the chart, but work over four threads instead of two.
• For the herringbone, work the top row in 3740 followed by 676 offset by one stitch.
• For the somersault stitch, work two rows of hem stitch following the chart. Working from the centre of the hem-stitched box, carefully snip each horizontal linen thread down the centre line once and using a needle, un-pick the linen threads back to the two outside edges and carefully weave the threads into the fabric thus forming a selvedge. You should be left with vertical threads only.
• Referring to the diagrams on page 113 work one row of somersault stitch as indicated on the chart.

Work the Hardanger as follows:
• Work the Kloster blocks using one strand of perlé cotton No. 5, counting over four threads of the linen. Keep checking that the blocks are directly opposite each other, referring to the diagrams as necessary.
• When all the Kloster blocks are complete, use very sharp, pointed scissors to cut across the ends of the blocks. Take this section slowly, counting and cutting two threads each time.
• Needleweave the remaining linen threads using one strand of perlé cotton No. 8 adding spider's web filling stitch as indicated.
• The diagonal threads included in the two bottom, outer Hardanger motifs are added as the bars are wrapped (as the first stage of the spider's web filling shown on page 121).

Working The Projects

These project instructions are intended for the less experienced stitcher, particularly those who have in the past stitched mainly from kits or perhaps chart packs. The idea of starting a project from scratch is sometimes very daunting so I have included the most useful instructions here so that you can find them at a glance. Refer also to Starting to Stitch on page 16 for further information.

Which Threads Do I Need?

• Each design is charted in the Motif Library with the colour key listing the threads needed to work the project.

Which Fabric and How Much?

• The fabric used, the design size and stitch count of the design is included in the caption under the colour picture.

• If you are working the design exactly as photographed just add a margin of 12.5cm (5in) to the design size and you can move on to 'Where Do I Start'.

• If you wish to use alternative fabrics you must check the thread count of the material and if this is different to that of the stitched sample you must work out the finished design size. To check the thread count of a particular fabric, lay a ruler on top of the material and using a needle

✳ Winter Gable Cottage ✳
Stitch Count: 60 x 80
Design Size: 11.5 x 5cm (4½ x 2in)
Fabric Selection: Grey Jobelan 27/28 threads to 2.5cm (1in)
Tapestry Needle Size: 24

This charming design was stitched in two strands of stranded cotton (floss) for the cross stitch and one strand for the back stitch outline. The chart is on page 159 of the Motif Library. See Working the Projects.

count the number of threads or blocks to 2.5cm (1in) and this will tell you the stitch count. (A larger thread count will produce a larger stitched design.) To work out the design size refer to Calculating Design Size on page 17.

Where Do I Start?

• Start stitching in the middle of the design to ensure an adequate margin for stretching and framing.

• To find the middle of the fabric, fold it in four and press lightly. Open out and work a narrow line of tacking (basting) stitches following the threads to mark the fold and the centre. These stitches are removed when the work is completed.

Before You Start

• Rule a line on the chart (if using a copy) to match the tacking (basting) stitches on the fabric.

• Check you have all the colours you need and mount all the threads on a piece of card alongside its shade number (see page 15).

• Sew a narrow hem or oversew the raw edges to prevent fraying. This can be removed on completion. Avoid sticky tape and any clear glues as they have a habit of creeping and will attract grime to your fabric.

• Work one large cross stitch at the top of your work away from the stitching to remind you which is the top and which way the work is facing.

How Many Strands?

• If the chart you wish to stitch does not indicate how many strands of stranded cotton to use, check by carefully pulling a thread from the edge of the fabric and comparing it with the strands of cotton. The threads on the needle should be a similar weight to the threads in the fabric.

• If using alternative threads to the ones used in the stitched sample, try working a few stitches in the fabric margin to check the effect you will achieve.

Finishing Work

• When you have completed the stitching, check the work for missed stitches and press ready for mounting or making up.

Motif Library

I have used a variety of stitched pieces in the book to illustrate a stitching technique or unusual type of thread and you will find the chart within this section of the book.

- The Motif Library charts are illustrated in colour with a black or white symbol added to aid colour identification and to make photocopying possible.
- Each square, both occupied and unoccupied, represents two threads of evenweave or one block of Aida unless stated otherwise.
- Each occupied square on a chart equals one stitch.
- A three-quarter cross stitch is shown as a triangle occupying half a square.
- All that determines the size of a cross stitch

design is the number stitches up and down and the choice of fabric.

- All of the designs in the Motif Library may be worked in cross stitch but you may like to experiment using other stitches.
- DMC stranded cottons were used but alternatives are given where appropriate, such as Anchor stranded cotton or Beadesign.
- Some of the designs are charted over two pages: there is no overlap, just continue stitching. You could photocopy the two parts of the charts and stick them together.
- Back stitches are shown by an arrow pointing to a solid line, with the DMC colour beside it.
- The four small arrows on each chart will help you find the centre quikly.

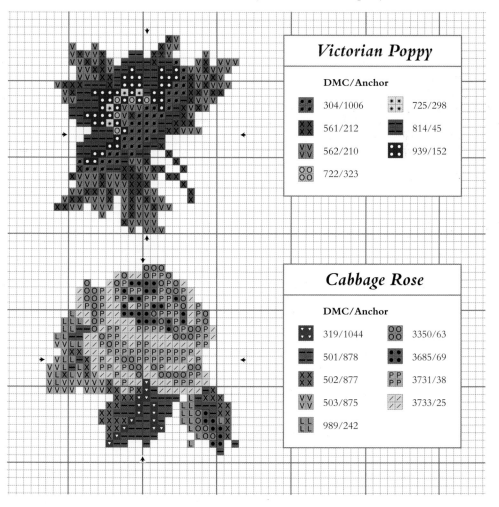

Victorian Poppy

DMC/Anchor

304/1006		725/298	
561/212		814/45	
562/210		939/152	
722/323			

Cabbage Rose

DMC/Anchor

319/1044		3350/63	
501/878		3685/69	
502/877		3731/38	
503/875		3733/25	
989/242			

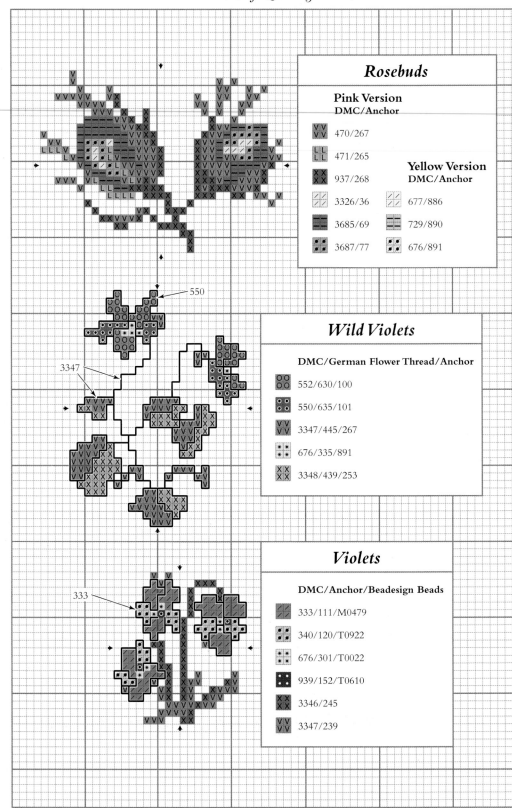

Rosebuds

Pink Version
DMC/Anchor

470/267

471/265

937/268

3326/36

3685/69

3687/77

Yellow Version
DMC/Anchor

677/886

729/890

676/891

Wild Violets

DMC/German Flower Thread/Anchor

552/630/100

550/635/101

3347/445/267

676/335/891

3348/439/253

550

3347

Violets

DMC/Anchor/Beadesign Beads

333/111/M0479

340/120/T0922

676/301/T0022

939/152/T0610

3346/245

3347/239

333

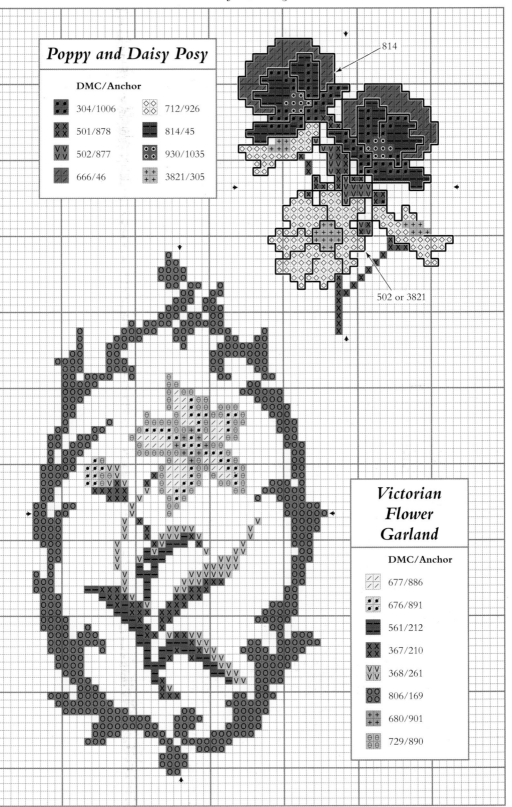

Poppy and Daisy Posy

DMC/Anchor

■	304/1006	◇◇	712/926
✗✗	501/878	■	814/45
ᴠᴠ	502/877	∘∘	930/1035
▨	666/46	✦✦	3821/305

814

502 or 3821

Victorian Flower Garland

DMC/Anchor

⁄⁄	677/886
∷	676/891
■	561/212
✗✗	367/210
ᴠᴠ	368/261
∘∘	806/169
✦✦	680/901
θθ	729/890

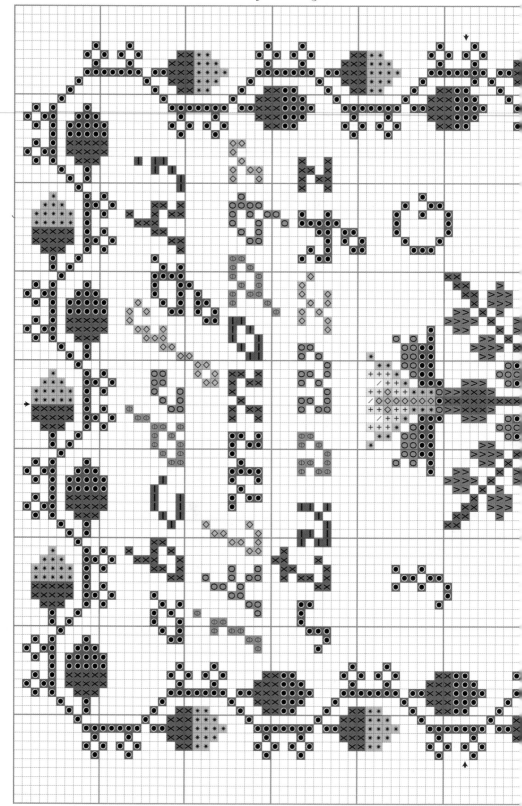

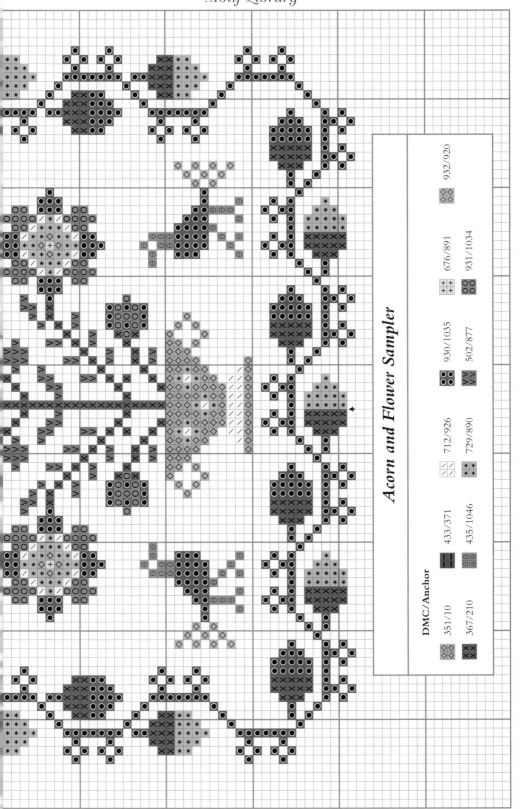

Acorn and Flower Sampler

DMC/Anchor			
351/10	433/371	712/926	930/1035	676/891	932/920
367/210	435/1046	729/890	502/877	931/1034	

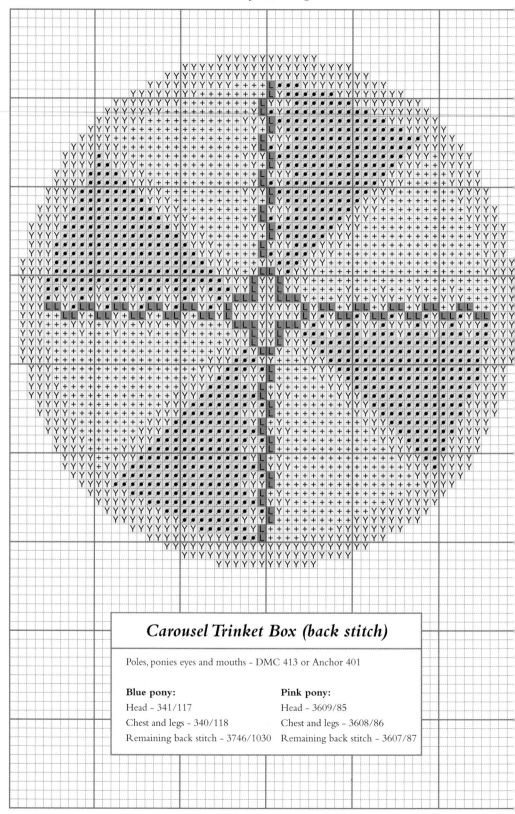

Carousel Trinket Box (back stitch)

Poles, ponies eyes and mouths – DMC 413 or Anchor 401

Blue pony:
Head – 341/117
Chest and legs – 340/118
Remaining back stitch – 3746/1030

Pink pony:
Head – 3609/85
Chest and legs – 3608/86
Remaining back stitch – 3607/87

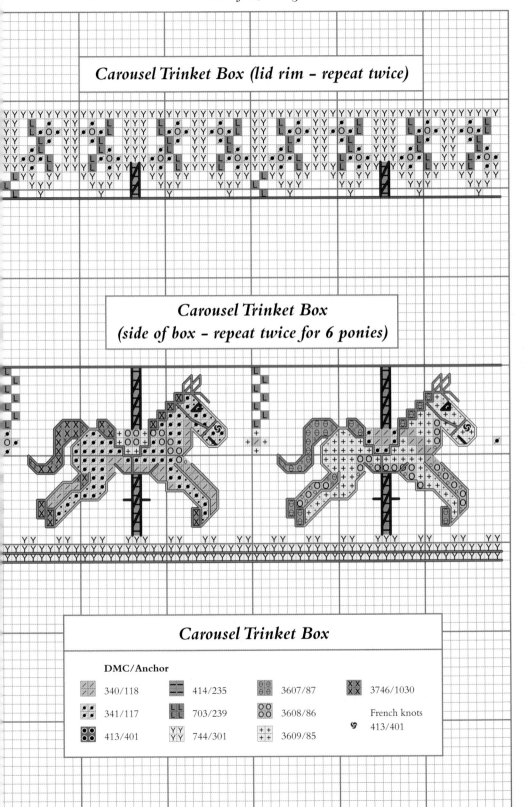

Carousel Trinket Box (lid rim – repeat twice)

Carousel Trinket Box
(side of box – repeat twice for 6 ponies)

Carousel Trinket Box

DMC/Anchor

340/118	414/235	3607/87	3746/1030
341/117	703/239	3608/86	French knots
413/401	744/301	3609/85	413/401

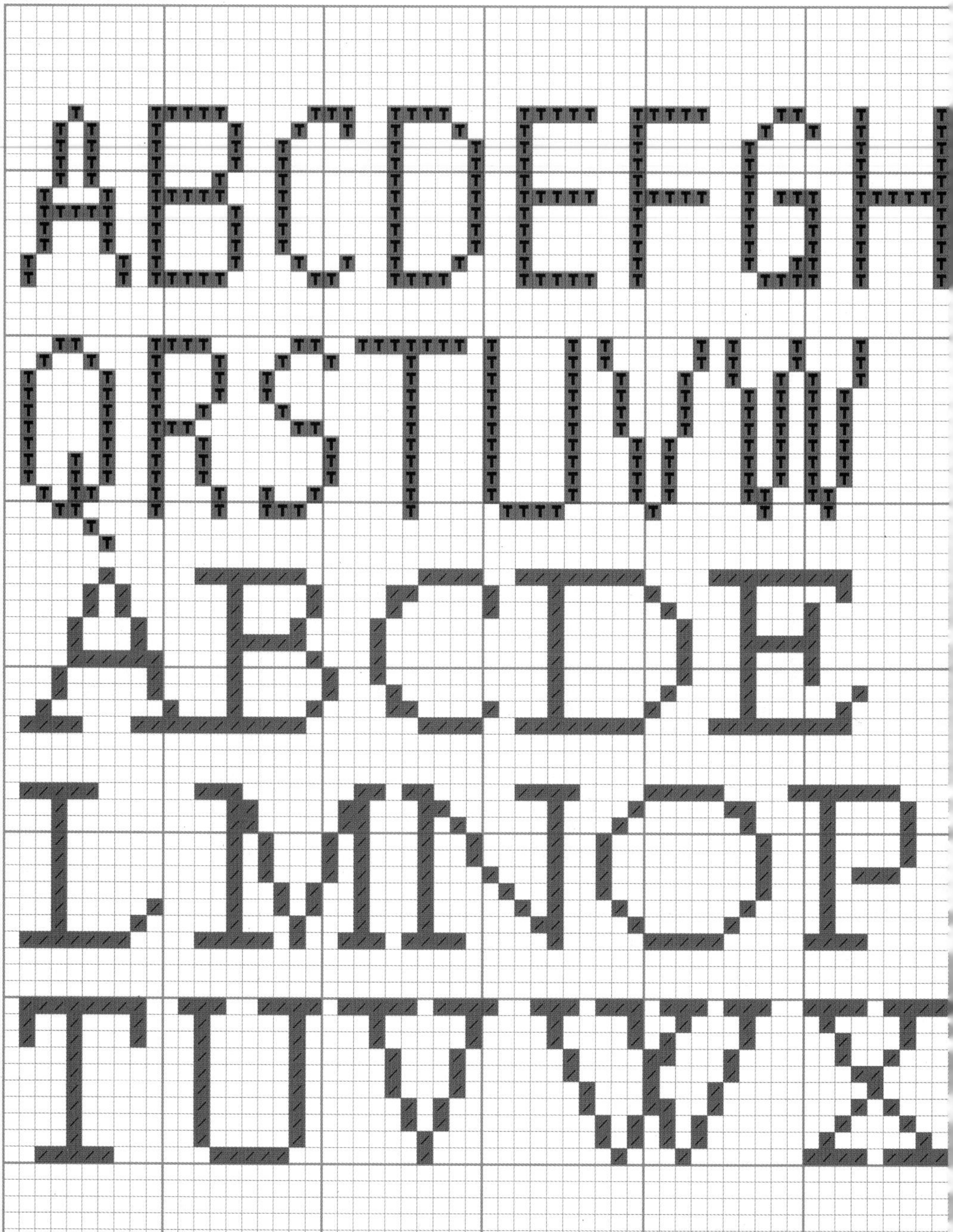

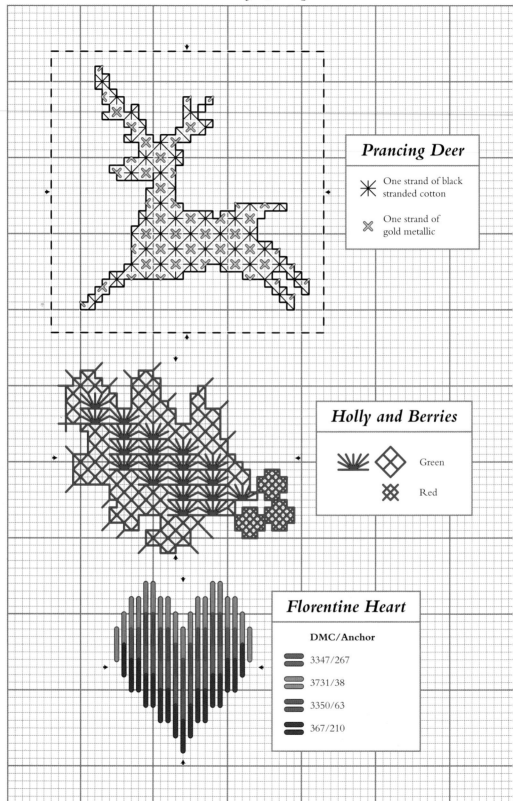

Prancing Deer

✳ One strand of black stranded cotton

✕ One strand of gold metallic

Holly and Berries

◇ Green

✕ Red

Florentine Heart

DMC/Anchor

▬ 3347/267

▬ 3731/38

▬ 3350/63

▬ 367/210

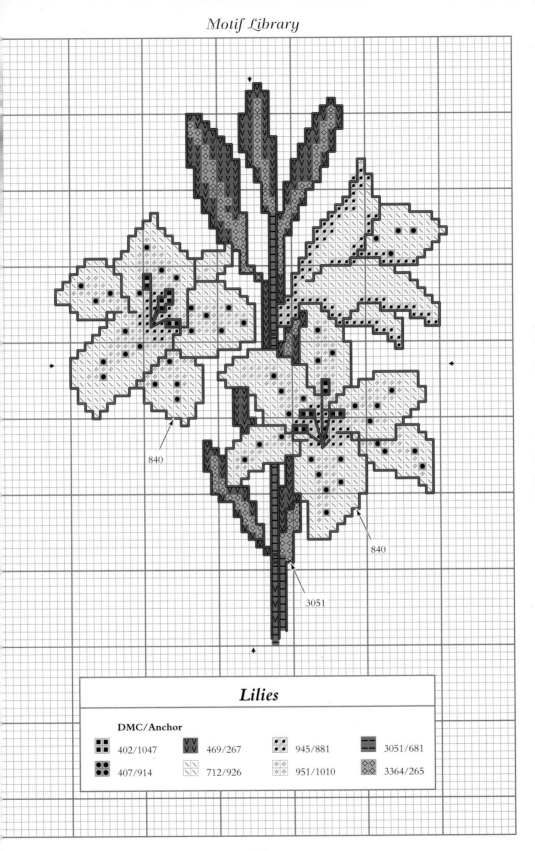

840

840

3051

Lilies

DMC/Anchor

402/1047	469/267	945/881	3051/681
407/914	712/926	951/1010	3364/265

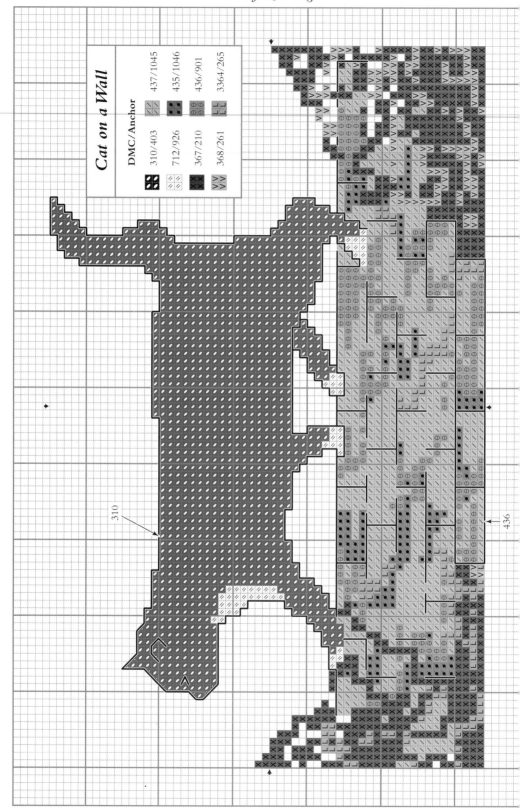

Cat on a Wall

DMC/Anchor

310/403 | 437/1045
712/926 | 435/1046
367/210 | 436/901
368/261 | 3364/265

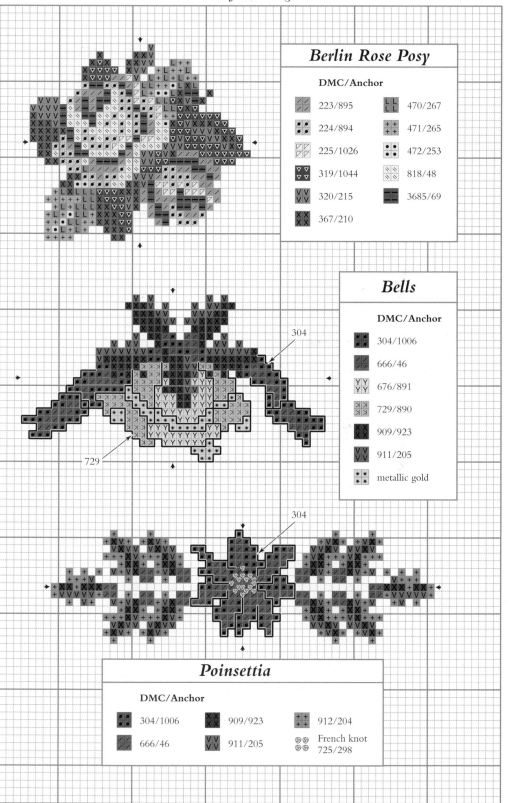

Berlin Rose Posy

DMC/Anchor

223/895			470/267
224/894			471/265
225/1026			472/253
319/1044			818/48
320/215			3685/69
367/210			

Bells

DMC/Anchor

304/1006	
666/46	
676/891	
729/890	
909/923	
911/205	
metallic gold	

304

729

304

Poinsettia

DMC/Anchor

304/1006		909/923		912/204	
666/46		911/205		French knot 725/298	

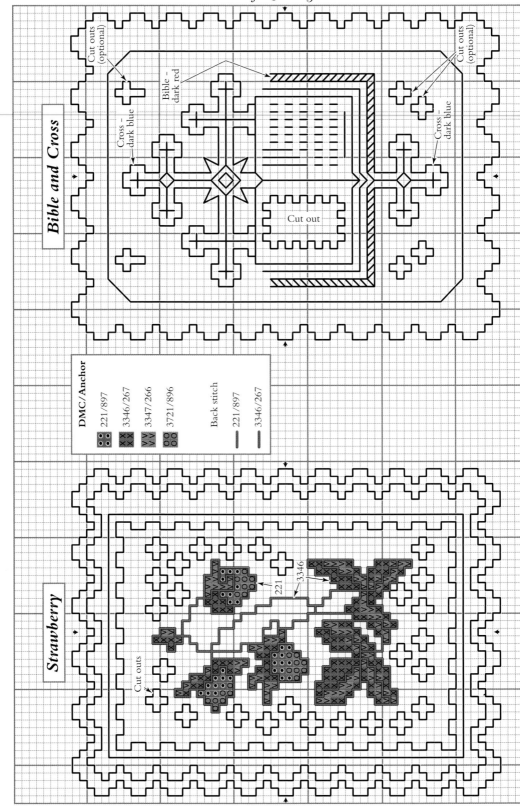

Bible and Cross

Cut outs (optional)

Cross – dark blue

Bible – dark red

Cut out

Cross – dark blue

Cut outs (optional)

DMC/Anchor

221/897
3346/267
3347/266
3721/896

Back stitch

221/897
3346/267

Strawberry

Cut outs

221

3346

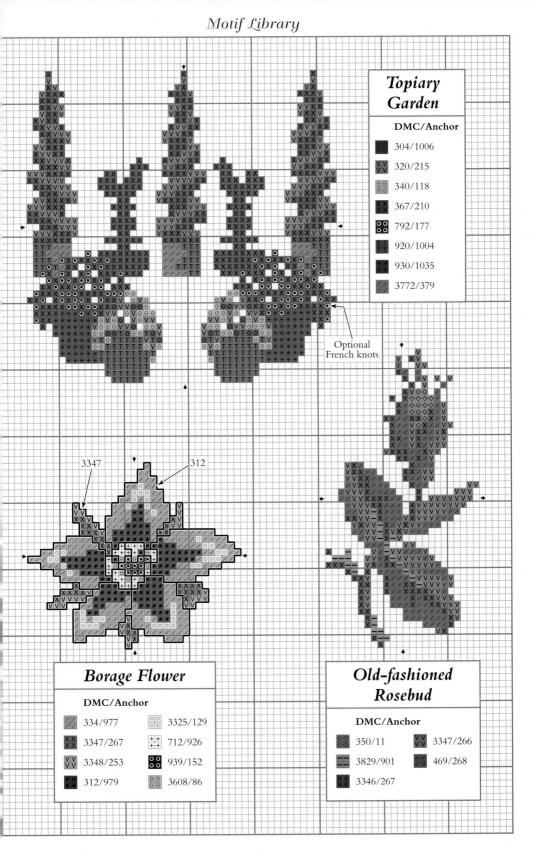

Topiary Garden

DMC/Anchor

	304/1006
	320/215
	340/118
	367/210
	792/177
	920/1004
	930/1035
	3772/379

Optional French knots

3347

312

Borage Flower

DMC/Anchor

	334/977		3325/129
	3347/267		712/926
	3348/253		939/152
	312/979		3608/86

Old-fashioned Rosebud

DMC/Anchor

	350/11		3347/266
	3829/901		469/268
	3346/267		

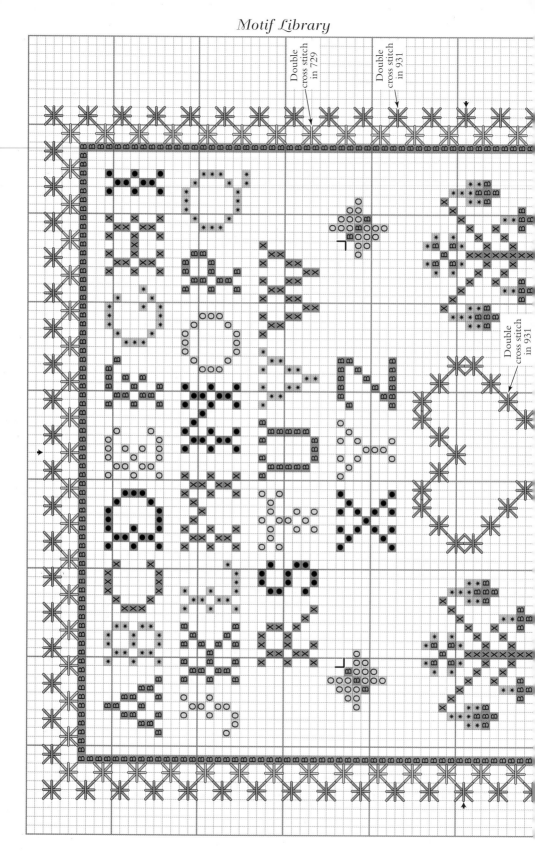

Double cross stitch in 729

Double cross stitch in 931

Double cross stitch in 931

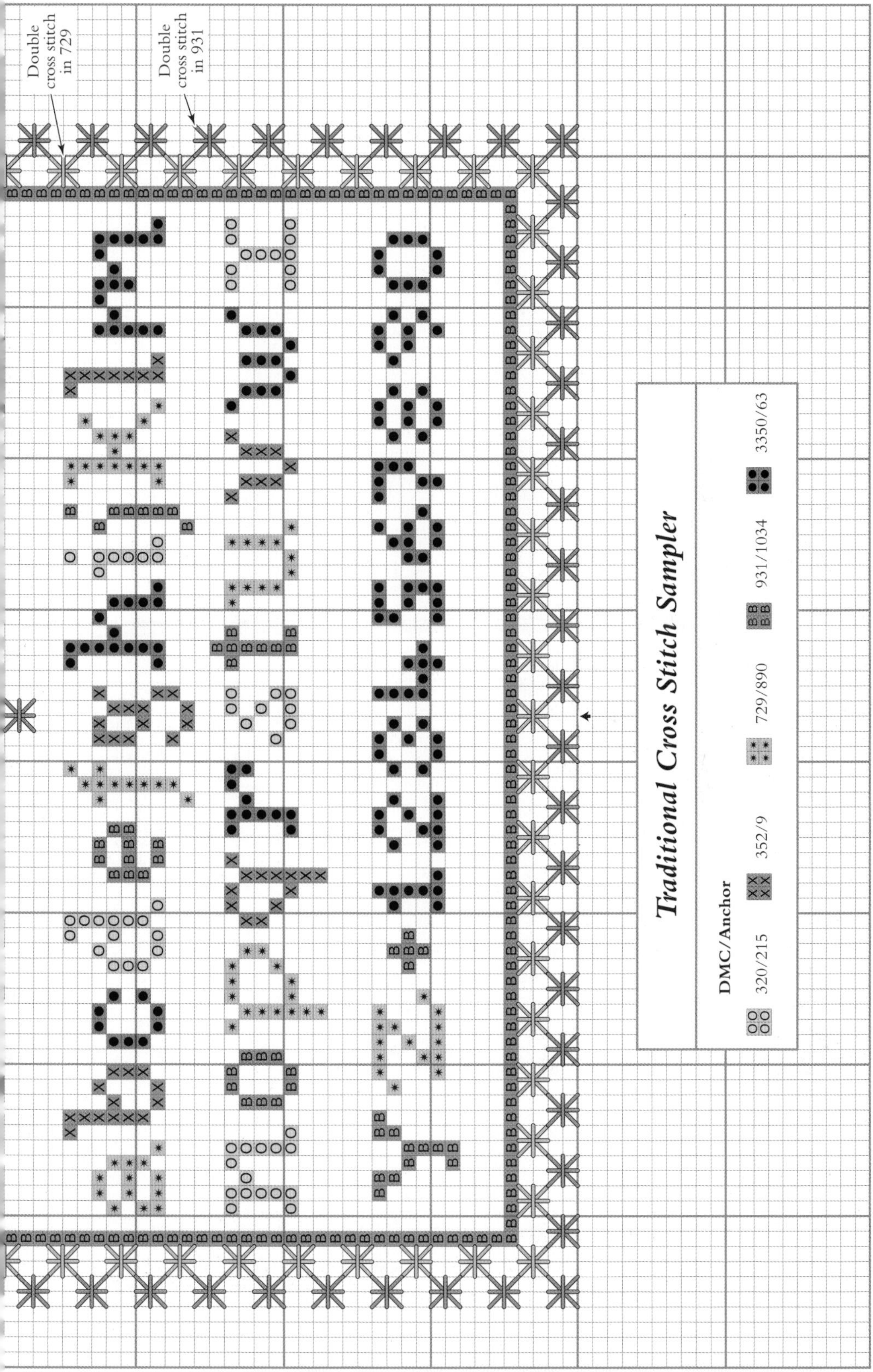

Double cross stitch in 729

Double cross stitch in 931

Traditional Cross Stitch Sampler

DMC/Anchor

OO OO 320/215	XX XX 352/9	** ** 729/890	
	BB BB 931/1034	●● ●● 3350/63	

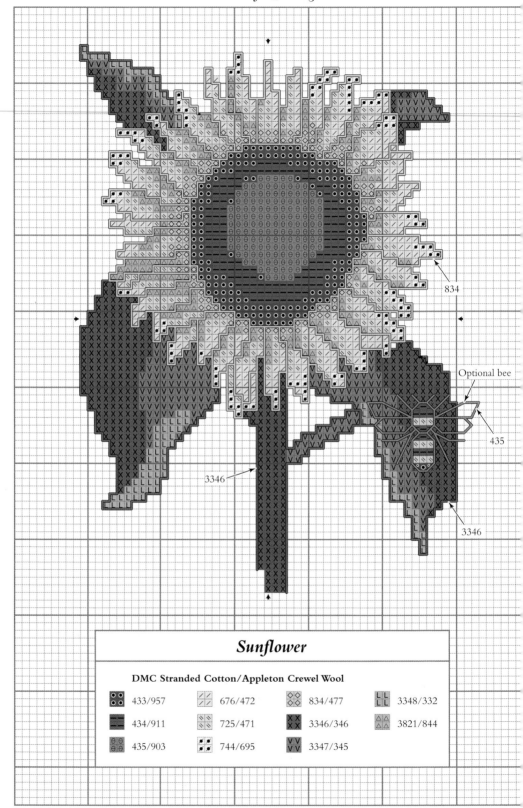

834

Optional bee

435

3346

3346

Sunflower

DMC Stranded Cotton/Appleton Crewel Wool

● ● 433/957	⁄ ⁄ 676/472	◇ ◇ 834/477	L L 3348/332
434/911	§ § 725/471	X X 3346/346	△ △ 3821/844
⊕ ⊕ 435/903	∴ 744/695	V V 3347/345	

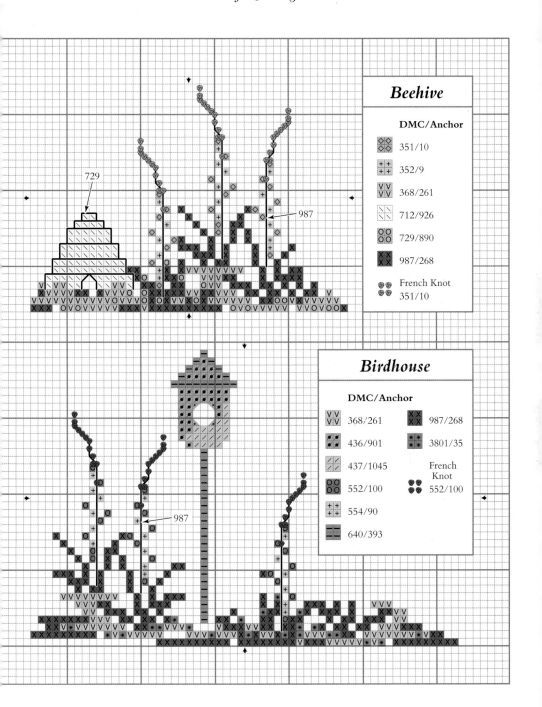

Beehive

DMC/Anchor

◇◇	351/10
++	352/9
VV	368/261
NN	712/926
OO	729/890
XX	987/268
French Knot	
	351/10

Birdhouse

DMC/Anchor

VV	368/261	XX	987/268
	436/901		3801/35
	437/1045	French Knot	
OO	552/100		552/100
++	554/90		
	640/393		

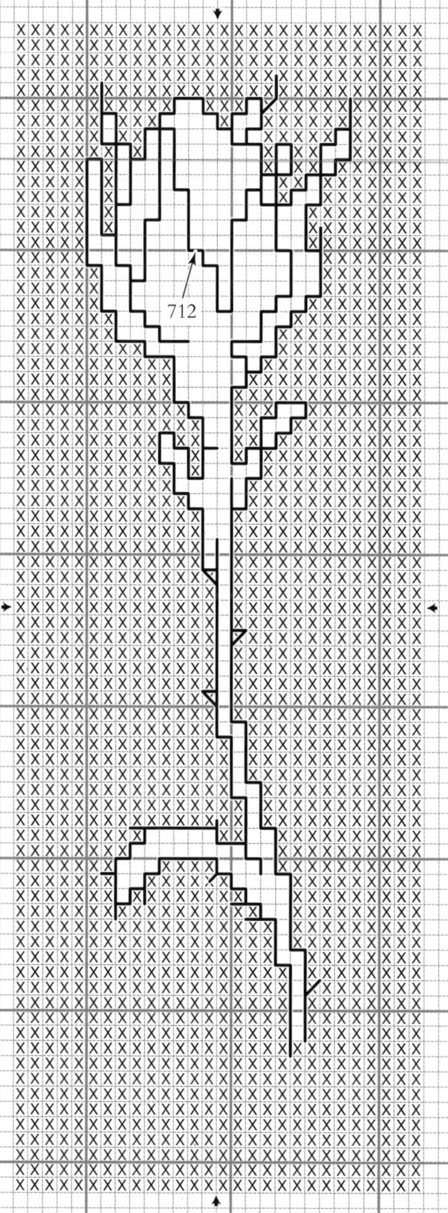

712

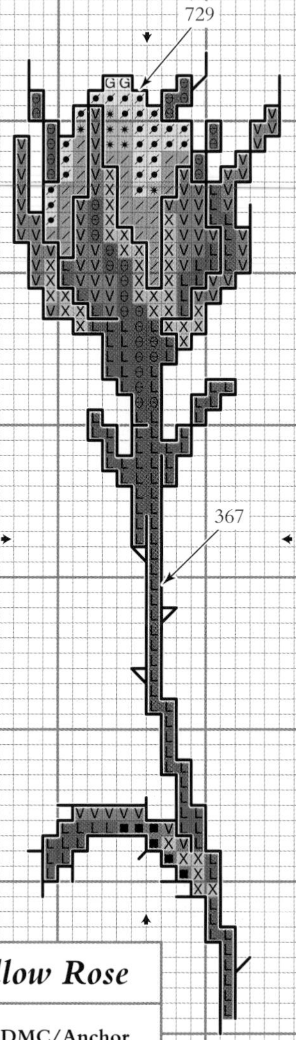

729

367

Yellow Rose

DMC/Anchor

367/210
676/891
G G / G G	677/886
680/901
729/890
3051/681
X X / X X	3053/261
L L / L L	3346/267
V V / V V	3347/266

Assisi Rose

DMC/Anchor

X X / X X 712/926 – or Caron Waterlilies 115
All background stitching

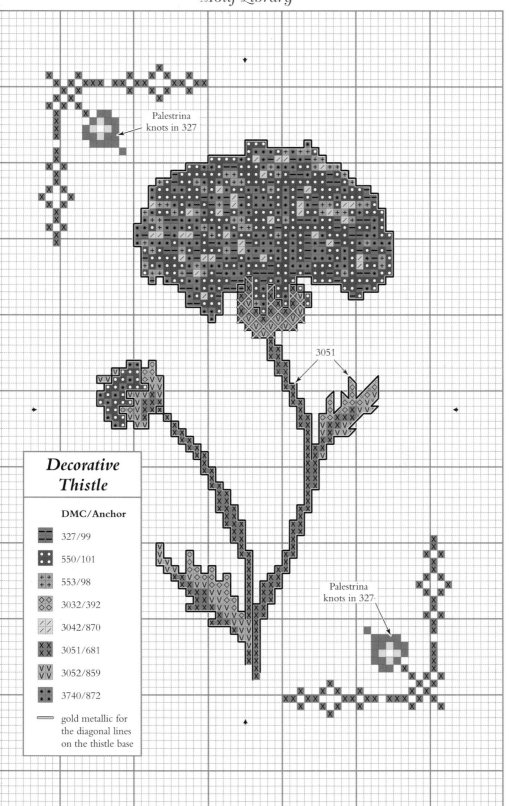

Palestrina
knots in 327

3051

**Decorative
Thistle**

DMC/Anchor

	327/99
	550/101
	553/98
	3032/392
	3042/870
	3051/681
	3052/859
	3740/872
—	gold metallic for the diagonal lines on the thistle base

Palestrina
knots in 327

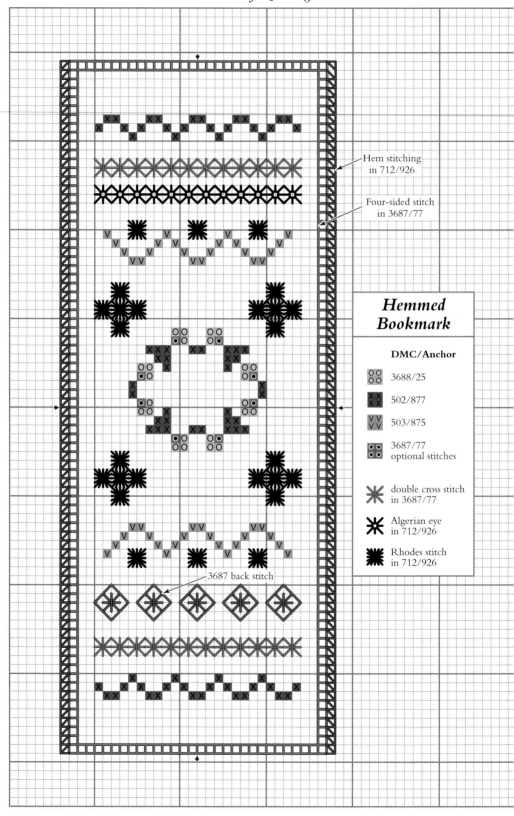

Hem stitching
in 712/926

Four-sided stitch
in 3687/77

Hemmed Bookmark

DMC/Anchor

3688/25

502/877

503/875

3687/77
optional stitches

double cross stitch
in 3687/77

Algerian eye
in 712/926

Rhodes stitch
in 712/926

3687 back stitch

Simple Sampler

DMC/Anchor

436/901	501/878	502/877	754/1012	931/1034	3350/63

436

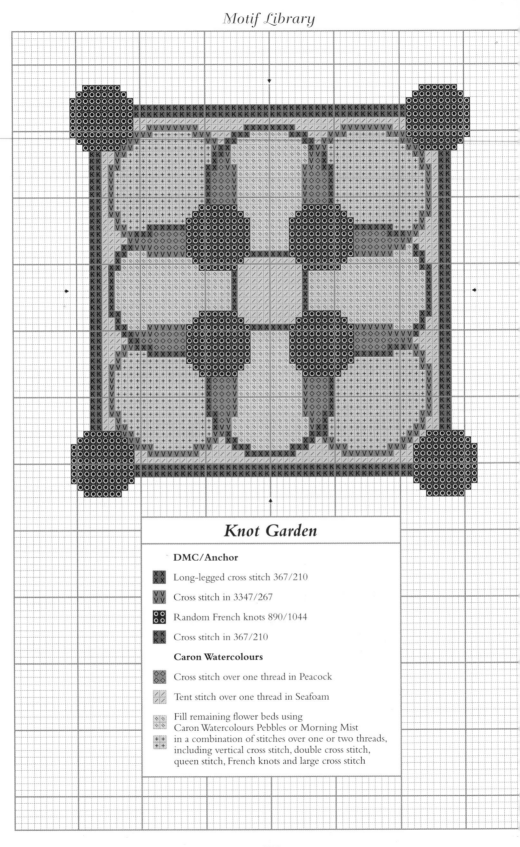

Knot Garden

DMC/Anchor

Long-legged cross stitch 367/210

Cross stitch in 3347/267

Random French knots 890/1044

Cross stitch in 367/210

Caron Watercolours

Cross stitch over one thread in Peacock

Tent stitch over one thread in Seafoam

Fill remaining flower beds using
Caron Watercolours Pebbles or Morning Mist
in a combination of stitches over one or two threads,
including vertical cross stitch, double cross stitch,
queen stitch, French knots and large cross stitch

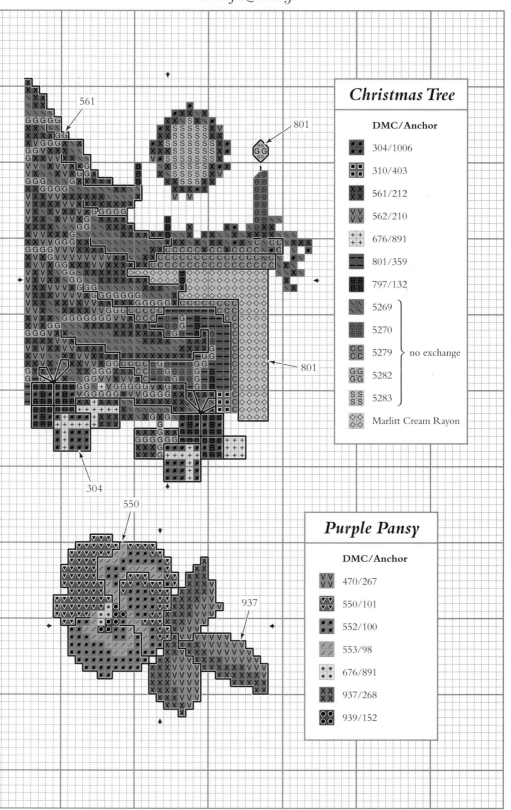

Christmas Tree

DMC/Anchor

	304/1006
	310/403
	561/212
	562/210
	676/891
	801/359
	797/132
	5269
	5270
	5279 no exchange
	5282
	5283
	Marlitt Cream Rayon

Purple Pansy

DMC/Anchor

	470/267
	550/101
	552/100
	553/98
	676/891
	937/268
	939/152

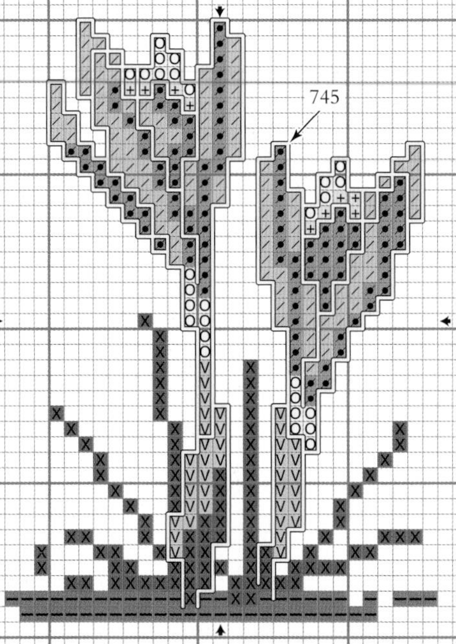

745

Purple Crocus

DMC/German Flower Thread

▨	208/3432	+	676/2084
▨	209/3332	○	745/3522
✕	367/3602	▬	840/3302
Ⅴ	368/2000		

Rhodes stitch

Satin stitch

Long-legged cross stitch

Long-legged cross stitch all round edge

Long-legged cross stitch

Long-legged cross stitch

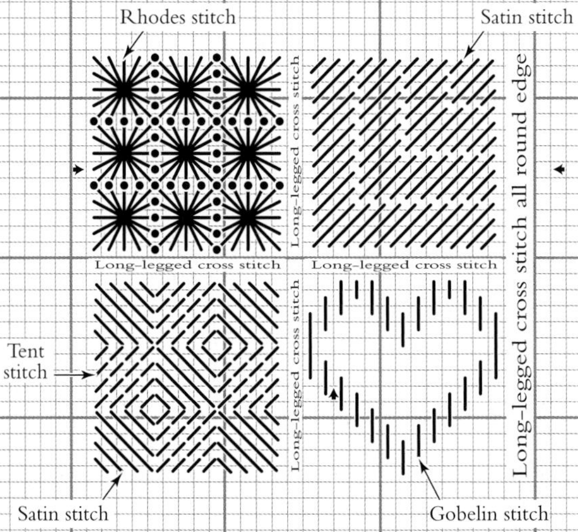

Canvas Stitch Sampler

Appleton Crewel Wool

205 - Pale Terracotta

722 - Dark Terracotta

335 - Green

692 - Pale Gold

695 - Dark Gold

Long-legged cross stitch –
select colours of your choice

Tent stitch

Satin stitch

Gobelin stitch

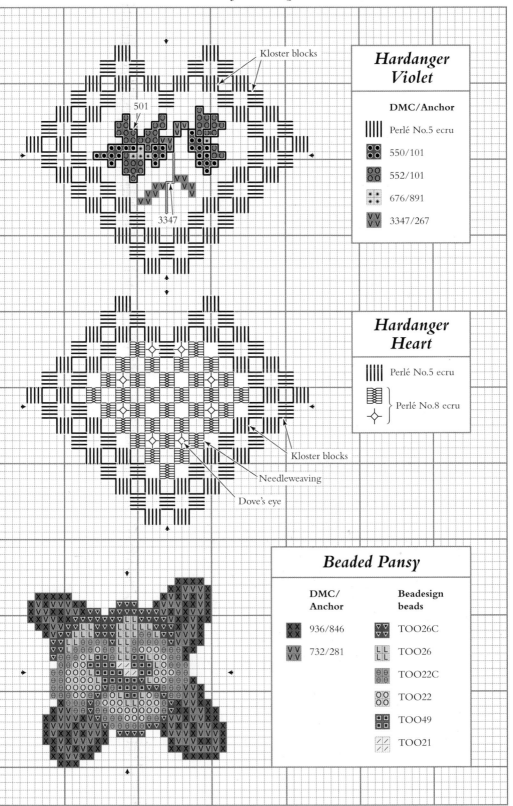

Kloster blocks

501

3347

Hardanger Violet

DMC/Anchor

|||| Perlé No.5 ecru

○○ 550/101

○○ 552/101

** 676/891

V V 3347/267

Hardanger Heart

|||| Perlé No.5 ecru

⊞ } Perlé No.8 ecru
◇

Kloster blocks

Needleweaving

Dove's eye

Beaded Pansy

DMC/ Anchor		Beadesign beads	
XX 936/846		▽▽ TOO26C	
VV 732/281		LL TOO26	
		⊖⊖ TOO22C	
		○○ TOO22	
		▣▣ TOO49	
		⁄⁄ TOO21	

840

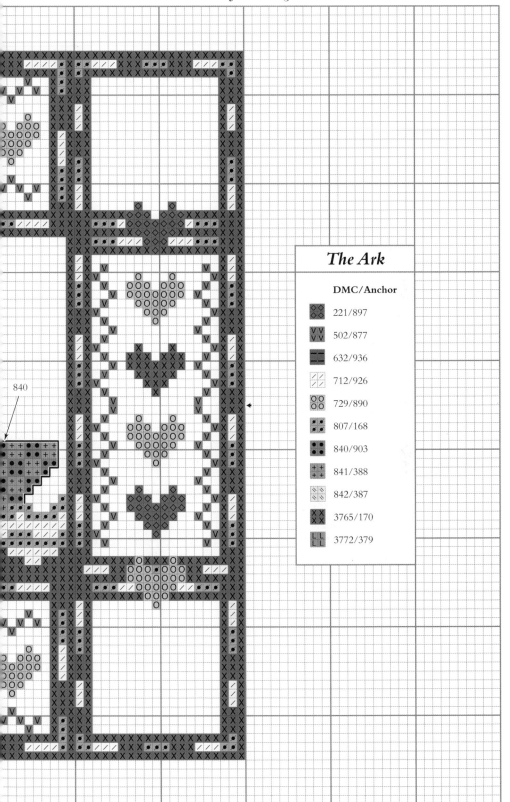

The Ark

DMC/Anchor

⬥ 221/897
V V 502/877
▬ 632/936
⁄⁄ 712/926
OO 729/890
:• 807/168
•• 840/903
++ 841/388
⁄⁄ 842/387
XX 3765/170
LL 3772/379

840

814

501

501

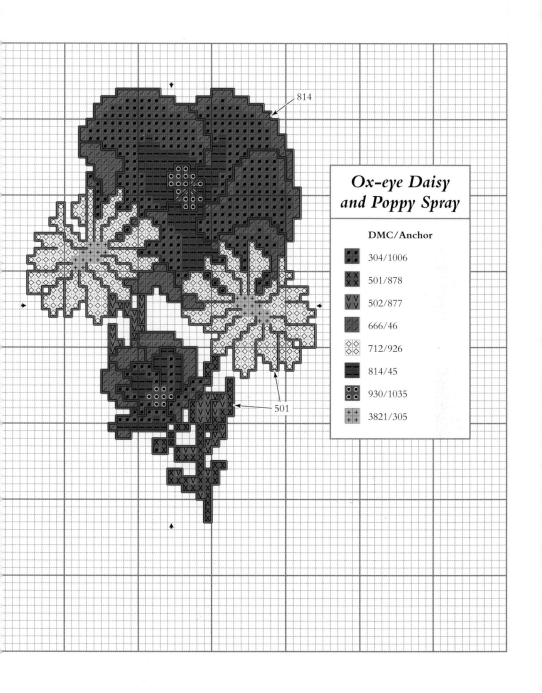

Ox-eye Daisy and Poppy Spray

DMC/Anchor

- 304/1006
- 501/878
- 502/877
- 666/46
- 712/926
- 814/45
- 930/1035
- 3821/305

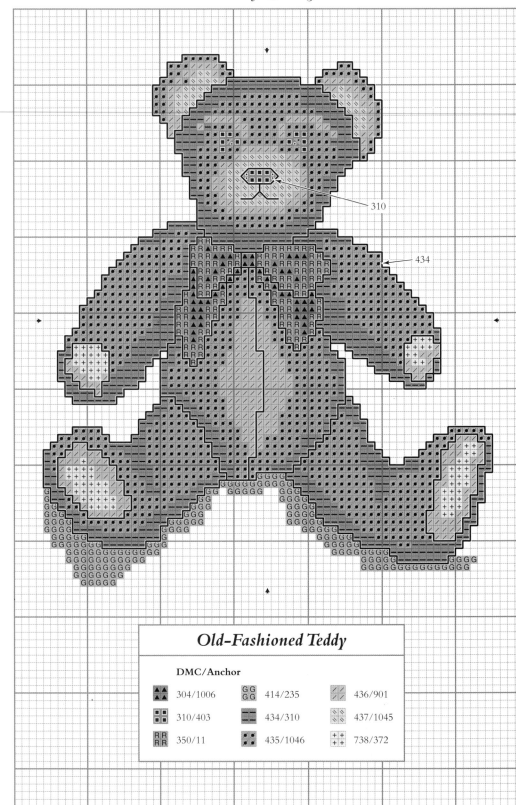

Old-Fashioned Teddy

DMC/Anchor

▲▲ 304/1006	GG 414/235	⁄⁄ 436/901
■■ 310/403	— 434/310	§§ 437/1045
RR 350/11	◆◆ 435/1046	++ 738/372

310

434

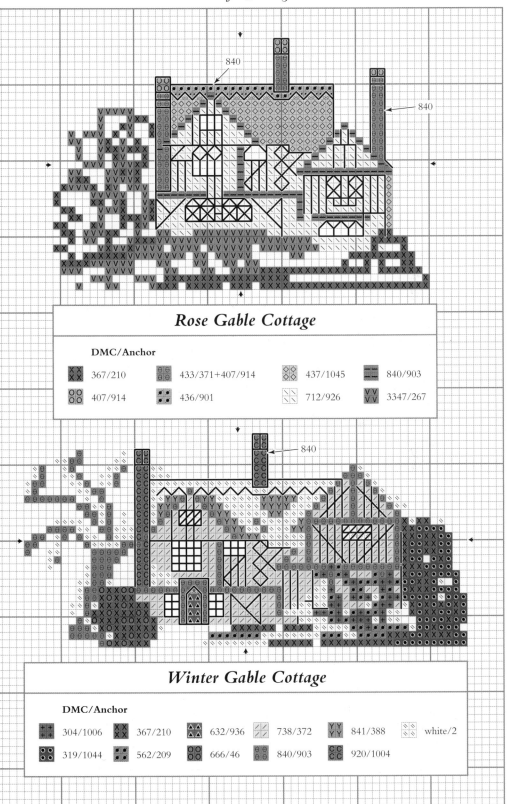

840

840

Rose Gable Cottage

DMC/Anchor

367/210	433/371+407/914	437/1045	840/903
407/914	436/901	712/926	3347/267

840

Winter Gable Cottage

DMC/Anchor

304/1006	367/210	632/936	738/372	841/388	white/2
319/1044	562/209	666/46	840/903	920/1004

841

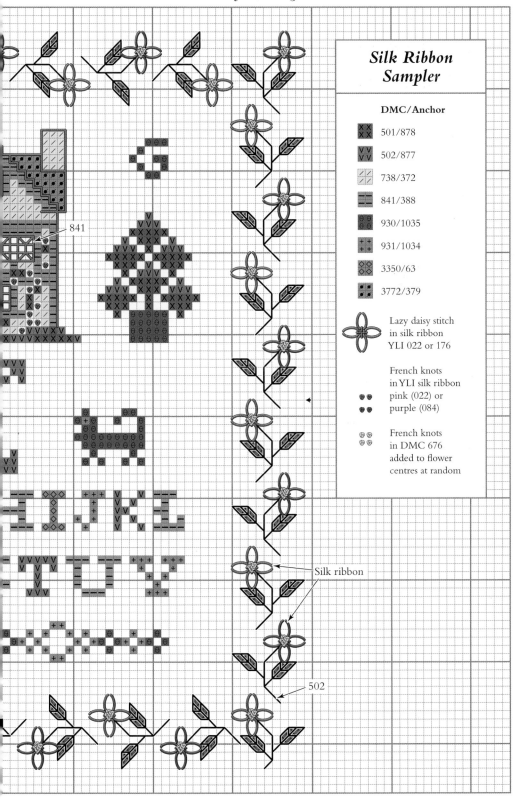

Silk Ribbon Sampler

DMC/Anchor

501/878

502/877

738/372

841/388

930/1035

931/1034

3350/63

3772/379

Lazy daisy stitch
in silk ribbon
YLI 022 or 176

French knots
in YLI silk ribbon
pink (022) or
purple (084)

French knots
in DMC 676
added to flower
centres at random

841

Silk ribbon

502

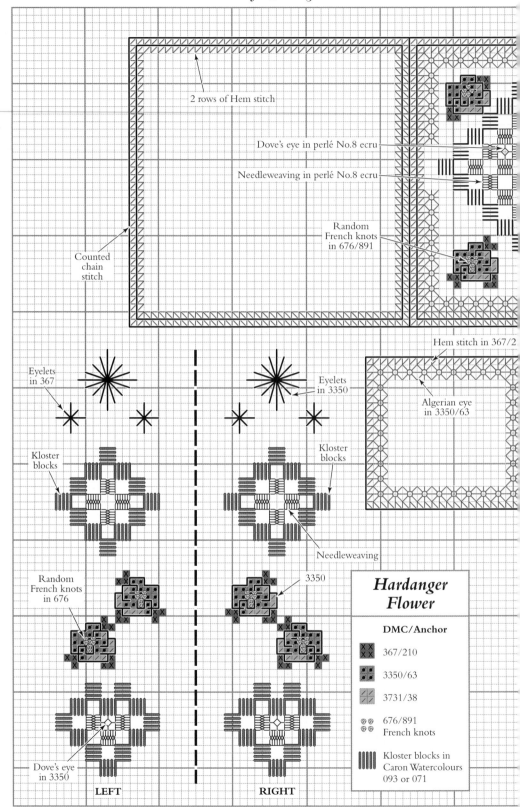

2 rows of Hem stitch

Dove's eye in perlé No.8 ecru

Needleweaving in perlé No.8 ecru

Random
French knots
in 676/891

Counted
chain
stitch

Hem stitch in 367/2

Algerian eye
in 3350/63

Eyelets
in 367

Eyelets
in 3350

Kloster
blocks

Kloster
blocks

Needleweaving

Random
French knots
in 676

3350

Dove's eye
in 3350

LEFT

RIGHT

Hardanger Flower

DMC/Anchor

367/210	
3350/63	
3731/38	
676/891 French knots	
Kloster blocks in Caron Watercolours 093 or 071	

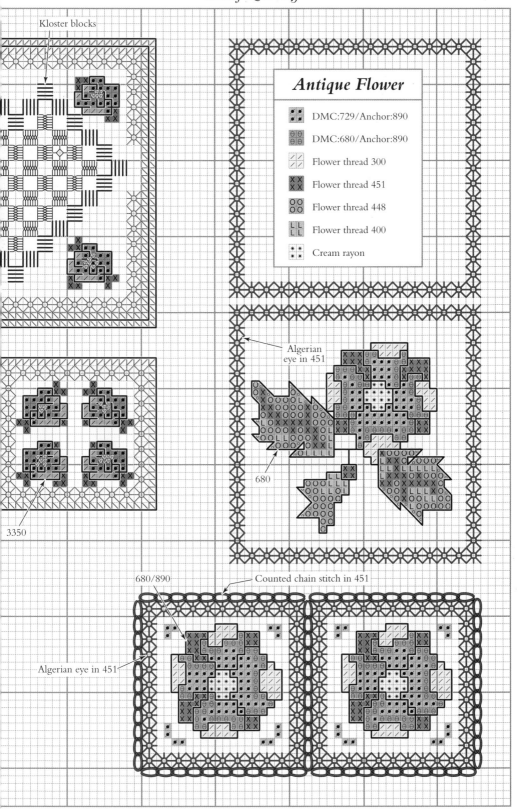

Kloster blocks

Antique Flower

- DMC:729/Anchor:890
- DMC:680/Anchor:890
- Flower thread 300
- Flower thread 451
- Flower thread 448
- Flower thread 400
- Cream rayon

Algerian eye in 451

680

3350

680/890

Counted chain stitch in 451

Algerian eye in 451

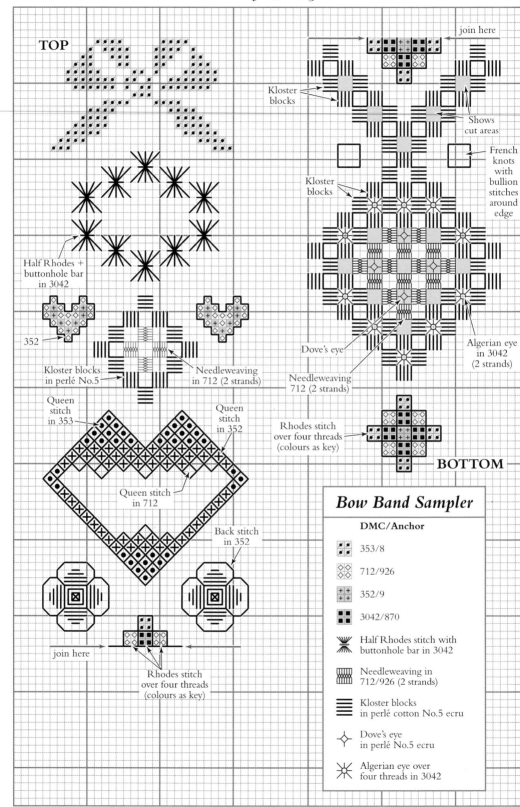

TOP

join here

Kloster blocks

Shows cut areas

French knots with bullion stitches around edge

Kloster blocks

Half Rhodes + buttonhole bar in 3042

352

Kloster blocks in perlé No.5

Needleweaving in 712 (2 strands)

Dove's eye

Needleweaving 712 (2 strands)

Algerian eye in 3042 (2 strands)

Queen stitch in 353

Queen stitch in 352

Queen stitch in 712

Rhodes stitch over four threads (colours as key)

BOTTOM

Back stitch in 352

join here

Rhodes stitch over four threads (colours as key)

Bow Band Sampler

DMC/Anchor

353/8

712/926

352/9

3042/870

Half Rhodes stitch with buttonhole bar in 3042

Needleweaving in 712/926 (2 strands)

Kloster blocks in perlé cotton No.5 ecru

Dove's eye in perlé No.5 ecru

Algerian eye over four threads in 3042

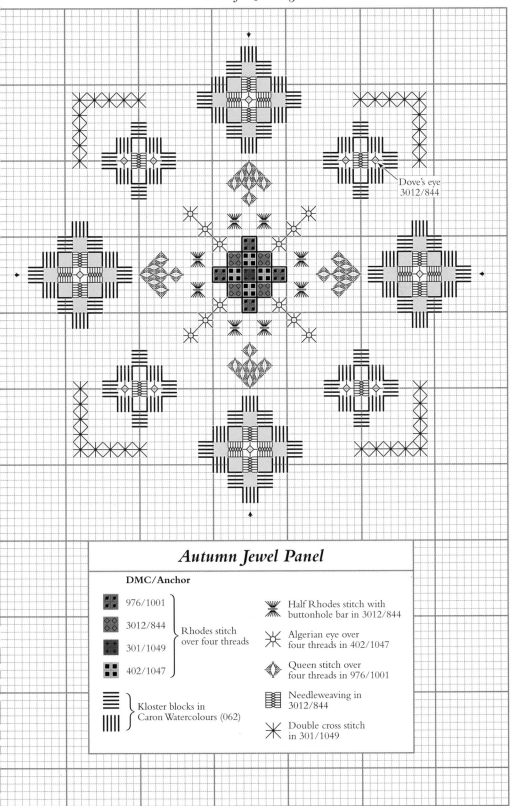

Dove's eye
3012/844

Autumn Jewel Panel

DMC/Anchor

976/1001

3012/844 } Rhodes stitch
301/1049 } over four threads

402/1047

} Kloster blocks in
Caron Watercolours (062)

Half Rhodes stitch with
buttonhole bar in 3012/844

Algerian eye over
four threads in 402/1047

Queen stitch over
four threads in 976/1001

Needleweaving in
3012/844

Double cross stitch
in 301/1049

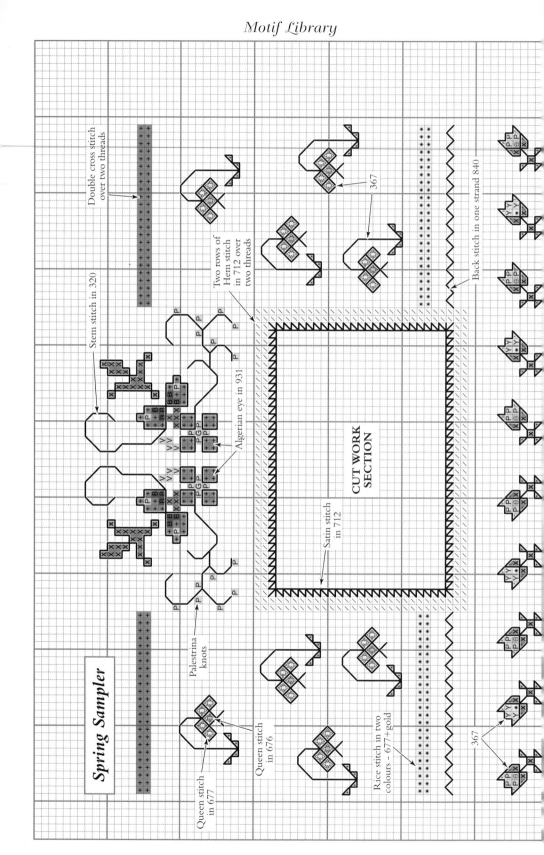

Spring Sampler

Double cross stitch over two threads

Stem stitch in 320

367

Two rows of Hem stitch in 712 over two threads

Back stitch in one strand 840

Algerian eye in 931

CUT WORK SECTION

Satin stitch in 712

Palestrina knots

Queen stitch in 677

Queen stitch in 676

Rice stitch in two colours – 677+gold

367

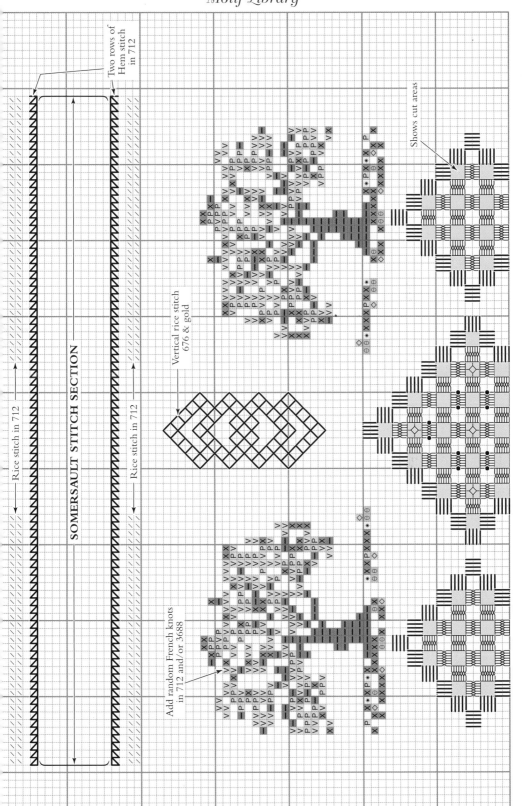

Two rows of Hem stitch in 712

SOMERSAULT STITCH SECTION

Rice stitch in 712

Rice stitch in 712

Shows cut areas

Vertical rice stitch 676 & gold

Add random French knots in 712 and/or 3688

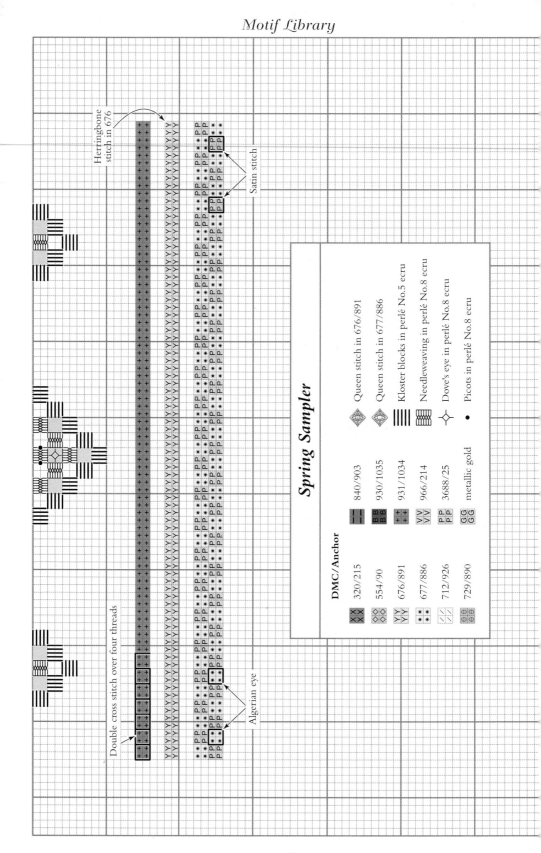

Herringbone stitch in 676

Satin stitch

Double cross stitch over four threads

Algerian eye

Spring Sampler

DMC/Anchor	
XX XX	320/215
◇◇ ◇◇	554/90
YY YY	676/891
** **	677/886
∕∕ ∕∕	712/926
θθ θθ	729/890
‖ ‖	840/903
BB BB	930/1035
++ ++	931/1034
VV VV	966/214
PP PP	3688/25
GG GG	metallic gold

◈	Queen stitch in 676/891
◈	Queen stitch in 677/886
‖‖‖	Kloster blocks in perlé No.5 ecru
▦	Needleweaving in perlé No.8 ecru
✦	Dove's eye in perlé No.8 ecru
•	Picots in perlé No.8 ecru

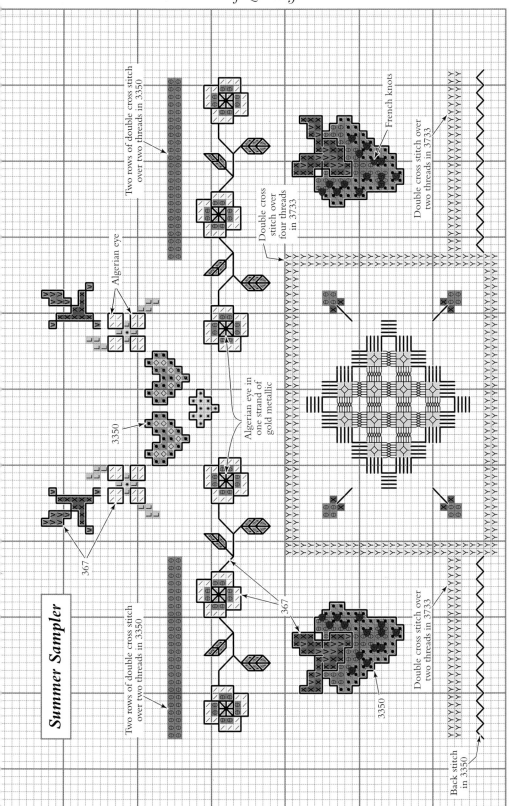

Summer Sampler

Two rows of double cross stitch over two threads in 3350

Algerian eye

French knots

Double cross stitch over two threads in 3733

Double cross stitch over four threads in 3733

Algerian eye in one strand of gold metallic

3350

367

367

Two rows of double cross stitch over two threads in 3350

3350

Double cross stitch over two threads in 3733

Back stitch in 3350

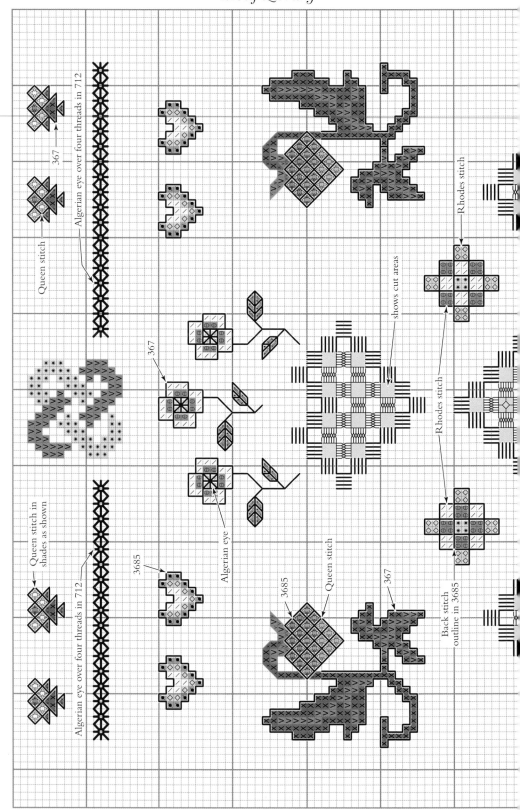

Queen stitch

367

Algerian eye over four threads in 712

Rhodes stitch

shows cut areas

Rhodes stitch

367

Algerian eye

Queen stitch in shades as shown

Queen stitch in shades as shown

Algerian eye over four threads in 712

3685

3685

Queen stitch

367

Back stitch outline in 3685

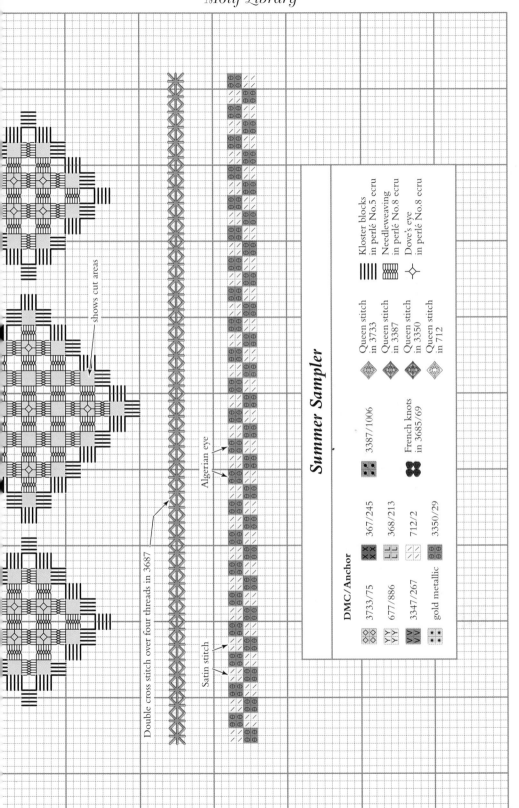

shows cut areas

Algerian eye

Double cross stitch over four threads in 3687

Satin stitch

Summer Sampler

DMC/Anchor

◇◇ ◇◇	3733/75	✕✕ ✕✕	367/245	
Y Y Y Y	677/886	L L L L	368/213	
V V V V	3347/267	∕ ∕ ∕ ∕	712/2	
✱✱ ✱✱	gold metallic	⊕⊕ ⊕⊕	3350/29	

⊕⊕ ⊕⊕	3387/1006
●● ●●	French knots in 3685/69

◈	Queen stitch in 3733
◈	Queen stitch in 3387
◈	Queen stitch in 3350
◈	Queen stitch in 712

‖‖‖	Kloster blocks in perlé No.5 ecru
▥▥	Needleweaving in perlé No.8 ecru
✧	Dove's eye in perlé No.8 ecru

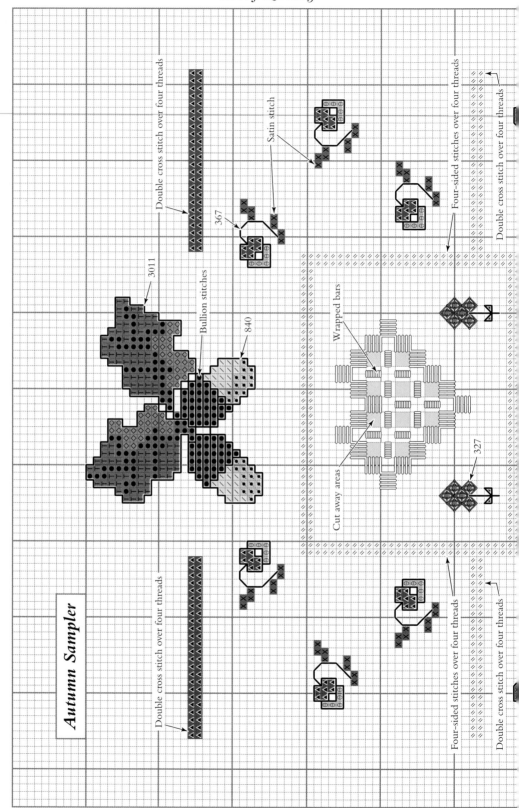

Autumn Sampler

Double cross stitch over four threads

3011

Bullion stitches

840

Double cross stitch over four threads

367

Satin stitch

Four-sided stitches over four threads

Double cross stitch over four threads

Wrapped bars

Cut away areas

327

Four-sided stitches over four threads

Double cross stitch over four threads

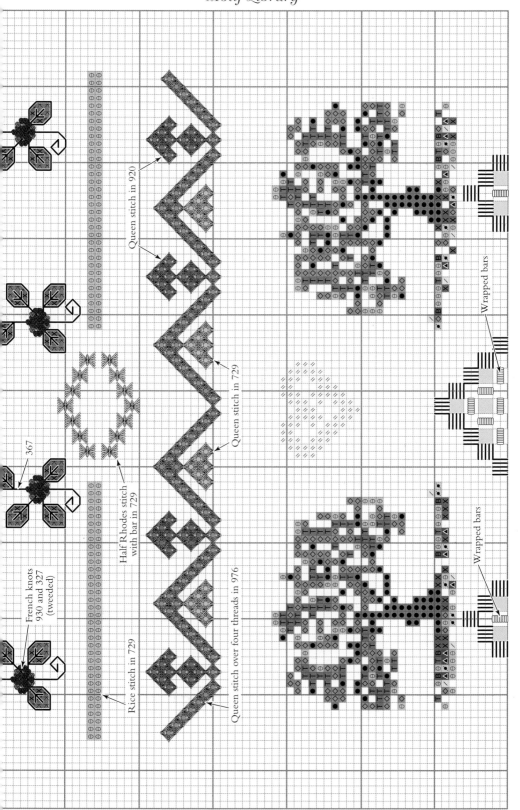

Queen stitch in 920

Queen stitch in 729

French knots
930 and 327
(tweeded)

367

Half Rhodes stitch
with bar in 729

Rice stitch in 729

Queen stitch over four threads in 976

Wrapped bars

Wrapped bars

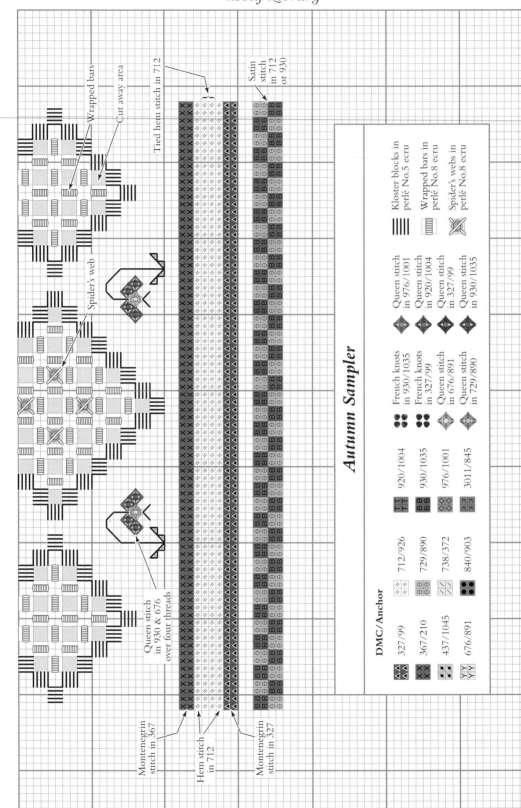

Wrapped bars

Cut away area

Tied hem stitch in 712

Satin stitch in 712 or 930

Spider's web

Queen stitch in 930 & 676 over four threads

Montenegrin stitch in 367

Hem stitch in 712

Montenegrin stitch in 327

Autumn Sampler

		Kloster blocks in perlé No.5 ecru
		Wrapped bars in perlé No.8 ecru
		Spider's webs in perlé No.8 ecru

Queen stitch in 976/1001	French knots in 930/1035	
Queen stitch in 920/1004	French knots in 327/99	
Queen stitch in 327/99	Queen stitch in 676/891	
Queen stitch in 930/1035	Queen stitch in 729/890	

920/1004   930/1035   976/1001   3011/845

712/926   729/890   738/372   840/903

DMC/Anchor

327/99   367/210   437/1045   676/891

174

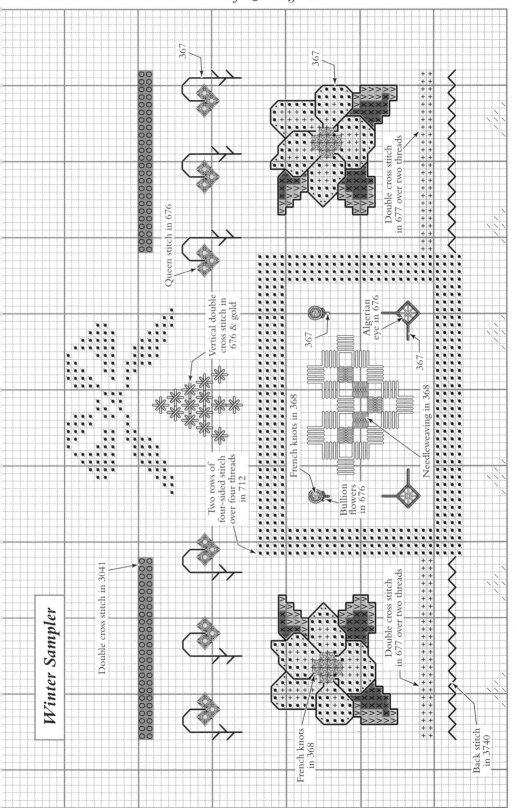

Winter Sampler

Double cross stitch in 3041

Queen stitch in 676

Vertical double cross stitch in 676 & gold

Two rows of four-sided stitch over four threads in 712

French knots in 368

Bullion flowers in 676

367

367

Algerian eye in 676

Needleweaving in 368

367

Double cross stitch in 677 over two threads

French knots in 368

Double cross stitch in 677 over two threads

Back stitch in 3740

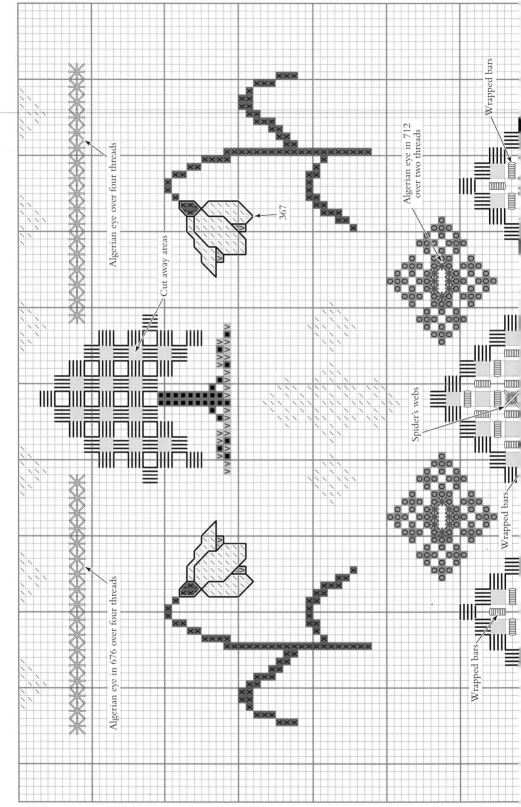

Algerian eye over four threads

Cut away areas

367

Algerian eye in 712 over two threads

Wrapped bars

Spider's webs

Wrapped bars

Algerian eye in 676 over four threads

Wrapped bars

Wrapped bars

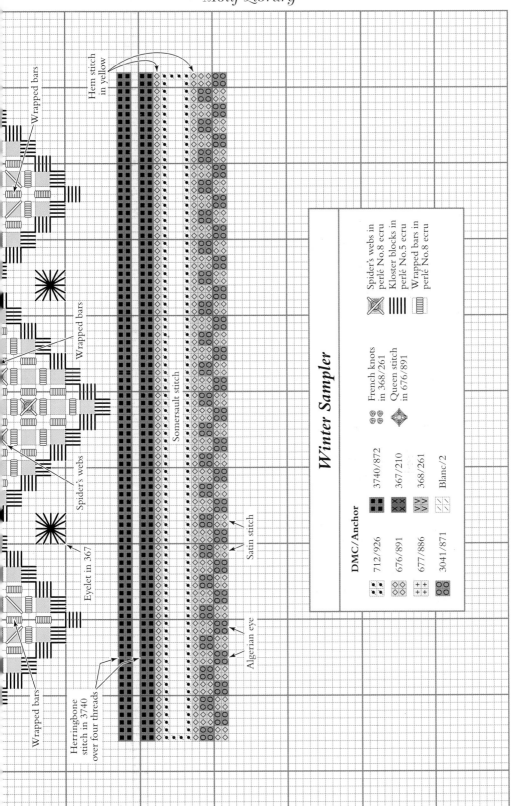

Wrapped bars

Hem stitch in yellow

Wrapped bars

Somersault stitch

Spider's webs

Eyelet in 367

Satin stitch

Algerian eye

Wrapped bars

Herringbone stitch in 3740 over four threads

Winter Sampler

DMC/Anchor

712/926	3740/872		French knots in 368/261	Spider's webs in perlé No.8 ecru
676/891	367/210		Queen stitch in 676/891	Kloster blocks in perlé No.5 ecru
677/886	368/261			Wrapped bars in perlé No.8 ecru
3041/871	Blanc/2			

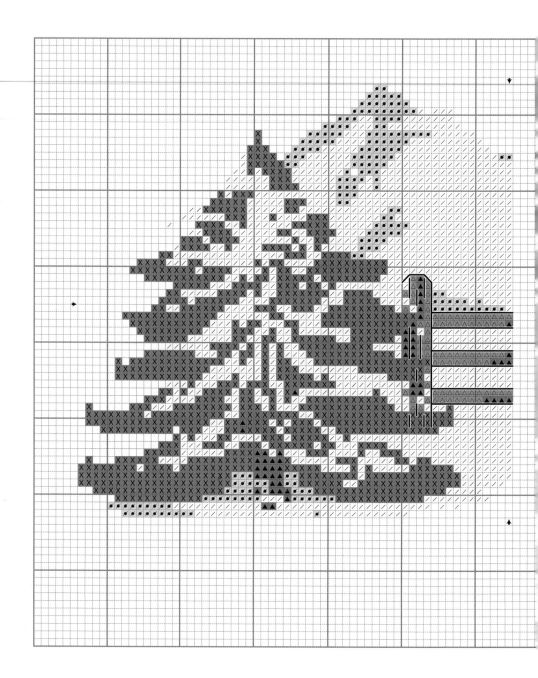

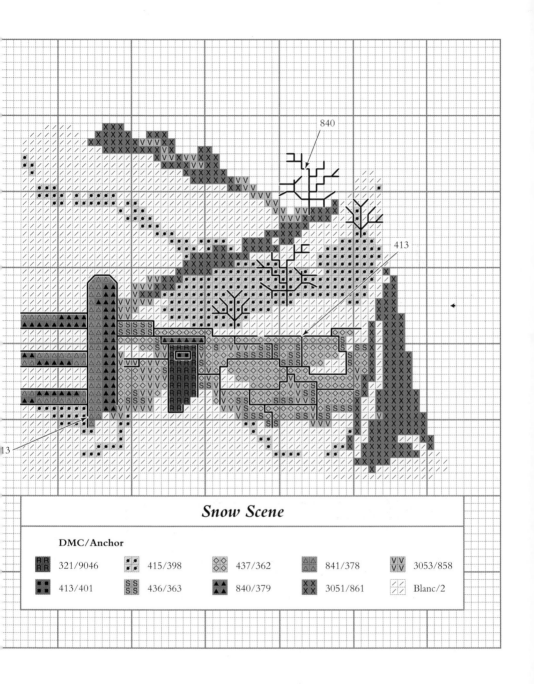

Snow Scene

DMC/Anchor

R R / R R	321/9046	• • / • •	415/398	◇◇ / ◇◇	437/362	△△ / △△	841/378	V V / V V	3053/858
■ ■ / ■ ■	413/401	S S / S S	436/363	▲▲ / ▲▲	840/379	X X / X X	3051/861	╱╱ / ╱╱	Blanc/2

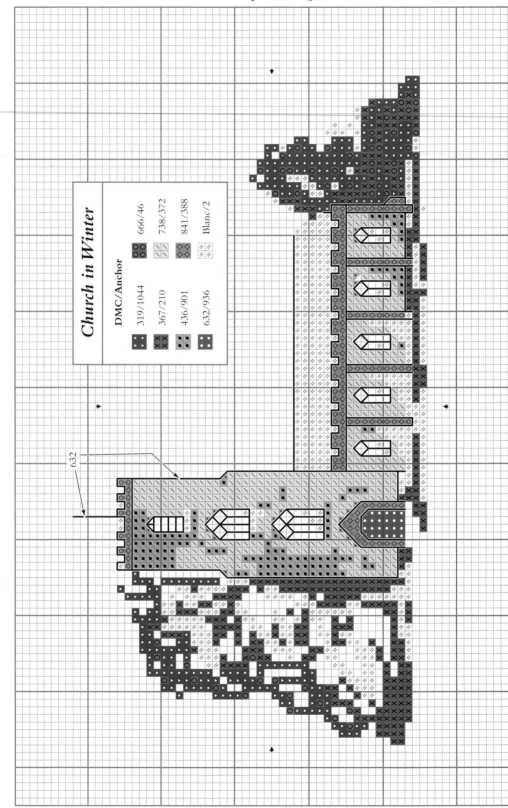

Church in Winter

DMC/Anchor

319/1044	666/46
367/210	738/372
436/901	841/388
632/936	Blanc/2

632

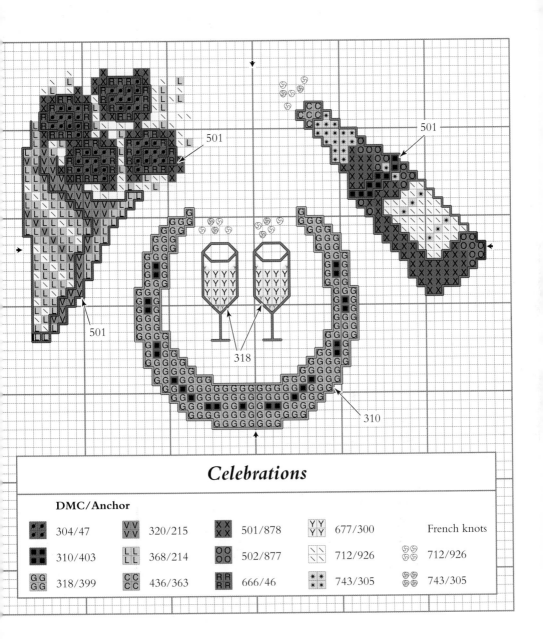

Celebrations

DMC/Anchor

304/47	320/215	501/878	677/300	French knots
310/403	368/214	502/877	712/926	712/926
318/399	436/363	666/46	743/305	743/305

Finishing Techniques

Embroidery designs can be made up into a wonderful range of objects, both practical and decorative and how they are made up or completed makes a great deal of difference to the look of the finished piece. This section describes some of the basic finishing techniques used in the book and suggests ways of displaying your embroidery.

If you are unable to find any items mentioned – don't panic! – there are always alternatives on the market. Experiment!

Washing and Ironing Your Work

If it becomes necessary to wash your embroidery, hand wash the stitching in bleach-free soap, rinse well and remove excess water by squeezing gently in a soft, clean towel. Dry naturally.

To iron a piece of embroidery, first cover the ironing board with four layers of bath towel and press the work from the wrong side using the steam button if your iron has one. Take extra care when ironing work containing buttons and charms and avoid ironing metallic threads.

Stretching and Mounting

Professional framing can be very expensive, but we all feel that our larger projects deserve the professional touch. It is a great shame when after spending hundreds of hours stitching a precious piece of cross stitch, the finished piece is just poked in an unsuitable frame without any further attention. By following the method explained below for padded mounting, you will be able to produce a very good result and have the pleasure of knowing that you completed the whole project on your own. The advantage of a padded mounting for embroidery is that any slightly 'lumpy bits' on the back of your work will be pushed into the padding rather than appear as raised areas on the front of the embroidery.

- Take time to make sure that you have centred the work carefully and that the edges are really straight, otherwise it will show when you put the completed piece in the frame.
- Pad all your completed pieces, even cards, as the padding raises the embroidery, which displays it to better effect.
- Use foamcore board which consists of two layers of thin card with a layer of polystyrene

between. This construction makes it easy to cut the board and to pin into the edge as the pins are actually inserted into the polystyrene. You will probably have to buy foamcore board at an artists' supply shop rather than a needlework shop.

You Will Need

3mm foamcore board, or acid-free mounting board
Double-sided adhesive tape, or strong thread for lacing
Polyester wadding (batting) for padding
Glass- or plastic-headed pins

1 Using a sharp craft knife, cut a piece of foamcore to fit your frame (cut round the piece of glass that fits the frame).

2 Attach a piece of wadding (batting) to the foamcore board using two or three strips of double-sided adhesive tape, then trim the wadding to exactly the same size as the foamcore.

3 Position your embroidery on top of the padding and centre it carefully in relation to the padded board. Fix the embroidery in position by pinning through the fabric into the edges of the foamcore board. Start in the middle of each side and pin towards the corners. Make sure your pins follow a line of Aida holes or a thread of linen so that your edges will be really straight. Adjust the fabric's position until you are completely confident that it is centred and straight.

4 Turn the work over, leaving the pins in place, trim the excess fabric to about 5cm (2in) all round and fold it to the back.

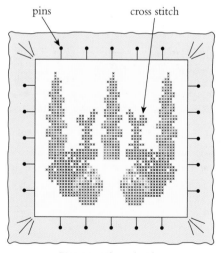

pins   cross stitch

Pining out the embroidery

5 Fix the edges of fabric in place using either double-sided adhesive tape or by lacing across the back using strong thread (see diagram). As the pins remain in place, it is still possible at this stage to adjust the position of the fabric and replace the tape or tighten the lacing. When you are completely satisfied with the result, remove the pins and assemble the frame.

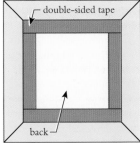

The taping method

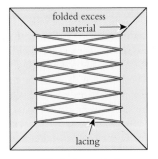

The lacing method

Stretching and Starching Canvas Work

It is the nature of canvas work to distort especially when worked in tent stitch, so it is necessary to stretch and starch the needlework. You will be able to use the board and squared paper many times and will soon master the technique.

You Will Need

A flat, clean board (e.g. chipboard)
Squared paper (e.g. dressmaker's graph paper)
Nails 2.5cm (1in) long
Hammer
Cold water starch (e.g. wallpaper paste without preservatives or anti-fungal agent)
Masking tape
Kitchen palette knife

1 Cover the board with the squared paper and stick down with masking tape.

2 Place the embroidery right side down on the paper. You should be able to see the squares on the paper through the unstitched canvas. Start at one corner and begin nailing down the canvas about 5cm (2in) from the embroidery, hammering in the nails far enough to hold the fabric firmly. Following the line in the canvas, align the canvas with the squared paper, placing nails about 2.5cm (1in) apart (any further apart and the needlework may acquire a scalloped edge). When you have completed the first side, go back to the corner and repeat for the side at right angles to it. In order to square the work, draw a pencil line on the canvas from the first nail you inserted, to the diagonally opposite corner. Work out where this line should end in relation to the lines on the graph paper. Pull the embroidery to this point and nail this corner and then complete the nailing of the last two sides. If your stitching is very distorted it may help to dampen the embroidery.

3 When the last nail is in position the work should be completely square. Mix a small quantity of the starch to the consistency of soft butter and spread it evenly but sparingly with a knife over the canvas, avoiding the unstitched areas. Allow this to dry completely and then remove the nails to remove the work from the board. Not only will the work be completely square but the starch will have evened the tension so your stitches should look even better!

Framing

Needlework generally looks better framed without glass. If you prefer to use glass with this method, you must ensure that the embroidery does not touch the underside of the glass. Insert very narrow strips of board (spacers) into the edges of the frame, between the glass and the mounted embroidery to hold them apart, before you assemble the frame. Always check that both sides of the glass are completely clean. Before adding the final backing board to the back of the picture, line the back of the work with aluminium tin foil to discourage small insects.

When the frame is assembled, seal the back using gummed paper tape, gently pushing the tape into the rebate. The tape will shrink slightly as it dries thus sealing the picture.

Noahs Ark (see page 53) – finished with a frame

Painting Frames and Mounts

When choosing a frame for a particular project, select the largest moulding you can afford and do not worry if the colour is not suitable. Ask the framer to make up the frame and a coloured or gold slip for you, but buy the frame, glass and so on in kit form (most framers do not mind!) and then decorate the frame yourself.

You can use readily available products for this, for example car spray paint (available from car repair or body shop suppliers). There are hundreds of colours in the range, but if you have no luck, try bicycle paints which include even more colours! For subtle matt shades, explore endless possibilities with emulsion paints from DIY shops, often available in tiny tester sizes, ideal for trial and error.

Before you begin to paint a piece of moulding, take care to cover all nearby surfaces with paper or dust cloths, If the moulding is completely untreated, rub down gently with fine sand paper, clean with white spirit on a soft cloth and allow to dry completely before painting.

Making a Bag

A bag or sachet is easy to stitch, can be made in any size and has many different uses – holding small gifts, pot-pourri or wedding mementoes. A bag could be made entirely from Aida or an evenweave fabric, with the design embroidered directly onto the fabric, or it could be made from an ordinary dressmaking fabric with an embroidered panel sewn on. The instructions which follow are for a bag made with stitching fabric with an embroidery design worked on to the fabric. You will need sufficient fabric for the front and back of the bag and a piece of cord or ribbon for a tie.

1 Cut out two rectangles of fabric according to the size you wish your bag to be, and allowing 4cm (1^1/2in) seam allowance all round. Stitch your embroidery design onto the front piece and the back too if you wish.

2 With right sides of the bag rectangles together, pin and stitch both sides and the bottom of the bag, matching the edges for a neat finish. Press the side seams open.

3 To make the top of the bag, fold the top edge over to the wrong side by 6mm (^{1}/4in), press, then fold over again. Pin in place and sew two rows of stitching around the top to form a casing. Turn the bag to the right side. Snip the side seam between the lines of parallel stitching, binding the cut edges with small buttonhole stitches or over-stitching.

4 To finish the bag with a tie, thread a piece of cord or ribbon through the channel and knots the ends to secure.

Making a Band

Stitching a border or a selection of motifs on a band is a lovely way of embellishing all sorts of objects, such as cakes, hats, tie-backs and flower pots. There are many ready-prepared bands available in various widths and with different coloured edgings, or you could cut a length of Aida or linen and hem the edges.

1 Measure the length or circumference of the object to be decorated with the band. Stitch the length of border or row of motifs required, from the centre of the band outwards. When the embroidery is finished, stitch side seams to neaten the ends of the band. If you are using a length of Aida or linen, you will need to stitch seams along the lengths of the band.

2 Sew on pieces of Velcro for fastening the ends or stitch the band to the item being decorated.

184

Making a Bell Pull

A bell pull is another useful way of displaying cross stitch. You could use one of the designs charted in the Motif Library or design one of your own. A simple rectangular bell pull shape is the easiest to make up but you could make one with a pointed bottom end if you prefer. First, decide on the size of your bell pull – the length of the bell pull hanging rod determines the width of the fabric you need, so buy the bell pull ends and rods before you start stitching. You will also need cotton backing fabric and decorative braid.

1 Work your cross stitch design onto your stitching fabric.

2 Turn under the edges of your evenweave fabric so that your design is central. Fold your backing fabric to the same size and press the turnings.

3 Place the embroidered piece and the backing fabric wrong sides together and pin. Slide the rods in position top and bottom, and add the bell pull ends, then slipstitch the fabric pieces together, adding decorative braid around the edges if desired.

Making a Bookmark

Bookmarks make quick and useful gifts. You could make one of your own (described below) or mount your work in one of the commercially made bookmarks available.

1 Decide on the size of your bookmark and stitch your design onto the fabric.

2 Trim the fabric to within 1cm (1/2in) of the stitching all round. Hem all the sides. If you want to create a shaped point at the bottom, don't hem the bottom but turn it under by about 6mm (1/4in) and tack (baste) (make sure none of the embroidery is included). Find the seam centre point and bring the two corners together so they meet at the back then slipstitch these two edges together. A tassel at the point would finish the bookmark off nicely.

Mounting Work in Cards and Gift Tags

There are many, many blank cards and gift tags available from needlecraft shops and mail-order suppliers. The following method describes mounting work in a card and should be applicable to tags too.

1 When your piece of stitching is complete, press the design on the wrong side and set aside.

2 Open the folded card completely and check that the design fits in the opening. Apply a thin coat of adhesive or double-sided adhesive tape to the inside of the opening (see diagram below). Add the design, carefully checking the position of the stitching before pressing down firmly.

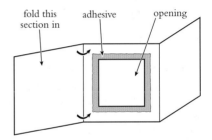

fold this section in   adhesive   opening

Mounting work into a card

3 Fold the spare flap inside and stick in place with either double-sided adhesive tape or another thin application of adhesive. Leave to dry before closing. Add ribbon trims as desired.

Mounting Work into Commercial Products

There are many items available today which have been specially designed to display embroidery such as trays, stools, fire screens, mugs, boxes, mirrors, trinket pots and coasters.

To mount work in these products, you generally only need to follow the manufacturer's instructions, but it helps to back the embroidered work using iron-on interfacing as this strengthens the stitches and prevents fraying. Interfacing is available from needlework supplies shops and good craft shops. Cut a piece of interfacing a little larger than your stitched fabric, set the iron to a medium heat, or as indicated on the interface instructions, and iron it onto the reverse side of the stitching. Trim the fabric to size before mounting.

Making Cushions, Pincushions and Scissors Keepers

Your cross stitch embroidery can be made up into cushions, pincushions and scissors keepers following the same principles. Basically, two pieces of fabric the same size and shape are joined together, with stuffing inserted into the centre. The fabric may be embroidered on one side or both. There are two main ways of joining the fabrics, using counted chain stitch or normal hand or machine sewing.

To join using counted chain stitch (or long-legged cross stitch), the two fabric sections are joined wrong sides together using counted chain stitch (see page 103) and the stuffing is inserted through an opening before the last side is completed. If a cord for scissors or to attach to a chatelaine is required, insert this immediately after stuffing and anchor it in place as the last side is stitched.

To join using normal hand or machine sewing, proceed as follows. Pin the back and front pieces together, right sides facing (A).

Stitch the pieces together, by hand or machine, leaving an opening to fill with polyester filling (B).

Turn right sides out, insert the filling and slip stitch the opening to close. Make a twisted cord as described on page 187 and slip stitch to the seam, using matching thread and making a join at the bottom and tucking the raw edges inside. Alternatively, you could use a ready-made cord for an edging.

Making a Tassel

Tassels are useful for adding a finishing touch to many projects, including cushions, cards and bookmarks. Tassels can be made from various threads, usually from stranded cottons (floss) to match the cross stitch design, but you could also use metallic threads or tapestry wools.

Decide on the length of tassel you require and cut a square piece of stiff card to this size. Wrap the thread round and round the card (A) to form the body of the tassel, in whatever thickness you require.

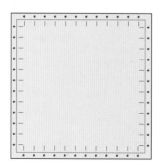

A *Pin front and back together*

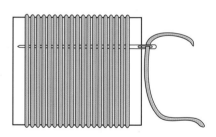

A *Wrap thread around card*

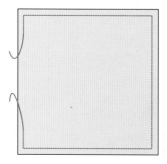

B *Stitch around cushion*

B *Cut bottom threads*

Whilst holding tightly to the top of the tassel, cut across the threads at the bottom and take the tassel off the card (B). Pinch the threads together at the top and tightly wrap a length of thread just below the loop at the top (C). Knot this and thread the ends through to join the other lengths. Trim the tassel ends if they are uneven. To attach the finished tassel, use a length of matching thread through the loop at the top.

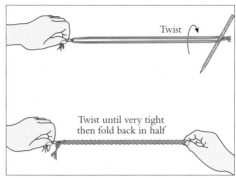

C *Knot the neck*

Making a Twisted Cord

A twisted cord is perfect for finishing off or embellishing many projects. Choose a colour or group of colours in stranded cottons (floss) to match the stitching. Cut a minimum of four lengths, at least four times the finished length required and fold in half. Ask a friend to hold the two ends whilst you slip a pencil through the loop at the other end. Twist the pencil and continue twisting until kinks appear. Walk slowly towards your partner and the cord will twist. Smooth out the kinks from the looped end and tie another knot at the other end to secure.

Bibliography

DE DILLMONT Therese,
Encyclopedia of Needlework (DMC)

EMBROIDERERS' GUILD,
Making Samplers (David & Charles, 1993)

LOVE Janice, *Basics and Beyond*
(Love 'n' Stitches, 1992)

O'STEEN Darlene, *The Proper Stitch*
(Just Cross Stitch, 1994)

SEBBA Anna, *Samplers* (Weidenfield &
Nicholson, 1979)

*The Anchor Book of Hardanger
Embroidery* (David & Charles, 1997)

*The Anchor Book of Ribbon
Embroidery* (David & Charles, 1997)

*The Anchor Book of Counted Thread
Embroidery Stitches* (David & Charles, 1987)

Acknowledgements

A special thank you to my husband Bill and my two special children, James and Louise who have put up with this for the last time!

To Michel Standley, our administrator, who makes it possible for the business to continue whilst I write books; my secretary, Helen King, who writes my lists and makes me follow them, and Sharon Reynolds our housekeeper, who makes it all possible!

A special thanks to all my stitchers, pattern checkers and testers: Hanne Fentiman, Sue Moir, Barbara Webster, Jill Vaughan, Su Maddocks, Glenys Thorne, Michelle Daniels, Susan Bridgens, Ann Sansom, Hanne Lise Stamper, Amanda Lake, Joan Dewar, Violet Holland, Janet Jarvis, Joan Hastewell, Margaret Pallant, Liz Burford, Margaret Locke, Lesley Clegg, Margaret Cornish, Linda Smith, Mary Miles, Doreen Ely, Ann Dudley, Jenny Kirby and Barbara Grenville.

Thanks to all the generous suppliers of the materials and equipment required for this book, particularly Malcolm Turner of Fabric Flair and Rainer Steimann of Zweigart for lovely fabrics,

DMC Creative World and Coats Crafts UK for stranded cottons and metallic threads and Ian Lawson Smith for his wonderful I.L.Soft computer programme.

To Cheryl Brown at David & Charles for thinking of me for this title and Linda Clements for editing and sorting out this complicated manuscript. To Brenda Morrison for all her hard work and design flair. To Ethan Danielson for all the excellent technical stitch diagrams and beautiful charts that make this book so special.

Thank you to all the wonderful stitchers who have supported and encouraged me over the past fifteen years and who have made it possible for me to earn a living from my cross stitch passion.

My grateful thanks for help and advice from Mary Jenkins, Brenda Keyes and Moira Blackburn (see Suppliers). Last, but certainly not least, my love and thanks to Sue Hawkins (Technical Director of the Cross Stitch Guild) who has taught me so much and never laughs at my silly questions! This book would not have happened without her.

Jane Greenoff's Inglestone Collection

Jane Greenoff's kit company based in England, supplies cross stitch kits, gold-plated needles, stitching paper and stitchers' gifts. For more information, web site address or Jane Greenoff's classes write to: The Inglestone Collection, Yells Yard, Fairford, Gloucestershire GL7 4BS. Tel: 00 44 1285 712778. Fax: 00 44 1285 713799. E-mail: greenoff@easynet.co.uk

---

Suppliers

Moira Blackburn
PJA Crafts, 96 Denbrook Avenue, Bradford
BD4 0QN
Cross stitch kits

Coats Crafts UK
PO Box 22, Lingfield, McMullen Road,
Darlington, Co. Durham DL1 1YQ.
Tel: 01325 394394
E-mail: coats.crafts@coats.com
Stranded cottons and Kreinik blending
filaments, Glow in the Dark and Fine braids

Daylight Studios,
89–91 Scrubs Lane, London, NW10 6QU.
Tel: 0208 964 1200
Daylight bulbs and lamps

DMC Creative World,
Pullman Road, Wigston, Leicester, LE18 2DY.
Tel: 0116281 1040
Stranded cottons and perlé thread

Fabric Flair (and Beadesign)
Northlands Industrial Estate,
Copheap Lane, Warminster, Wiltshire
BA12 0BG. Tel: 01985 846400
E-mail: mail@fabricflair.com
Beads and charms, linens and other evenweaves,
Zweigart products, blunt beading needles

Framecraft Miniatures Ltd,
372 Summer Lane, Hockley, Birmingham,
B19 3QA.
Tel: 0121 212 0551
E-mail: sales@framecraft
Web-site: framecraft.com
Silk gauze, trinket pots and brooches

Hantex Ltd,
Unit 8–10, Lodge Farm Business Units,
Wolverhampton Road, Castlethorpe, Milton
Keynes MK19 7ES. Tel: 01908 511331
E-mail: sales@hantex.co.uk
Novelty buttons and charms

Sue Hawkins (Technical Director of the
Cross Stitch Guild, designer and David &
Charles author)
Needleworks
The Old School House, 67 Hall Road,
Leckhampton, Cheltenham, Gloucestershire
GL53 0HP. Tel: 01242 584424.
E-mail:SueHawkinsNeedleworks@
compuserve.com
Counted cross stitch canvas work and crewel embroidery

Inglestone Collection
Yells Yard, Fairford, Gloucestershire GL7 4AR.
Tel: 01285 712778
E-mail: greenoff@easynet.co.uk
Stitching paper, stitch catchers, gold-plated needles

Mary Jenkins (designer, author and teacher)
22 Alfreda Road, Whitchurch, Cardiff CF14 2EH

Brenda Keyes (designer and author)
The Sampler Company
Holly Tree House, Lichfield Drive, Prestwich,
Manchester M25 0HX. Tel: 0161 773 0914
Cross stitch kits, charts, motif books, thread organisers

Macleod Craft Marketing,
West Yonderton, Warlock Road, Bridge of
Weir PA11 3SR. Tel: 01505 612618
Caron Collection Threads

Quilt Direct,
11 Iliffe House, Iliffe Avenue, Oadby,
Leicester LE2 5LS. Tel: 0116 271 0033
E-mail: sales@quiltdirect.com
Pure silk ribbon (YLI)

Sewing Basket Card Co.
14 Kensington Industrial Park, Hall Street,
Southport, Merseyside, PR9 0NY.
Tel: 01704 549754
Three-fold cards

Zweigart & Sawitzki,
PO Box 120, D–71043 Sindelfingen,
Germany. Tel: 0049 7031 7955
E-mail: info@zweigart.de
Linen, Aida and all other evenweaves

Index

star struck

pamela anderson

ATRIA BOOKS

New York London Toronto Sydney

ATRIA BOOKS

1230 Avenue of the Americas
New York, NY 10020

ISBN 13: 978-0-7434-9283-6
ISBN 10:   0-7434-9283-8
ISBN 13: 978-0-7434-9374-1 (Pbk)
ISBN 10:   0-7434-9374-5 (Pbk)

First Atria Books trade paperback edition June 2006

10 9 8 7 6 5 4 3 2 1

ATRIA BOOKS is a trademark of Simon & Schuster, Inc.

For information regarding special discounts for bulk purchases,
please contact Simon & Schuster Special Sales at 1-800-456-6798
or business@simonandschuster.com.

Manufactured in the United States of America

To my mom—
the nut doesn't fall far from the tree.

acknowledgments

THANKS

To Mom and Dad for having a sense of humor and supplying me with one in the face of life's ups and downs.

To my brother, Gerry Anderson, for being there for me through thick and thin, and for helping me with this manuscript and supplying great advice and direction/confirmation—huge help! He's such a talent—writer, producer, and director . . . watch out!

To my children, Brando and Dilly, whom I love desperately, for giving me the idea and inspiration for staying home and writing so I could spend more time with them . . . the universe *does* validate good decisions.

To Eric Shaw Quinn—of course . . . my partner in crime on this project—are you me or am I you? The lines have blurred and you are wearing my shoes . . . and they're trashed—you've walked more than a mile!

To my editor, Brenda . . . you have always been a great supporter and believed in this from the start . . . another best-seller to add to your list? Thank you for everything.

To Judith—the boss at Simon and Schuster!—thanks for

allowing me to be creative and not forcing me into a "Pammyland" concept! I'm on to you—all is forgiven.

To Hefner, for helping to build interesting adventures in our lives, empowering women . . . and for just being you!

To David LaChapelle, Luca, and Jesus . . . talented, genius, eccentric, and honest! My favorite people—friends whom I lean on and who put me out if I catch on fire You remind me of what's important besides family: *art*.

To all the people I love and work with . . . and whom make life easier . . . or just more interesting . . . especiailly: everyone at PETA, and Dan Mathews (my other gay husband), everyone at MAC, Melanie Arthur, Lori and Kylie Anderson, Michael Ullman, Barry Tyerman, Steven Pranica, Amanda, Tommy, Chef Jay, Charisse, Sue, Harper and Michael, Jamie, J. P., Steve Levitan, and everyone at *Stacked*, Spade, Stern, Leno . . . and/or whoever I'm . . .

Don't try this at home!

star struck

1

you shook me all night long

Why do my nipples hurt? was Star's first thought as she woke from a strangely deep sleep, her hands gliding along her naked body to the tender nipples that had awakened her. She winced as she made contact, realizing only belatedly that she was naked. Star tried to open her eyes but couldn't; the room was too bright. She raised her hand to shield her view, only to be blinded by a huge diamond ring that hadn't been on her finger when she went to sleep.

When *had* she gone to sleep? And where?

Stretching, Star reached up to push back her hair as she tried to get her bearings and she struck herself on the forehead with the chrome handle of the Colt .45 she was holding in her right hand. She screamed and fell off the dresser on which she'd been perched. The gun went off, taking out a glass table top that shattered into four-carat chunks of safety glass.

Star stared at the revolver in her hand. She'd never even touched a gun before, but here she was, naked except for a pair of Gucci boots, a strange diamond ring, and a gun welded to her hand.

What the hell was going on?

Why did everything feel so strange? So blurry?

She was hungry but didn't have an appetite. Her skin felt alive, vibrating gently against her every nerve ending. The sun was so bright she could hardly see and the carpet was so soft it tickled her bare ass where she sat, puzzled, on the floor.

Looking around, Star was relieved to see that she was still in her hotel room in Cabo. Well, what was left of her hotel room. Pictures had been torn off the wall and defaced; cushions from the chairs and sofa had been built into a fort in the middle of the room; tables were stacked to the ceiling; and dozens of empty Cristal bottles, scattered everywhere, prompted her to wonder if the damages would be covered under the "incidentals" clause in her modeling contract.

As she further surveyed the damage, Star noticed the unmade bed that was a confusion of sheets, pillows, and strangely chosen items from around the room—a candlestick, an ice bucket, and a selection of well-placed objets d'art. Condoms, some used, some blown up like balloons, also littered the space. "Well, I'm glad we played safe," she said with a little laugh, swatting one of the oddly shaped balloons out of her way. That's when she saw the tiny video camera and a few dozen tapes strewn across the coffee table, along with the remnants of several lines of cocaine. How odd, Star reflected. I don't do drugs. I wonder who's been here? Her musings turned to panic as she saw a pair of bare feet sticking out from beneath the tangle of Frette sheets, next to a blender that must have been taken from the room's wet bar. Actually, the blender was working double duty because its cord had been used to bind the mysterious pair of ankles to the bedposts.

A modern-day Goldilocks, Star crept closer. Who are these feet attached to? And what are they doing in my bed? Tentatively, she reached out and touched a big toe with the barrel of the gun. A small, strangled cry escaped her throat as the toe responded, wiggling as if to get away from the cold steel barrel. Star put her hand over her mouth, felt the strange diamond against her cheek, and pulled it away.

She felt so naked.

Well, aside from the boots and the ring, she was naked. But it wasn't just that she didn't have any clothes on. She felt vulnerable—raw and exposed. Try as she might, she could not remember what had happened last night, could not remember how she'd wound up asleep on the dresser, and could not guess who this might be in her bed. She stood frozen for a minute, listening to the muffled cries coming from under the sheets.

Star made her way around the bed looking for clues to identify the stranger. She found nothing. It was a man; that much was clear from the rather sizable tent pole raised under the sheets. But who? Surely, she would remember an erection like that, she thought with a playful giggle, reaching out and giving the massive morning wood a tap. The moans changed, a different tone now, at least an octave lower.

Finally, she could stand it no longer. She reached for the hem of the crumpled sheet, ready to expose the identity of the well-endowed stranger . . . but then her phone rang, startling her as it played its version of "You Shook Me All Night Long."

Star pulled back, oddly frightened by the old AC/DC song that had shattered the silence.

Should she answer it?

The phone rang again. It echoed in the room and in her head.

Would it seem suspicious not to answer it?

It rang.

And rang.

What time was it anyway?

Taking a deep breath, Star answered it.

"Hello?" she said softly, moving away from the body in the bed.

"Star? Honey, is that you?"

"Who is this?"

"It's Rufus," the caller said with a startled laugh.

She considered the information for a moment. Everything seemed so strange. She felt dizzy and medicated.

"Your boyfriend?" he said, when she didn't answer, an edge in his voice.

"Hi, baby, I'm sorry," she said, scratching her nose with the gun. "I just woke up and I'm not feeling right."

"Not feeling right?" he said, curious at her strange choice of words. "What do you mean, 'not feeling right'? And *why* are you whispering?"

"Are you working for the CIA?" she asked sharply, closing the bathroom door behind her.

"What?"

"Well, I just thought, what with the third degree you were interrogating me," she snapped.

"I'm sorry," he said gently. "You just seem so strange."

"Well, I *feel* strange," she continued. "Isn't that what I've been trying to tell you?"

"Is everything all right?" he asked, genuinely confused.

"I'll have to get back to you when I know, but thanks for your concern." Star clicked off the phone, regarding it irritably for a moment before dropping it into the toilet.

Her captive was waiting patiently for her when she returned to the bed.

"What did I do last night?" she asked herself.

And then, with a child's impatience on Christmas morning, she tore off the sheet and found herself staring into the face of the rock-and-roll musician Jimi Deed, bound, gagged, and tied to her bed. Star hadn't seen Jimi since she threw him out of her trailer back on the California set of her TV show, *Lifeguards, Inc.* The only way she'd been able to convince him to leave had been to agree to go out with him when she got back from Cabo, though he'd called persistently and threatened to follow her. She was *still* in Cabo, and yet here he was.

"What are you doing here?" she demanded, unconsciously waving the gun at him.

Jimi winced, crying out in fear as the barrel of the shiny pistol passed near his nose.

"Oh, sorry about that," she said, embarrassed and apologetic, although continuing to wave the gun around. "It's not mine," she explained. "I'm not sure how it got here. For that matter, I'm not sure how *you* got here. I'm not really a gun person; I don't even know how it works, really. I mean, I guess you just pull on . . ."

And with that, the room was suddenly and violently filled

with feathers raining down like the first snow of the season.
Jimi screamed through his gag and writhed wildly on the bed,
his head next to the blackened remains of the pillow she'd
shot out from under him. She looked like an angel with a .45.

"Oh . . . I'm so very sorry," she said, putting the gun on
the bedside table. "You don't look too dangerous. Well not
most of you, anyway," she said, lifting the sheet for a peek
under the big tent he was pitching. She gave a low appreciative whistle. "Looks like you've got a bigger pistol than me."

Jimi struggled vainly against his bonds, startling Star. She
dropped the sheet, frightened, but soon realized that he was
no threat to her in his present condition.

"So how did you wind up here?" she said, sitting down beside him.

Jimi made some rather defiant noises through his gag.

"Oh, right, the gag," she said, knocking herself in the forehead with the heel of her hand. "My bad. Now, no screaming.
I doubt anyone would hear you or, judging from this room,
care. But I've got a really bad hangover from all this champagne, so, shhh."

Star unbuckled the very professional ballgag that was in
his mouth, allowing him to spit out the orange ball.

"What the fuck?" he demanded.

"What do you mean?" Star said, rising. "And what the
hell are you doing in my hotel room?"

"I'm tied to the bed and you've got a gun," he said. "Two
plus two."

"When did you get here?" she asked, still puzzled. "What
happened last night?"

"I've been here for three days," he said. "Last night just
made it clear I should have left after two. Or killed you. Now

will you let me go? I was supposed to be somewhere last night."

"You've been here with me for three days?" Star asked, not really paying much attention to what he'd said after that. "How is that possible?"

"Are you going to let me go?"

"I don't know. Do you promise not to tell anyone about all this?"

"I promise I'll visit you in Mexican jail," Jimi snarled, straining at his bonds.

"Now you have to promise me that you won't get me in trouble," Star said, rising, alarmed by his belligerent attitude even in his present circumstances.

"Are you fucking kidding me?" he said with a snort of laughter. "You kidnapped me and tied me up at gunpoint."

"Oh that's ridiculous," Star said, laughing. "I've never had to tie a man up, unless he wanted me to."

"Well, it seemed hot at first," Jimi admitted, doing what he could to shrug. "But then you wouldn't let me go, and that's kidnapping."

"You seem pretty glad to see me this morning," she said, reaching out and playfully tweaking the persistent erection, tenting the sheets in front of him. "Maybe we could work something out."

"Work something out?"

"Well, used to be you wanted to date me pretty bad, as I remember."

"That was before I married you and you tied me up and kidnapped me!" he roared. "Now all I want to do is see you behind bars."

"M-m-m-married?" Star stuttered. "I'm married?"

"Since yesterday."

"My mom is definitely not going to approve of this."

"She was pretty pissed," Jimi laughed.

"She was here?"

"No, you called her to tell her," Jimi nodded smugly.

"Oh my God."

"What else happened? How did you get here?"

"You really don't remember, do you?"

Star only shook her head in answer.

"I'll make you a deal," Jimi said. "You untie me and let me go to the bathroom, and I'll tell you what happened."

"No, I don't think I can trust you yet."

"We're married," Jimi said with a touch of self-righteousness.

She looked at him.

"Okay, so that doesn't count for much," he agreed. "But I really do have to pee."

She looked around the room and found the solution—an ice bucket, filled with slush and an upended bottle of Cristal. She arose from the bed where she'd been sitting, grabbed the bucket, and, marching out onto the balcony of her top-floor rooms, dumped the contents down the combined heights of the high-rise hotel and the steep cliffs on which it sat, into the Pacific, hundreds of feet below.

Leaving the French windows open, she walked back to the bed where he lay and pulled back the sheets.

"I can't believe I don't remember this," she said, taking his cock in her hand and guiding it into the ice bucket.

"You can't be serious!" he snarled.

"Roll over as much as you can," Star said playfully. "It's time for a little game of fireman and hose."

"Fuck you."

"Suit yourself," she shrugged, taking the bucket away.

"I'll piss right here," he said defiantly.

"And you'll lie in it," she said, folding her arms under her naked breasts.

"Mother fuck," he said, turning his hips as much toward her as he could, bound to the bed as he was.

"Oh, you want the bucket back now?"

"Just put it over here."

"Say please."

"Please," he said through gritted teeth.

Once again she took his cock in her hand and guided it into the bucket.

"Wow," she observed, looking at the almost-full bucket.

"Well, I've been tied up since last night."

"Okay then . . ." Returning from the bathroom where she'd emptied the bucket, Star took a seat on the bed, legs folded Indian style beside Jimi's naked body. "So, tell me what happened."

"You didn't untie me," he said, turning his head away.

"Tell me," she said, reaching out and toying with his now deflated cock.

"No," he said. "Cut it out."

"Tell me," she coaxed, stroking him back to erection.

He shook his head violently from side to side.

"Come on," she said, stroking harder.

"Get the fuck off of me," he protested.

"If you tell."

"Fuck you."

Laughing, she grabbed some hand cream from the bedside table and slathered it onto her hands and his erection. Mercilessly she began again, stroking and stroking until his balls tightened and he neared the brink. Abruptly she stopped and let him subside. As his orgasm faded she resumed her tease, stroking, sucking, and riding him near to orgasm. Again and again she played, always stopping just before he finished, until he was screaming and begging for release.

"Please, please, now," he pleaded as she rode him once more to the edge.

"Will you tell?" she asked, slowing down and letting him subside again.

"No, fuck you!" he spat.

"Okay, then," she said, climbing off. She spotted the video camera on the coffee table and brought it back with her. "Smile for the camera," she said, straddling him once more. She taped the two of them as best she could from her position astride him. She was driving him slowly mad, and enjoying every minute of it.

"I'll do it, I'll do it, I'll do anything, just don't fucking stop!" he screamed as she brought him to the brink once more.

"How can I believe you?" she asked, turning to film his answer.

"I don't know," he said. "I give you my word."

"I must have tied you up for a reason," she said. "I'm not sure about your word. Tell me something that I can use against you if you go back on your promise. Something nobody else knows."

"I was involved in a hit-and-run accident a couple of years back."

"You're a rock star," she scoffed. "That's like a rite of passage. What else?"

"I used to pay for studio time by screwing the woman who ran the recording studio."

"You've probably been bragging about that one for years," she said dismissively, picking up the pace and riding him harder. "Tell me *real* secrets."

"I used to take tap and ballet classes in high school," he blurted out, desperate. "And I was really good. My mom has recital pictures in her living room."

"That's the stuff," she said, bearing down. She had managed to get herself off a few times in the process, but managed to score one more off of her captive before he lost it and erupted, screaming and writhing in his relief.

She fell to one side and they lay panting next to each other for a bit.

"You raped me," he said.

"Raped you? Me?" she said, rewinding the tape and playing it back for him in the viewfinder.

"Please, please, now," his voice rang out. "Oh fuck yeah."

"Yeah, you sound like a rape victim," she said, giving him a swat. "Now, tell me the story."

The trip to Cabo had seemed like the perfect escape. Between her simultaneous shooting schedules for *Hammer Time* and *Lifeguards, Inc.,* her public appearances to promote both shows, and keeping the investors happy at her nightclub, Ka Mano, while juggling a personal life that included dating both Rufus and Mando, Star was, as she liked to say, "blowing the candle at both ends." In her spare time, she was also building a reputation as a photographer's model. Star's gatefold debut in *Mann* magazine had provided the bare essentials to start her modeling career. While she had added clothes to her modeling with some success, "less is more" best described her career, much to her mom's chagrin.

The trip to Cabo had come to Star through her friend and mentor, Jayne. A designer-label suntan-lotion company had come to *Mann* for models. And once again, Jayne's position as the magazine's executive editor and Star's dear friend had been a godsend to Star. As usual, Star's manager had arranged things and taken the credit along with his percentage, but it was her old friend who'd not only hooked her up but pushed her to take the assignment.

And so Star headed south of the border, as much for the promise of a vacation as the work.

It was a promise kept. Each day she spent a few hours shooting with a group of other models. She was the centerpiece of the promotion, but the whole shoot didn't rest on her. After hours—aka early afternoon—she was free to while away her time at the fashionable seaside resort, where she had been put up in the top-floor El Presidente suite.

The water was brisk, refreshing, and as blue as she'd ever seen.

The hotel, perched atop steep cliffs above the Pacific, looked as if it had been bleached white in the sun, in sharp contrast to the lush tropical plants and flowers that grew like weeds.

Star's rooms at the Cabo Ritz were party headquarters for the crew and models. It was off-season and the town had turned back into a sleepy fishing village where there was little to do, so they made their own fun.

There was some nightlife, though it was pitched primarily

to the spring-break crowd and the sort of lowlifes who'd want to spend the evening at such dissolute debaucheries, and Star couldn't figure out why no one in the cast or crew seemed interested.

So, when the phone rang during yet another afternoon nap, more than anything she'd actually thought it was going to be the production manager, the only person who'd actually called the room since her arrival.

"Star?"

"Yeah."

"I was hoping it would be you."

"Who were you expecting?"

"You got no idea how many Estrellitas I've talked to in the last twelve hours."

"What?"

"It means 'little star.' "

"Who is this?"

"Let me give you a hint," he said, clearing his throat and singing. "Oh, my penis has a first name, it's L-A-R-G-E—"

She hung up.

The phone rang again.

"Goddamn it!" she screamed into the phone. "How did you get this number? I told you I'd see you when I got back from the shoot—"

"Miss Leigh?" the production manager asked tentatively, interrupting her tirade. "Is everything all right?"

"Oh, Herb, I'm sorry, I . . ." Star trailed off, embarrassed. "I thought you were someone else."

"Jeez, who's been calling your room?"

"Doesn't matter," Star said, laughing it off. "I think he got the message. What's up?"

They had a brief conversation about the schedule for her last day of shooting.

"Okay, I'll see you in the morning," Star said. "Adidas."

"Adios." Herb laughed as he hung up.

The phone rang again almost immediately, and she naturally assumed it was Herb.

"What did you forget?" she answered.

"Are you having a bad day?"

"Am I?" Star said, a warning in her voice. "Maybe I'm just confused, but I was sure we'd agreed that I would go out with you when I got back to L.A. and that you wouldn't bug me before I got back."

"Well, that was before this bad mood," Jimi explained reasonably. "Me and some of the boys just happened to be in Cabo—and not a minute too soon, it sounds like. So, if you'd just tell me your room number, we'll come right on up and get started on cheering you up."

"Here?" Star demanded. "You're here?"

"Well, the call's not coming from inside the house, but—"

She hung up.

Almost immediately, the phone began to ring again.

She stared at it.

She wondered how he could dial that fast.

It kept ringing.

She put it in the drawer of her bedside table.

It rang and rang and rang.

"What?" she said, snatching open the drawer and answering it at last.

"What's your room number. I can be there in—"

"Oh, no," Star said, curious but wary. "How did you find me?"

"Well, you told me you were going to Cabo," Jimi snorted. "And the rest was easy. I just called every hotel until I found you."

"Persistent."

"I think you're worth it."

"You do, hunh?" she said, at last intrigued.

"I'm here, aren't I?"

"Yeah, you are."

"Ninety-nine percent of success is showing up."

"What's the other one percent?" She giggled.

"Truly amazing talent," he said with a rumble of husky laughter.

"Are you talented?"

"You have no idea."

"No, I don't, actually." Star giggled.

And so it began.

It just wasn't possible to tell him no.

After talking with Jimi on the phone for three hours that first day, Star agreed that she and her friends from the shoot would meet him and his friends for drinks at the hotel bar. It seemed like innocent fun, and it was, at long last, something to do on her vacation that involved leaving her room besides work. Star had had just about all the rest and relaxation she could stand, and a little tequila and a lot of dancing sounded like just what her holiday needed.

Best of all, it was the first offer she'd made the others on the shoot that had drawn any interest at all. Missy, her makeup and hair girl, three of the other models—Diane, Cindy, and Kat—and Roberto, one of the boys on the crew who was also one of the girls, all jumped at the chance to come along to see what would happen that evening.

Just knowing that they were going out that night enlivened Star on the next day's shoot. She'd made quite the hit learning to windsurf for the cameras. Afterward, she'd snagged some of the summer line they were there to model and enlisted Missy, who'd been doing her makeup for the shoot, to help her get ready so she could make a real entrance at the bar that night. She made quite the project of it.

The truth of it was, Star hadn't been all that interested in Jimi. She didn't even intend to see him after she got back to L.A.

"Okay, Missy," Star said, making like she was cracking a whip as she emerged wearing a bikini top, Gucci short shorts, and stilettos. "Bring on the eyeliner."

"I'm sorry, but the señor will not be permitted in the hotel bar," the maître d' said with a little sniff. "You are not dressed properly for the Ritz. Perhaps the Hilton will be more to the señor's liking? They have no standards there that I can detect."

Star, Missy, and the others were enjoying the show from their table inside the Land's End, the bar to which the maître d' was attempting to refuse entry to Jimi and his scruffy lot. Clad more or less identically in saggy jeans, black Franken-stein shoes, and wife-beaters, they looked like someone's backup dancers.

"Which one is he?" Diane, one of the other models, whis-pered to Star.

"I honestly don't know," Star confided with a tiny shrug. "They all look alike. They're all hot."

"I noticed that. Is he in a rock-and-roll band or a marching band?" Missy teased, laughing at her own joke.

"I'm not so sure." Star shrugged. "But it looks as though he's not going to be in here anytime soon."

"Look, Jeeves," Jimi shouted loudly enough to be heard at Star's table. "We are supposed to be meeting guests at your foofy, uptight place. You should be happy we're here. Look around."

"That's him, the belligerent one." Star nodded disgustedly, recognizing the attitude from the fight he'd gotten into when he'd broken into her trailer only a week earlier and surprised yet another intruder who'd beaten him to it.

She smiled at herself.

She had broken up the fight in her trailer and gotten Jimi to leave by promising to go out on a date with him when she got back from Cabo if he stopped stalking her. She also agreed to read a movie script that the other intruder, Steph Golden, had broken in to leave for her. And there she was going out with Jimi in Cabo and she'd not read a word of the *Hy Voltz* script. Not my most successful negotiation, she thought ruefully.

"He seems very, um, persistent," Cindy fished for a compliment as she sipped at the straw in her fruity drink. "That's always a good sign, right?" Her head bobbed back and forth like a tennis spectator's as she watched Jimi trying to outflank the implacable maître d'.

"Yeah," Star said, bemused as security stepped in to prevent Jimi from coming to her table. "You've got to admire his determination."

"Sure, what the fuck?" Kat said, toasting with her coconut shell.

Star rose to rescue him before he wound up in some seedy Mexican jail.

"A man will follow his dick off a cliff." Diane shrugged, stirring her drink with the straw.

"Is there a cliff nearby?" Star called over her shoulder with a little laugh and a toss of her head that brought both Jimi and the security guards up short.

"Hi," Jimi said, twisting his goatee nervously, unable to manage much more than an adolescent croak. "You look fucking amazing."

"Is there a problem?" Star asked without addressing Jimi directly.

"Señorita e'Star," the maître d' fawned. "I am so sorry I did not realize, is this man a guest of yours?"

"Yeah. What's wrong?"

"I'm afraid that the Ritz has a very strict dress code," the maître d' said with an obsequious bow. "I can offer you and your guests a table by the pool perhaps? Or in the cabana? But I cannot allow gentlemen without jackets in the Land's End Club after six. My sincerest apologies."

"No worries," Star said, waving the nervous man in for a landing with a gentle gesture. "Tell you what. I haven't gotten to see much of Cabo. Perhaps you could recommend a night-club. Something local and not too touristy? Where we could go for a little drink in the company of gentlemen without jackets?"

"I'm sure Miss e'Star could get in anywhere in the world she cared to call," the man said with another bow. "But, per-haps Madre de la Perla?"

"What?" Star asked. The name brought her up short. "What's the name of the place?"

"Madre de la Perla," the man repeated. "In *inglés,* Mother of Pearl. It's an open-air *cantina de la ostra*—oyster bar."

"I'm home," Star said, flinging her arms around Jimi's neck and hopping up and down as she spun him around. "Shuck me, suck me, eat me raw!" she shouted.

"I thought you'd never ask," Jimi said, grinning as he took her in his arms.

"They're actually supposed to be a 'hypochondriac,' " Star explained to her mystified party as she drained the oyster shell of its contents and chased it with a shot of tequila. "That means they'll put lead in your pencil," she added with a confidential giggle. "Who wants an oyster shot?" she asked as she dropped the hollow shell into the gold, spray-painted coffee can that had been placed on their table to collect the empties.

The whole place had the same sort of makeshift feel to it. Formerly a dockside gas station and general store catering to local fishermen, with a little imagination and a lot of spray paint, the place had been converted into a dockside gas station, general store, *and* a bar. There were a few rough wooden tables, benches, and an odd assortment of old webbed lawn chairs, where local fish and seafood were served fresh off the fishing boats that bought gas and shopped for supplies there.

The fiberglass had been stripped from the old red-and-white promotional gas station awning, and the rusty, bare frame had been wound with old, loudly colored Christmas tree lights. Brightly hued scraps of cloth hung from the rafters to separate the *cantina de la ostra* from the Texaco. Local musicians serenaded Star and her party with their brassy music from the deck of a small pontoon boat, lashed alongside the dock.

It was quite perfect. Exactly what Star had been looking for. But it was the name of the establishment that got to her like a message from the universe and her late grandfather Papa Jens that tonight was the right thing to do. As she watched the waitresses, she remembered her life in Miami at Mother Pearl's Steak and Oyster Emporium, where she'd lugged beer and shucked oysters wearing a tiny T-shirt emblazoned with those immortal words: SHUCK ME, SUCK ME, EAT ME RAW. The memory made her smile.

Jimi had entertained by playing all the glasses at the table like drums, smashing most of them. His reckless abandon was appealing somehow, and Star couldn't resist the growing attraction as he tugged her out onto the dance floor. Water misted on them from pinholes in water pipes in the rafters to help keep the dancers cool, and soon the small dance floor was filled with wet, tanned half-naked bodies.

"It's time for instant margaritas," Jimi announced.

"Instant?" Star said, crinkling her nose. "In this place? I think scratch margaritas all you're likely to get."

"No, not instant like that," Jimi said, hopping up on the table and waving the waitress over. "*Un* bottle . . . how do you say *bottle* in *español*?"

"*Botella.*" She smiled.

"Cool. *Una botella* of tequila and *una botella* of triple sec and *una de* lime juice . . . how do you say *lime juice*?"

"*Jugo de cal,*" the waitress, who clearly spoke perfect English, answered.

"*Gracias.*" Jimi nodded, making quite the show of it.
"*Una botella* of *jugo de cal, por favor.*"

"Are you going to make margaritas at the table?" Star
asked, sure of the recipe for margaritas from her tenure
hawking cocktails.

"Sort of," Jimi said. "It's even more instant than that," he
explained, opening the bottles and lining them up. "Okay, I'll
go first. Star, you're in charge of tequila. Missy, you take the
jugo de cal. And it's Diane, right?"

"Right." Diane smiled despite herself.

"Diane, you have the easy job," he said, handing her the
remaining bottle. "You're on triple sec."

"Jimi," Star said, laughing at the production he was making of the whole thing. "What are we supposed to mix the
drinks in?"

"Ah," he said, lying back on the table and letting his head
hang off the end as he faced the canopy of garish Christmas
lights and stars. "That's what makes them instant margaritas.
They don't become margaritas until the instant they touch my
tongue."

"Got it." Star laughed.

As Jimi lay back on the table, the girls poured the contents
into his mouth. What his Mix-Mistresses lacked in technique,
they made up for in enthusiasm and quantity. Most of their
first batch wound up on the front of Jimi's shirt. But Jimi was
both a willing and eager coach. Before long, the whole cantina was in on it.

Star gave it a try. "Isn't it funny how tequila goes straight
to your nipples," she announced as she sat up. Despite the
fact that it was a warm night and she was still overheated
from the dance floor, they were obviously rock hard.

The night just kept getting stranger. One of Jimi's friend's dimples started to freak her out, and Star had to beg him not to smile. She began analyzing everyone, taking an interest in the strangest things. When she went to the ladies' to freshen up, she was taken by how hot it felt to pee. "I could pee for an hour," she told one of the girls who'd come with her. "That tequila must be really fresh or something."

At one point, Jimi borrowed a skull ring from "Dimples" and made quite the show of proposing, telling everyone who'd listen that Star was every young boy's fantasy, that it was love at first sight. She tried to say no, but he was having none of it, and so she just smiled and enjoyed the feel of the cool silver on her finger.

She didn't know what it was, but the night just kept getting better and better. The colored lights looked more vibrant against that sky. The stars kept getting brighter. The moon was blinding. The drinks couldn't have been tangier. Even the feel of the lawn chair was a treat against her skin.

"Oh, my God," she cried out, rubbing against the webbing. "This chair feels amazing."

Jimi exchanged a look and a laugh with his buds.

"X-cellent," he said, giving Star and his friends the thumbs-up. "Totally x-cellent. Maybe we should go for a walk on the beach, Star." He offered her his hand and she took it, only to marvel at the feel of his skin against hers.

"Your hands are so soft and yet so strong," Star said, rubbing his hand between both of hers. "It feels wonderful."

"And your hands feel awesome on mine," he moaned as she ran her hands up his arms.

The two could barely walk for grasping one another, and

Jimi's posse laughed at their awkward progress across the restaurant toward the beach.

"Ecstasy?" Diane asked elliptically.

Jimi's clones only laughed in reply.

"You fucker," Star said, striking the still-bound Jimi with the flat of her hand on his taut stomach. Like a belly flop it made a bigger noise than anything else. "You slipped me Ecstasy? Is that why I feel so weird?" she demanded, running her hand up and down the smooth naked skin of his stomach. It felt warm and velvety under her palm and she quickly became mesmerized by the sensation.

"Dude, I totally thought you'd have done X before," he said, pleading his case, her touch heating him up but his bonds keeping him from doing anything about the sweet torture of it. "Honest, I would never have slipped you anything if I'd known."

"Is that why I can't remember what happened," she said, tearing her hand away from the irresistible feeling of his skin.

"Well," he admitted, sorry but relieved that she'd stopped her stroking. "There were a number of substances involved. After the instant margaritas you just couldn't get enough."

"So you tricked me?"

"Well, you weren't exactly unconscious."

"But it's the same thing as forcing me," she said, strangely torn between the desire to feel his skin against her hand and her confused outrage at his revelation.

"You're not the one tied to the bed," he pointed out. "Wait and hear the rest of the story before you decide."

"So, you're saying that I wanted to do all these drugs?" Star said, recoiling, her hand clutched to her chest. The feel of her own skin was awesome, not to mention the sensation of her hand touching her naked breasts.

"You wanted a lot more than that," Jimi said with a dirty little laugh.

Their first kiss, though chemically enhanced, was electric and lasted, more or less, for two days. Star thought that there was a magical bond between them, above and beyond the attraction that she already felt.

There was something funny and sweet and, despite his outward ultrahip affectation, kind of nerdy about him. She couldn't quite put her finger on it, but Jimi Deed was charming in a way that made you want to take care of him.

And he knew how to kiss.

The Ecstasy just made her unable to resist more of a good thing.

"Oh, Jimi," she gasped, coming up for air but not really breaking contact with him. "You feel so . . . perfect against me." She groaned as she ground her hips into his.

"God, baby, that feels sooo good!" he howled, throwing his head back.

"Your T-shirt feels like velvet." She shivered, allowing the straps at her shoulders to fall away so that she could brush her bare nipples against the ribbed fabric. "Oh, feel the wind on your skin," Star said, turning and letting the warm sea breeze caress her naked flesh in the privacy of the night-darkened beach.

"You're so warm," he said, wrapping his arms around her

from behind and grinding his denim-encased erection into the silky fabric of the tiny black shorts sliding from her waist.

"I can't explain how I feel," Star said, reaching behind to grasp his thighs and urging him more tightly against her.

"Your body feels great," Jimi said, boldly running his hand up to fondle her breasts with such delicate finesse that there was only enough contact to create an arc of sensation.

Star shivered from the intensity.

Sensations fired through her body. The moist sand under her feet like walking on cooked oatmeal. The froth of the waves lapping at her ankles like lace cuffs. And Jimi's urgent and growing sexual need, like static electric shocks with each touch.

"You know what?" she said, turning back so abruptly that it startled him. "I think getting in the water naked would be so awesome right now. And I have a Jacuzzi in my room." She was so excited she was shouting.

"That is so cool," he said, embracing her, thrilled almost to the point of orgasm by just the idea of being naked in a tub with Star. He could feel himself begin to leak as little spasms rocked his body.

"Race you," she said, breaking away and running up the beach in the direction of the hotel.

Star was tearing off what was left of her clothes even before the door to her room closed. Jimi followed her as she filled the tub and climbed in.

The water felt like warm Jell-O against her skin, thicker somehow. More viscous. And then, Jimi was on her, rubbing against her, and they were naked together for the first time, in the warm, silky water.

His mouth sought hers out and the feeling of his tongue entwined with hers was almost too much. It was as if they were kissing in slow motion as each tried to seek out every bump and serration and indentation in the mouth of the other.

"What does this feel like?" he asked, trailing his fingers down her body and sliding them inside.

Star shrieked. The orgasm was instantaneous, swift, and fierce. Jimi merely brushed against that most sensitive spot and she went off like a gunshot. The effect was so intense she had to hang on to Jimi for support. But unlike a gunshot, it went on and on. As his fingers explored, it just kept happening, rolling over her like waves in a storm, too numerous to count and too frequent to regain her footing.

"Oh, God," she said, when at last she found words. "You've got about two days to stop doing that."

So he did it again.

The effect was exactly the same, or maybe even better, she couldn't decide because he didn't stop the second time until she forced his hand away, unable to endure the pleasure any longer. It was a delicious pain, like drinking something really cold when you're thirsty on a hot day. It burns so good going down. Sex with Jimi was like orgasms came by the gallon and she was drinking too fast.

She pushed him backward until he stumbled and ended up sitting on the enormous tub's silky marble steps. And, like the neck of the Loch Ness monster, his erection broke the surface even though the steps were submerged.

Wow, she thought.

"What?" he asked.

"You know what I'm really good at?" Star asked mischievously.

"What?" He grinned in reply.

"Holding my breath."

She took him into her mouth, her head underwater as she plumbed the depths.

"Oh, shit," his voice rang out in the marble room.

She almost drowned, but what a way to go.

They spent the next two days naked in the water. They rubbed, licked, sucked, fondled, and tasted each other to orgasm so repeatedly that their entire bodies were chapped and raw. After the first couple of hours they had discovered Star's video camera, and they began relentlessly filming each other, not only when they were rubbing each other raw, but in the bathroom or showering or eating breakfast.

They simply could not seem to get enough of each other. It was as though the camera allowed them to see more than just when they were looking at each other.

He was filming her when he said those words that reshaped their destinies.

"Marry me?"

She looked up at him with a nervous giggle and smiled. It was as though she was checking to see if he was kidding.

"Okay," she said.

"And the ring?" she asked, wiggling her upturned fingers.

"We stole it," Jimi admitted.

"Oh my God," Star gasped. It was quite the rock and she knew they'd be looking for it. She tried to pull it from her hand, moving toward the door to throw the ring into the ocean below, but his laughter stopped her. "What's so funny?"

"You," he said. "We didn't steal it. I bought it for you."

"That's not all that funny," she giggled, unable to resist his full and easy laugh.

"No," he admitted, still laughing. "It's not. But you wanted to."

"I did?" she asked in disbelief, crossing back over to him.

"That's why you bought that gun," he said. "I shouldn't have let you, but really, you buying that gun was the best thing ever."

"Excuse me," Star said to the clerk at Salvatore's. "Do you speak English?"

"Si, Señora," he replied, beaming at her. "What do you need today?"

"A gun," she said, looking through the glass case at the revolvers the store had on offer, while Jimi videotaped the scene.

"A gun?" the clerk asked, only a little surprised after years of American tourists. "What sort of gun?"

"I don't know," she shrugged. "The silver one is nice."

"Lo siento, Señora," the clerk corrected himself. "What will you be using the gun for?"

"I need to rob a jewelry store," Star said, looking up from the glass case and smiling into the man's startled face. She had counted on surprising him—and she succeeded.

"The, uh, silver one should be fine," he said, recovering as Jimi's laughter shook the camera. "Perhaps this is a little joke?"

"Oh no, I'm serious," Star assured the man. "Could I hold it?"

"Por supuesto." The clerk gave her a bow, took a key from his pocket, and opened the case. "Here you go," he said, handing her the gun.

"Heavy," she said, assuming her best Charlie's Angels' stance, tossing her hair back and posing both for the camera and for Jimi. "How many thingies does it hold?" she asked, looking down the barrel.

"Siete . . . seven thingies," the clerk said, glad that the gun was not loaded.

"Does it come with thingies?" she asked, sighting the clerk down the barrel.

"No, but we sell thingies as well." He ducked to get a box of bullets from below the counter. "May I?" he asked, extending his hand.

Star handed the clerk the gun, and he demonstrated how to insert the bullets into the magazine.

"Cool," she said. "I'll take it and a dozen of the thingies."

"A dozen?" the clerk asked. "We sell them by the box."

"Yeah, er, right," Star shrugged. "I mean a dozen boxes."

"This must be quite a jewelry store," the clerk said, playing along with the joke as he assembled the purchase.

"It's an amazing ring," Star said, leaning against Jimi. "We're going to be married."

"Congratulations," the clerk said. "Will there be anything else?"

"Does it need batteries?"

"But we didn't rob the store?"

"No, I'd already bought you the ring before you bought

the gun." Jimi smiled, remembering the exhilaration he'd felt in that moment, and pretty much every moment since he'd left with Star for Madre de la Perla.

"And the wedding?"

"At some club." He rolled his eyes. "We got the license and had a Mexican Elvis impersonator marry us after the bikini contest. The winner was your maid of honor. You both wore white."

"Bikinis?"

"Naturally."

"So, how did you get tied up?" she said, zooming in to film his answer.

"You convinced me to let you," he replied with as much of a shrug as he could manage under the circumstances. "It seemed like a good idea at the time. Kind of hot, actually."

"Why didn't I let you go?"

"To keep me from going back to work and leaving you here," he said, looking away.

"You're lying," she said, leaning in, the camera just inches away from the tip of his nose.

"No, I had a big concert I was supposed to do yesterday," he said. "They're pretty pissed. Turn on the news. They're looking all over the world for me."

"But that isn't why I wouldn't let you go, is it?" she said, reaching down and stroking his cock again.

"Don't start that again," he winced. "I'm sore all over after the last few days. Aren't you?"

"I wondered why my nipples hurt," she nodded, the camera bobbing. "So tell. Why wouldn't I untie you?"

"So I wouldn't go back to my girlfriend."

"Your girlfriend?" she said, jumping to her feet and dropping the camera, but not turning it off. "You have a girlfriend? But we're married."

"Maybe," he said. "I'm not sure about ceremonies conducted by Elvis impersonators. He did do a good 'Volare.' "

" 'Volare' isn't an Elvis song," she said petulantly.

"I'm just saying."

"So are we married or aren't we?"

"I think we get to decide that."

"And how do we do that?"

"Watch the tapes," he suggested. "You'll see what I got to see the past few days."

"Why did you ask me to marry you?" she asked, sitting again and placing the camera on the bedside table to film them both.

"We're good together."

"The sex."

"Hell yeah, but that's not it."

"Like what?"

"Like even now, I'm tied to the bed, you're holding me hostage at gunpoint and sitting there naked and, well, I don't know about you, but this just fits."

"I remember," she shrieked, leaping up and jumping on the bed. "I remember, I remember, I remember!"

"Everything?" he said bouncing uncomfortably.

"No," she said, stopping and letting the bed recede. "But I remember why I tied you up."

There was a long silence. She stood over him on the bed, staring out the window.

"Why?" he asked, finally.

"Why what?"

"Why did you tie me up?"

"I can't tell you."

"Why not?" he asked, puzzled.

"I don't know if I can trust you."

"Babe, in the last few days you've told me your whole life."

"Yeah, but I don't remember that. I just remember that you tried to leave me and so I tied you up."

"Because you love me?"

"I hardly know you."

"Because you were afraid to be alone?"

"Not exactly."

"What exactly?"

"Because I feel so at ease with you around," she said, trying to put words to it. "Being naked around you is like wearing a coat and gloves on a cold day."

"But you're Miss March," he said a little surprised. "And the world's favorite lifeguard."

"Being an exhibitionist is the best cover for being shy," Star said, reaching up to brush his long black hair away from his face. "No one suspects."

He turned his head to kiss her hand as she stroked his hair. They regarded each other a moment.

"What's left to hide?" he asked her.

"Me," she said simply. "The part I save for myself."

He shook his head, not understanding.

"There's this website," she said, folding her hands in her lap and looking out the window of the room. "This guy spends his whole life following me around and taking pictures of me and posting them on this website. It's like his career or something. He has pictures of me going to work.

Pictures of me going to the store. Pictures of me walking the dog, on the set, having lunch with friends, on dates, kissing, holding my mother's hand. He even has pictures of me sleeping. It's like he's stealing my life. Not the part that we all give the world, but the part I keep for me." The tears felt warm on her face.

They sat silent for a long time. Jimi looked at Star and she looked out the window at the late-afternoon light reflecting on the ocean below.

"Untie me," he said at last.

"So can you escape?"

"So I can hold you."

Star looked at Jimi a moment. Maybe he was telling the truth. Or maybe she just wanted to be held. Either way, she couldn't make much of a marriage out of it if she kept her husband tied to the bed. Eventually they'd have to change the sheets.

Looking around for something to cut the bonds with, Star spied some dagger-sized shards of glass from the table she'd shot earlier. She wrapped one of them in a towel so she wouldn't cut her hands, then sawed through the random bonds she couldn't untie or unbuckle.

"If you love something, let it go," she said, stepping back from the bed when he was free.

"I always thought that was such a stupid thing," he said, rubbing his wrists. "I mean, if you let it go, how will it know you love it?"

She laughed, still a little woozy from the afternoon and God knew what all else.

Jimi extended his arms and Star fell into them.

It was just them, naked in bed with a blender. No Ecstasy,

no special effects, just the two of them joined perfectly together like interlocking pieces in a puzzle.

Jimi ran his hands down her body, drawing her so tightly into him it was as if he were trying to merge them into one. When they kissed, it was the same. It wasn't just sex, it was as if they were trying to become one person, two halves fused together. When she took him in her mouth, or he was inside her, the passion turned them into a single being, if only for a perfect instant.

When it was done, they lay sweating together, still united, unwilling to separate. Star writhed against her husband, moving to excite him, to extend their union and . . . and that's when she heard the noise, the excruciatingly familiar sound of a camera's auto rewind. She saw only a man's shoe under the curtains. That's all she needed before she was up, gun in hand, running for the balcony.

"You son of a bitch!" she screamed, running toward the sound. The shoe disappeared and she saw the man run for the rope ladder he must have used to climb down from the rooftop onto her balcony.

Jimi was too blissed out to realize what was going on, but when he heard Star's shouts and screams he followed her out onto the balcony, where he found her holding a gun on a man hanging from the railing—dangling, really—hundreds of feet above the jagged rocks of the coastline below.

"Get the camera," she directed.

"What's going on?" Jimi asked, unsure of what he was witnessing or what he should do.

"This is the guy," Star said by way of explanation, brushing away angry tears. "You know . . . this is the one with the website."

"Star?" Jimi said, unsure of what she wanted.

"It's time for a little confession," she said, prodding the photographer's ribs with the toe of her Gucci boot. "Get the camera."

A smile split Jimi's face. "You got it, babe."

He returned with the camera, and the two spent the next few minutes forcing the intruder to admit what he was doing and how he got into his present predicament. While the man pleaded for his life, Star got his name and ID as a souvenir.

Satisfied, they were at a loss for what to do next.

The idea seemed to occur to the two of them at once.

"On three?" Jimi said, taking her hand in his.

Star nodded.

"One," they said together, each peeling a finger from the railing as Jimi continued to film. "Two . . ." Another finger. "Three!"

With a scream and a wail the man fell from view, past the twenty stories of the hotel, down the cliffs and into the rocks hundreds of feet below. The crashing waves swept him out to sea.

Jimi filmed for a while, unable to think of anything else.

Star scanned nearby balconies to determine whether anyone had witnessed the photographer's fall.

They looked at each other. Did anyone see? Did anyone hear? Dare they breathe?

And with that thought came a pounding on the door.

"Oh shit," Star said.

"Get the tapes," Jimi instructed as they dashed back into the room.

Star raked their videos into a pillowcase and knotted it.

More pounding.

She stepped awkwardly into a pair of bikini bottoms and barely grabbed the top while Jimi, clad only in a pair of jams and a tank, grabbed her hand and dragged her out onto the balcony.

As the knocking continued, they climbed the photographer's rope ladder up to the roof and pulled it up behind them, just as the door to their room opened.

"Room service," the maid called from the door. "Ay, dios mio."

2

sweet peace
and time

How did I get here? Star wondered as she looked around the harbor at Cannes. Dressed in formal black rubber, laced up the front, and cinched at the waist, she rode at the prow of a yacht the movie studio had hired to create her entrance at the film festival. She was excited about attending. She was excited about being in the movie. She'd read the script for *Hy Voltz* with Jimi and fallen in love with the idea of being an action hero. The studio had been amazing, putting everything together. It helped take away a little of the fear she felt about being catapulted up onto the big screen.

But that morning truly took her breath away.

To this almost too perfect small town on the ocean were added that morning the perfect mix of fluffy white clouds and sunshine, a gentle breeze, and hundreds, possibly thousands, of smaller boats dotting the harbor, each laden with photographers and video crews poised to capture the moment of Star's arrival at that year's film festival.

How had this happened?

She laughed as she waved at the well-wishers and paparazzi who bobbled in her wake. She looked up at Jimi, who sat next to the captain on the bridge, and shared a secret smile as if to confide a bit of her disbelief.

They exchanged a wary glance. Ever since Cabo they'd been looking over their shoulders. The body of the photographer who had fallen from their hotel balcony had washed ashore in Migrino, just up the Baja coast. There had been speculation about his death, but most thought he'd simply fallen scaling the cliffs in search of his prey. And it really was that simple, he had fallen. But Jimi and Star were a little paranoid about hiding out since their marriage had made them the targets of even more media attention. Plus, Jimi was being sued for missing the show, though insurance was covering it.

Their secret, not to mention their tormentors, had provided them with a common enemy. They became inseparable. So when Star had accepted the movie role and the promotional debut at Cannes, Jimi was right there at her side.

He grinned.

It was all the encouragement that she needed. She turned back to the crowds and the eyes of the world and waved. She could hear the shouts and cheers over the roar of the massive engines that powered her toward the red carpet that had been rolled out all the way down to the water's very edge to receive her.

She felt a strange swelling inside, as though she might cry

or run for cover. Perhaps it was joy or pride or ego or just fear
or paranoia or a little bit of all of the above. She stood alone
on the deck of a ship arriving in a city where she had never before been to promote a film that had not even been shot or, for
that matter, even fully scripted. But here was the world waiting to welcome her, watching her every move. It was her they
had come to see, and she knew it for sure for the first time that
perfect morning, she just didn't know why.

The weeks with Jimi leading up to Cannes had been a
whirlwind. Like a honeymoon on crack. They had returned
from Cabo to Jimi's Malibu beachfront of a bachelor pad.
The multimillion-dollar home was still only sparsely fur-
nished with a few well-chosen pieces and some art. Warhol's
pink camouflage hung above the bed, which was just a mattress on the floor, albeit a really, really nice mattress. A bed-
sheet partially covered the plate-glass window with the
money-shot view of the golden sands of Malibu.

"Were you robbed?" Star asked warily as she regarded the
interior of their new home. "The morons. Isn't that a Warhol?"

Jimi laughed, sluicing through the art and architecture
books. "When my ex-girlfriend left, I told her to take what she
wanted, and she wanted a lot. I just haven't gotten around to
it. But, this way we can make it our own. It won't be like
you're moving into my place, it'll really be ours."

"Yeah, I guess," Star said, realizing how little she knew
about this man. "It's my favorite Warhol ever."

"Then I must have bought it for you," he said quietly. And
then, "Oh, dude!" he exclaimed suddenly, striking himself on
the forehead. "I totally spaced on this one." Without further

explanation or intimation, he dragged Star out the front door, swept her into his arms, and carried her, not only across the threshold but back up the stairs and to the mattress by the window in his bedroom.

As they tore the sheets from the window, the magic of sunset poured into the room, and the spartan surroundings were forgotten as the forces of their need for each other once again overpowered them.

He couldn't get inside her fast enough.

"Oh, hell, yeah." Jimi heaved, driving himself inside her. It had been all the time since the hotel room in Cabo that they'd had their last fix, and both were glad the wait was over.

Star clawed at his back, matching his urgency as she tore at him.

It was beautiful, efficient sex, and both were taken care of more than once before the sun slipped below the horizon. If true love is when you come at the same time, this was it always.

Jimi fell away and they lay gasping, bathed in sweat and the pinkish gray twilight that spilled up from the ocean below and poured over the room through the massive unmasked window.

"I do love a good sunset," Star sighed contentedly.

She awoke to the harsh glare of morning from the unshaded window.

She clasped the sheet around her as she arose and then giggled as she realized what she was doing. In truth, it was stranger for the pair to be dressed in each other's company than nude.

Laughing, she cast the sheet aside and bounded out of bed to find her husband. As she padded down the second-floor landing, which was in effect the upstairs hallway, she heard Jimi singing the lyrics to "Rapper's Delight."

Following the sound of his voice, Star walked naked through several expansive but otherwise unidentifiable empty rooms.

She sang back to him, joining in the words to the song.

"In here, honey pie," his voice came from behind a pair of double swinging doors.

She smiled as she passed through the mahogany doors and into a vast commercial-scaled kitchen, all stainless steel and black tile. At the far side, bent over a range larger than the one they had back at Mother Pearl's, was her new husband.

"What are you doing?" she asked as she made her way around the archipelago of utility islands that dotted the unfathomable interior of the immense room. "And what's with this room? Will we be shooting a cooking show or are we opening a cafeteria?"

"Bowling alley," he said, still not looking at her.

"Too big." She laughed. "We'll never find the balls. So what's up? Coffee?"

"Ta-dah," he proclaimed, wheeling to greet her, stark naked and presenting a rather splendid breakfast tray. "The most important meal of the day—breakfast."

She dissolved into fits of laughter as she looked at the tray.

"You can cook!" Star said with delight, clapping her hands, pleased to know something practical about him. In fact, pleased to know anything about him at all.

"Let's eat outside," he suggested, strolling out of the house onto the patio.

"And do the neighbors care that we're not formally dressed?" Star asked, following him out to the pool.

"It's one of the reasons I got this place," he explained, setting out the food on a wrought-iron table near the pool. "It's right next to a nature preserve on one side and a cliff on the other. So there are no neighbors."

Star had to admit that he was a very good cook. Granted, fruit, fried eggs, and toast weren't that challenging, but nothing was burned and the presentation was imaginative. The two grapefruit halves had cherries in the center. "Hmm," she said, holding them up to her chest. "Freudian. Got something on your mind?"

"Just breastfast," he grinned.

"It's a great house." Star looked around for a chair to pull up to the iron table. "Lots of potential," she added, mentally decorating the place when Jimi leaped abruptly into the pool, reemerging with first one, and then a second wrought-iron chair to match the table. Placing each on the deck, he leaped adroitly from the water and made his way over to Star with the chairs. More amazing to her than his behavior was the fact that the chairs actually matched the table.

"What else is down there?" she asked, peering tentatively over the side.

"Not much now," Jimi shrugged. "For a couple of weeks there was a 1967 Cadillac convertible after a kick-off party we had for one of our albums, I forget which."

"Whose car?" she asked, taking her chair. The wet iron was chilly against her bare skin.

"Not sure," he said, toying with the left grapefruit. "Seems almost painful to break up the set now."

She gave a little rumble of laughter. "So, how'd the car wind up there?"

"Parking," he said with a vague air.

Breakfast in the warm morning sun was easy and pleasant; their worries were soon forgotten as they laughed and talked together.

"Do you want anything else?" he asked as the plates were pushed aside.

"Umm-hmm," Star grinned, slipping under the table and taking him in her mouth.

Jimi was impressed with Star's place. It was filled with French antiques. Though some, like the "real Parisian sidewalk," were of dubious origin, none was of the distressed and pickle-white American type. It was girly, but he had to admit it was well put together. Lots of cool stuff like the PlayStation and the big-screen TV, an excellent stereo system, video game system, and lots of furniture that was more about how it felt than how it looked. And it looked great. Too much pink for his taste, but otherwise, a thumbs-up. And two thumbs-up for the fully stocked bar that he hit hard.

Star was relieved to be home for the first time in three weeks. She immediately called Engel, her buddy from the *Lifeguards* crew who was dog-sitting with Mutley, to check on her beloved pooch and to get him over to the house as soon as possible. Then she hit the showers to wash off what was left of Cabo.

Jimi snooped around a bit, getting to know more about her, but if you look for something long enough, you'll find it.

He had been looking for more game cartridges. What he found was a drawer full of men's clothes.

Star had decided that the shower was not quite enough and was just sinking into a tub full of gardenia-scented bubbles when the door to the bathroom flew open and Jimi began emptying the drawer full of clothes into the tub with her.

"What the hell are these?" he demanded.

"Um, I don't know," Star said, unsure of just how to react.

"The question is, whose clothes are these?" Jimi screamed, leaning down closer as though she might not hear him.

"Is there some kind of prize?" Star asked, trying for humor.

"You think this is funny?"

"Not anymore," she sighed, getting out of the tub full of wet clothes and crushed gardenia bubbles. "So what's the problem, Jimi?"

"They're men's clothes!" he leaned in and shouted again.

"Yeah?" Star said, losing patience. "Come on, you think you're the first?"

She shoved her way past and stepped back into the shower to wash off the remains of her ruined bubble bath.

Jimi was stunned and chastened. Her complete lack of intimidation or even reaction to his bullying startled him.

"I'm sorry, hon, it just freaked me out," he said, sitting on the side of the tub, still holding the drawer.

"Duh," her voice echoed inside the shower.

Jimi didn't know exactly what to do. With his ex-wife there had never really been anything to deal with. She'd done things pretty much her way, and he'd either gone along or been left behind. They'd never really fought, but then they'd never really talked either. She'd never given him reason to be jealous, and frankly, he'd never really paid her that much attention.

"Look, Jimi," Star said gently, emerging from the shower. "I'm in love with you. I've never felt like this before. And I can't explain it. But I don't know a damned thing about you. And you don't know anything about me. This is just something to know about me. Did I see other men before we met? Yes. But it's over now, I married you. The end. Okay?"

"Okay," Jimi said, taking the towel from her and gently drying her off.

"Did you?"

"See other men before we met?" Jimi asked.

She laughed.

"I've taken full advantage of being a rock star. I've been mostly single for the past two years," he said with a little shrug. "I had a serious girlfriend. And I was married. Twice."

"Really? Well, then, you already know how this works."

"If I did I'd still be married, right?"

She laughed. "So, does it bother you that I've been with other men?"

"No," he shrugged. "When I think about it, it seems kind of hot. Like I'd like to watch."

"Yeah," she giggled, and then caught his eye and stopped. "Really?"

"Yeah." He grinned. "Like live porn."

"We can do anything we want," she said, climbing onto his lap and licking the side of his face as he'd done to her the first time they met. "Anything?"

They laughed at their shared secret for a moment, and then he buried his face in her breasts.

The doorbell rang.

"Mutley!" Star shouted, snatching a robe from the hook behind the bathroom door. "Mutley's home. Why don't you clean this mess up and then come meet the only competition you've got."

The wet towel smacked him on the side of the head.

The pictures were a sensation. The shots of two of them, breakfasting naked at Jimi's, Star's feet sticking out from under the table, her head in his lap, began appearing on the cover of every questionable publication on the planet, and even a few fairly respectable ones, almost before they'd done the dishes.

Star was at a loss.

The press had always been persistent, but this was a whole new dimension. This kind of coverage was like breaking and entering. Jimi took it even worse than she did. They'd been walking back to Star's after breakfast at The Omelet Shoppe when they'd passed a newsstand virtually plastered with the pictures. They froze for a second as they realized what they were seeing. And then Jimi began railing and shredding the papers and magazines.

Of course, the next day, everything at that and every other newsstand was covered with pictures of him tearing up the pictures the day before. Even more chilling was that neither had had any idea they were being watched. The secret weighed on them more.

In a way, it began to bond them together. At a time when they were looking for common ground on which to build their relationship, the constant perception that they were being watched and pursued bound them together as nothing else could have. It was "us against them."

Even in the first few days of their marriage, it became clear that more was afoot than simply the normal attention and curiosity surrounding a celebrity couple.

They were besieged.

One benefit was that there was never any wait for the official garbage pickup. All the trash was stolen within minutes of its being put out by the curb. The downside was that within days the press was filled with even more "trash" about them than usual, from speculation about their carb and alcohol consumption to their magazine subscriptions and product preferences.

Star then hired a private service to clean the house, as well as shred, destroy, and haul away all the "evidence."

The afternoon before the cleaning crew was scheduled, Jimi insisted that Star come with him to their place at the beach.

"There's something I want to show you," he said. "Besides, what else do you have planned?"

It was true. When they weren't making love, they were spending every waking moment together. Jimi even went with her to Skip and Billy's to get her hair done. The only reason Star hadn't wanted to go was because it meant more spy pictures and lurking "reporters."

As it turned out, there didn't seem to be anyone around, and Mutley greatly enjoyed his first visit to their new home. The three of them got into a game of tossing the round cardboard insert from an empty pizza box.

"Ewwww," Star had groaned when Jimi pulled the disk out of one of the empty boxes stacked and awaiting the cleanup crew.

"Relax," Jimi guffawed. "It was a cheese pizza."

Star was too amused to resist, and they played until nearly sundown.

"Mutley is falling for you too," Star said as they made their way back up to the house from the beach.

"Then my evil plan is working," Jimi said, twirling an imaginary mustache and laughing a sinister laugh.

"So, what is it that you wanted to show me?" Star asked, hugging him around the waist as they walked. "This cardboard disk is special, but I'm thinking that we could have ordered in back at the other house."

"Oh, yeah," Jimi said, picking up his pace. "I was having such a good time I almost forgot. The safe."

"What?"

"Well, what with the cleaning crew coming tomorrow," he explained as he led her into the garage, "I just thought it would be a good idea to lock things up. And I figured you should know about the safe too. In case you ever needed it."

The garage had been semiconverted into a practice space for the band. The walls had been lined with carpet-covered baffles to muffle the sound on the outside and improve it on the inside of what was otherwise just a concrete box.

"Over here," he said, taking her to a spot just behind his keyboards. "Put your hand right in here." He guided her hand into a fold in the carpet and she felt the handle and instinctively pulled it.

The false wall swung away to reveal the door of a rather large safe that had been set into the wall behind it.

"Jeez, Jimi. That's huge. I thought it was going to be like one of those wall safes behind a picture that you see in the movies."

"Nah," Jimi chuckled. "You can't put anything in them. And besides, they're too easy to steal."

"Steal?"

"Yeah, you just cut 'em out of the wall and take 'em home to break into at your leisure. This baby," he said, patting the huge, black steel door, "this is here to stay. You'd need a crane and a Mack truck to get it out of here. Leastwise, that's what it took to put it in. Now here's the combination."

Star practiced opening the safe a couple of times until she was proficient.

"And here we go," Jimi said, swinging wide the door to reveal a closet-sized space. There was even a light inside. "It's fireproof and waterproof. So I keep things like family photos and important papers in here. My gun collection. Masters from some of the band's albums. Stuff like that."

"And here I thought it was going to be filled with gold bullion and uncut diamonds," Star said, charmed to find the safe filled mostly with items of sentimental value.

"Nope." He shook his head. "Hell, we don't even have wedding rings."

Mutley lost interest and began exploring the largely empty house, which was like buried treasure as he went sniffing from room to room. Eventually Star came looking for him, but not before he'd had quite the time of it. To Mutley, the house was perfect and Star and Jimi's plans would ruin everything.

"Come on, you," she said, wrestling Mutley out of the empty hall in which she'd envisioned a dining room once the *Hard Luck* album-tour loadout stored there could be relocated. Mutley, who was not going to be taken so easily, had spent the last few hours exploring the huge, empty house and was prepared for quite the game of hide-and-seek, slipping away from Star and taking off.

Star chased him from room to room, finding herself in

what would make a nice nursery one day. Away from the street and the pool, the room had loads of windows, a southern exposure, and more camping equipment than she'd seen in one place outside of the sporting goods section at the Wal-Mart back home in Sunrise City.

She was amazed. In this house, where it seemed no one lived, and with this man who seemed to have no interests outside of his music and the party, here was a room devoted to what, exactly?

"Jimi?" she called. "Jimi, what is all this stuff?"

No answer.

"Jimi," she called, returning to the central atrium and hallway, her voice echoing throughout the house.

She heard a muffled sound, and a moment or so later, Jimi came into the hall in reply.

"What is all this stuff?" she asked, pointing toward the door.

"Oh, it's my Y2K preparedness room." Jimi shrugged. "It seemed like a good idea at the time."

"Camping at the end of the world." She smiled, remembering all the fuss.

"Sounds like a song lyric," he said, picking up the words and singing them to her. "Camping at the end of the world, that's where we could just be."

"Not a bad idea," she said, leaning down to pat Mutley, who'd brought her a tent stake he'd found. "We might get some privacy there."

"You think?" he said, excited by the idea. "What do you think about houseboats?"

"I grew up on an island," she said with a little laugh. "I drove a boat before a car."

"Let's do it. I know the perfect place."

"When?"

"How about now?"

If Jimi had been unsure he loved her before that moment—
and he had not been—he knew it for sure right then.

It was the perfect plan.

They would go away for a few isolated days together, and
by the time they returned, the house would be ready to begin
the renovations. Meanwhile, Star and Jimi had a project and
a secret plan and they were ready to depart within twenty-
four hours of their decision to go. They told no one, they
would simply go missing.

On the evening before their disappearance, Jimi took Star
for sushi at Matsuhisa Miyasi's on Sunset Boulevard.

Best of all, though, the famous sushi bar was just down the
street from Reggie's. Little more than a trailer on stilts hanging off the side of the ridge that shelved Sunset Boulevard,
Reggie's was directly across the street from what for years had
been rock and roll's unofficial headquarters, the Sunset
Hilton. The often-renovated old hotel had been home to
every rock-and-roll band to play every venue on the Strip.
Owing to the strategic location and his natural talent, Reggie
had become the personal ink artist to the stars and Reggie's
one of the most privately famous tattoo parlors in the world.

"Okay," Jimi said over champagne after dinner. "I
brought you here for a reason."

"To get me plastered on champagne and take advantage of
me?" Star giggled as the bubbles tickled her nose. " 'Cause if
you did, you blew it, you're way more plastered than I am."

"No, that's only part of my plan for world domination,"
Jimi said, taking her hand and kneeling beside their table. "I

don't think we ever did this properly. Star," he said, looking at her with such naked sincerity that she fell silent, "I knew the first moment I met you, and I'm more sure every day, that I love you and I want you to be my wife."

"I, um, am." Star said, puzzled.

"Yeah, but we need wedding bands," he said, still kneeling.

"Oh Jimi," she smiled, wagging the huge diamond on her finger. "This ring is plenty for me."

"Well, I was thinking that just a ring, well, that's not permanent. Besides, what ring would ever be beautiful enough for your hand anyway?" he asked as they made their way down the boulevard. "And any ring we got would be the same as thousands of other rings on the fingers of thousands of other people. And then I knew. Permanent, original, and beautiful enough to be on your finger? It had to be Reggie's," he concluded, opening the door to the tattoo parlor.

"Jimi," Reggie called, looking up from the ass of the young woman he was inking with a rather sizable butterfly.

"A tattoo?" Star said. With only one small tattoo on her instep, she wasn't quite the expert.

Now, Jimi had more drawings on him than a subway station in Spanish Harlem. She was taken with the originality of it, and then it hit her.

"Just our names around our fingers," she said. "It's perfect, I love it. Bring it on, Reggie."

Later, as they made their way into a nearby club for a couple of celebratory drinks, they had their double-ring ceremony as they flipped off the press with their newly inscribed ring fingers. Of course the pictures wound up in the papers, but somehow it mattered less.

"Where are you taking me?" she asked, catching Jimi in the viewfinder of their trusty video cam as he merged their SUV onto the freeway and headed east. She hadn't bothered to ask where they were going; it didn't much matter to her as long as they were going together.

"We're heading for London Bridge," he declared, checking over his shoulder and weaving his way left as he picked up speed.

"London Bridge, huh?" she said skeptically. "We're driving to London to go boat camping?"

"Not a bit." He grinned. "Though I'd be really stoked to go up the Thames and the canals on one of those skinny English houseboats. We should totally do that. You can tour the whole country on the canal system they built before they invented trains. They call them narrowboats. They used to be pulled by horses that walked along towpaths they built on the canal banks. It was like a wonder of the world at the time. A single horse could pull a hundred tons. Now they preserve them like parks. We should go."

She never ceased to be amazed by the information that came spewing out of him. With all his *dude*s and *babe*s and *awesome*s and *totally*s he came off as one of the lesser bulbs on the marquee. But his knowledge could be blinding if you flipped the right switch. He had already gotten her a computer, set it up, taught her how to use it, and gotten her online. Not to mention designing and building his own sound studio, doing much of the electronics work himself. In complete contrast to the metal maniac he showed the world, he was a total tech geek, a Boy Scout, and regular Cliff

Clavin about a whole range of topics, like the canals in England.

"Hey," he said, reaching to his waistband and popping his fly. "Check this out."

His erection sprung free of his pants and he stroked it a couple of times for effect.

"Party ready, twenty-four/seven."

"Let's see if I can zoom in enough so people can see that at home," Star teased, zooming in on the formidable erection.

"That's not right, babe," Jimi snorted with indignation. "They can see this from home without a camera."

"I think I'm picking up something." Star giggled, leaning in toward her subject.

"You just need a closer look," Jimi said, taking the camera from her and pushing her head down.

Star had developed some oral talent over the years, and with Jimi's big cock she had really honed her skills. She took a dive and went face-to-face with his shaved balls, swallowing the sword whole.

"Oh, God, babe, you're the best," he said, filming her progress as he continued to rocket them down the freeway into the desert and toward London Bridge.

According to the Guinness book of world records, at $2.4 million the London Bridge was, at the time of its sale, the costliest antique ever purchased. But more outrageous than the price was that it was moved from London, where it had spanned the Thames River for over 140 years, and plopped down across a narrow part of Lake Havasu in the Arizona desert.

"There it is," Jimi said, pointing out the landmark as they cruised across the bridge toward their destination. "London Bridge. You owe me a blow job."

"How can it be London Bridge if it's in Lake Havasu City, Arizona?" Star said, folding her arms defiantly.

"They brought it here brick by brick from London," Jimi said triumphantly, slowing as they made their way through the faux-English tourist trap on the other side.

"I understand that," Star said firmly. "But what made it *London* Bridge was that it was in London, not the bricks it's made out of. Now that it's here, it's Havasu Bridge."

Soon he pulled the car onto the highway that would lead them down the banks of the massive lake to Smackwater Jack's landing, where they'd hired a boat for the weekend. The place was a sort of all-purpose marina for the busy, tasteless tourist on the go. Gas station, grocery store, car park, restaurant, and souvenir shop all under one corrugated-steel roof over a cement-slab floor. The floating docks were covered with bright green AstroTurf that in no way blended in with the muted hues of the desert surrounding them. Best of all, the only news anyone cared about was the weather report. No self-respecting paparazzi was within a hundred miles of the place.

Jack was short for *Jacqueline,* and Smackwater had inherited the place from her Native American father. They'd had to close the rattlesnake zoo after an incident a few years back, but she'd kept the family tradition and the family name alive. Jimi had first seen the place when he was a kid and his family had stopped in to see the rattlesnake zoo. He'd seen the houseboats then and thought what a perfect party they'd make.

And when his garage band had turned into superstars and he could afford to party anywhere he wanted, he'd come back to Smackwater Jack's. It was a great spot for a private party. Jack had respected his privacy and Jimi had paid for the damages. It was the perfect combination.

Much to Star's delight and surprise, after they'd loaded all of Jimi's equipment on board and parked and locked the car, they were on their own.

Jimi knew the lake, or so it seemed to Star, and they were soon in the eerie moonscape surroundings of a massive lake in the middle of the desert. Bounded by stark rock formations carved by the Colorado River, the place felt to Star as though they were boating in the Grand Canyon. The peaks of the canyons and arroyos that had been flooded to contain the eighteen-thousand-acre lake thrust up through the lake's surface at odd angles like broken glass, forming improbable islands as forbidding as mountaintops.

They had been out about an hour and had lost sight of all signs of civilization when Jimi cut the engine. The boat, aside from a slight drift, hung motionless in the middle of the vast lake.

"What is it? Why are we stopping?" she asked.

"This is the deepest point in the lake," he said, catching and holding her eye as the boat rocked in its own wake.

"Here?" she said.

"Here," he nodded.

They dug into the gear and pulled out the huge duffle bag, dragging it to the edge of the deck.

"He's heavy," Star said, as she helped pull the deadweight toward the water.

"He wasn't really," Jimi laughed as they dropped the bag.

"I put weights in it so it would sink to the bottom. Okay, together on three."

"One, two," they chanted together. "Three."

They rolled the bag into the lake and watched it sink, leaving only a few bubbles on the surface in memory.

"Okay, now for the best part." He stood up, pulled his shirt over his head, and shucked his pants. "Freedom," he said with a contented sigh.

"You mean . . ." Star's eyes lit up.

"We won't see anyone and no one will see us," he said with a wink and a nod. "If someone's coming, you'll be able to tell." He gestured at the wide expanse of water on all sides of them.

"Woo, hoo," Star howled, leaping from her seat on the prow and twirling her shirt over her head as she danced a little dance of freedom.

And for the most part, that's how they spent the next ten days. At one point three menacing black helicopters flew silently overhead like huge metal dragonflies as they lay naked on the deck of the boat below. Again, the fear that they had been seen swept over Star like a chill. But the helicopters took no heed of the tourists below, leaving Star and Jimi on their own. No one heard from them and they didn't hear from anyone. No press, no photographers, no agents, no nothing. In fact, if they hadn't brought the camera, there would have been no proof that they were ever there. They were on their own. It was a cherished vacation. By day, they swam and sunned and made love on every flat surface in the boat—and some of the slanted ones too. By night, they pulled the boat into private coves, cooked over fires Jimi built, and slept under the stars.

It was the happiest they would ever be.

Jimi, the gadget fiend, was once again possessed by Star's little video camera and began obsessively documenting their every move. From Star—who'd smoked only one joint ever in her entire life—awkwardly learning to roll joints, to their opus sex cookbook featuring the BreakFuck sandwiches with extra wiener, Ten Inch T-Bones, and Don't-Forget-Where-You-Came-From Mac and Cheese, Jimi got it all on tape. And of course, he captured a scene or two of their lovemaking, including one particularly adventurous session at the ship's helm.

Jimi had been lazily guiding the boat south toward the dam. Star had blended up some fresh strawberry-daiquiri antidote for the afternoon heat. "I have a surprise for you," she called as she climbed up the ladder from the lower deck.

"It's the miracle cure," Jimi said, letting go of the wheel with one hand and taking up the camera to capture her rising from the lower deck, like a blond Venus. He honked the horn with his dick in appreciation of her efforts. He was paying more attention to Star than to steering, the boat lurched, and Star's naked body was covered with strawberry daiquiris.

Never one to be wasteful, Jimi began licking the sweet, sticky nectar off her, following the ruby rivulets of melting ice down her body. Lower and lower, he followed the strawberry trails until they converged in the valley created by her thighs. The daiquiris forgotten and the camera nearly slipping from his hands, Jimi drove his tongue into her hungrily. Star caught the camera and then nearly dropped it again as his tongue hit home and she was hit with her own ecstatic waves. The camera, still running, wound up wedged on a console in front of the throttle, capturing all as Jimi drove Star mad with his attentions.

She cast her head back and held on to Jimi's head as much to support herself as to encourage him as she grew dizzy and light-headed from the heat of the afternoon and Jimi's fevered attentions.

"Yes, oh, damn it, yeah," Star screamed as she wound her fingers into his hair.

At last, able to stand it no longer, she grasped his shoulders, drawing him up to her and pleading with him for release. He was lost in his passion and drove himself mercilessly into her again and again with such force that Star had to hold on to the throttle to avoid being knocked off the console and falling to the deck below.

The throttle thus engaged, the boat's wheel got kicked, steering the boat hard to port so that they began making left turns at full speed. The boat made crazy circles around and around as the wails of its occupants rose and crescendoed. It was like a very adult theme-park thrill ride, spinning around and around as the passion of the moment took them both. The only thing missing was costumed characters.

Spent, they lay in each other's arms on the floor as their world continued to spin around them.

Eventually the camera and boat were switched off, and the two continued to feast on their daiquiris and each other as they lay in the warm spring sun.

"You know what?" he said coyly, flicking at one of her nipples idly with his thumb.

"Not yet," she pleaded, too blissed out in the moment to want to stir herself for another round.

"No, not yet," he agreed, taking a nibble. "I was just going to say that it was these that I first fell in love with."

"What?" She half-laughed.

"Your nipples." He tweaked one between a thumb and a forefinger. "When I saw a magazine photo of them poking holes through your sweater."

She laughed at the idea. The photos were just work for her, so she never thought about them as sexy.

"A, E, I, O, U," she said, laughing.

"What the fuck?" Jimi asked, amused but confused.

"It's what they had me say when they were taking the gatefold shots of me for *Mann* magazine. Supposed to make your mouth look sexy." She laughed harder. "They said, 'Say the vowels,' and I said, 'A, E, I, O, U, and sometimes Y.' "

He was laughing with her.

"But that's not the funniest," she went on. "Mars has this thing about pussy hair. It's his little kink—I guess he misses the seventies—and since he's the publisher, what he likes is what he gets. And he likes girls with a little hair down there. Well, I don't really have any."

"Thank you." Jimi chuckled.

"Just naturally, and I don't encourage what's there." She shrugged. "So Mars saw the test shots and ordered a two-week halt so that I'd have time to grow some. But he could wait the rest of my life and he'd never get what he was looking for from me. Anyway, we waited, and when it came time to go back into the studio, what do you know, I still didn't have any," she said, laughing harder.

"As if having a roomful of strangers talking about the hair on my twat wasn't humiliating enough, they decided they'd get me some. So, they brought in this little old man who specialized in making fake beards and mustaches, and I had to lie on a table like I was at the doctor's office while this poor little man crawled between my legs and glued crepe hair onto me so I'd look like I had something I don't and Mars would get whatever it was that he was looking for."

Jimi couldn't stop laughing.

"So I'm lying there, wrenching my spine, dislocating a shoulder, with a beard glued to my coochie, going, 'A, E, I, O, U, and sometimes Y.' "

They lay in each others arms until their laughter became a quiet periodic rumble.

The afternoon of their last day on the lake, Star and Jimi pulled into one of the lakeside gas stations to fill up as they'd done often enough before. But this time would be different.

During the day the station was run by a lone jockey, Earl, who pumped gas and took money. Business was slow enough that he could usually manage on his own. Besides, it wasn't as if a boat could get very far if a customer decided not to pay. The atmosphere at the gas station was as informal as Earl's uniform. Twentysomething, with shaggy sun-bleached hair and a permanently peeling nose, Earl had long ago torn the sleeves off the light blue attendant's shirt embroidered with his name, which he wore with cut-offs and beat-up sneakers with no socks. Earl had clearly been checking Star out on previous visits, so when she emerged completely naked and strolled over to say hello, she and Jimi knew they had a captive audience.

"How's it going?" she asked.

Earl stood frozen to the spot. It was Miss March. And she was talking to him.

"Uh, fine," he answered, his voice cracking.

"Kinda hot today for all those clothes," Star said, running her hand inside his loosely buttoned shirt.

"Yep," Earl said, not talking about the weather.

"What time do you get off?" Star asked suggestively, her hand sliding slowly down toward his waistband. "Wanna go for a ride?"

"What about your husband?"

"I'm pretty hot too," Jimi said, stepping up behind Star and trailing his fingers up her naked body.

"So, you coming?" Star asked Earl again. "I bet I can cool you both off."

"I get off at sundown," Earl managed to say at last.

"Tonight sundown is just the beginning," Star said, withdrawing her hand and slipping it through Jimi's fingers.

"We'll be back to pick you up," Jimi said, paying Earl for the gas.

"You sure you want to do this?" Star asked Jimi as they watch the gas dock recede, Earl staring after them in amazement. They'd talked about it before. Since they were leaving the next day, and Earl was cute and would be oh-so-grateful, they figured it was a good time to try.

"It'll be so hot watching you get off," Jimi said, chewing on her ear.

Just the idea got Jimi going. They didn't want to wait until they returned later for Earl, so they let the boat drift as they made love all afternoon. But the idea of a third was hot enough to have them both going again that evening when they picked him up.

"Hi," Star called, as Jimi navigated the boat expertly up to the dock.

"Hi," Earl said, hopping aboard without tying the boat off. "You need gas?"

"We're good to go," Jimi called down, pulling the boat away from the dock.

"Why don't you slip this off," Star suggested, flicking Earl's collar. She and Jimi were already naked.

Earl was clearly uncomfortable, but not so much that he'd miss out on an opportunity to have a woman like Star—and with her husband's encouragement. He shucked his shorts and kicked off his shoes as Star tugged him toward one of the padded benches that surrounded the rear deck.

Taking a seat, Star pulled Earl over to her. He gently kissed her lips and then, with Miss March guiding his head, dropped his lips lower to kiss and suckle her breasts. Jimi watched as he brought the boat into a secluded cove that he had picked for their little ménage. A bit off the beaten path, it afforded a little extra privacy on the vast lake.

By the time Jimi came downstairs, the video camera loaded and in hand, Star was nursing at Earl's hard cock, tickling his balls with her long nails.

"Ah," Earl cried out, his head and upper body jerking forward each time she hit a nerve, which was pretty often.

Jimi stroked himself and shouted encouragement as he filmed.

But as Star fitted Earl with a condom and pulled him on top of her to guide him inside, something in Jimi shifted. No longer was it a hot and erotic scene. It was someone getting ready to fuck his wife.

"No," Jimi said, setting the camera aside and moving toward them. "I don't think so."

And before he could slide into home, Earl was thrown out,

his clothes and shoes tumbling after him into the shallow water of the cove. He was treated to the sound of their laughter and the fumes of the boat's engine as they powered away, leaving him naked and treading water a long way from anyone.

As with all good things, the trip to Lake Havasu came to an end. It was time to return to their lives and to the obligations of the world. Star had promised the *Hy Voltz* people an answer on the script she was supposed to be reading, and on the trip home she actually read the script, or what there was of it. It was really just an overgrown version of what Star had come to understand was called a treatment. Kind of like someone was just telling the idea for the story with a few scenes written out to give the impression.

But the idea was irresistible, and both she and Jimi took to it as she read it to him in the car. It had started as a project that they were in together. His enthusiasm and confidence that she could play the part had been the main reason she'd said yes in the first place. He had even sat with her when she'd made the decision to get the tattoo of cable around her upper arm.

It was something new to do together. They had been virtually inseparable since that night they'd gone to Madre de la Perla in Cabo. In that moment on that May morning, Star stood on the prow of that yacht rolling into the harbor at Cannes like a tsunami engulfing everything in her path.

3

three little birds

The good news was that, due to Star's overwhelming reception at Cannes, *Hy Voltz* was the most hotly anticipated film of the year. The bad news was that, due to Star's overwhelming reception at Cannes, *Hy Voltz* was the most hotly anticipated film of the year.

Star's little summer movie project was rapidly turning into a big-budget action-adventure film, and the quirky little script was being turned into a formula-one, high-performance blockbuster. The original director had been replaced by someone with big-budget-movie credits. So, an untried Star and an untried studio were rushing to supersize the production, trying to keep their original production date so that Star could resume shooting her two television series in the fall.

As preproduction hurtled toward the commencement of principal photography, the only thing higher than the expectations was the tension.

And so it was fortuitous that Theresa had called with her "bad" news.

She and Star had spoken since Cabo and the wedding, but they were taking their time warming back up to each other after a few sharp words over the trip and the wedding and Jimi. Star had wanted to pick up the phone so often, just to vent about some crazy day or other on the *Hy*-way, as she and Jimi had taken to calling it, so, when the call came, Star was glad to hear from her best friend.

"Hello, Star?" Theresa said, her greeting almost a plea.

"Theresa!" Star trumpeted. "Hi! How great. What's up, you sound a little stressed!"

"He fired me! Can you believe that?"

"What?"

"Mother fired me," Theresa said, breaking down again for the umpteenth time since she'd gotten home from her former job at Mother Pearl's. Despite the name on the door, the place belonged to Bernie Weintraub, whom everyone called Mother.

Theresa had paced, cried, eaten all the sweets in the house, and, when that had failed, remembered what she'd done in every crisis since Eddie Greenleaf had kissed her behind the equipment shed in third grade. She called Star.

"I can't believe it," Star said, sitting heavily on the lowest step on the main staircase at the Malibu house. "What happened? Did you two fight?"

"No, he said it was for my own good," Theresa wailed.

"For your own good?"

"Well, I was planning to go to school at Manatee Community this fall," Theresa explained, sniffling but getting the better of her tears for a moment. "They have that accelerated dental assistant's program that I've been thinking about."

"Right," Star said, leaning against the railing to avoid being trampled by a workman who was carrying painting equipment and scaffolding up the stairs, which concerned her, as she hadn't arranged for anything on the second floor to be painted.

"So anyway, Vanda ran off and got married," Theresa said.

"No!" Star gasped. "Not that stripper? Isn't he gay now?"

"That was last month. He switched back after the sugar daddy dumped him, and she wanted to stake a claim before he changed back again," Theresa clarified sadly. "So we're not only shorthanded, but since Vanda took off to follow his dance troupe, I'm senior girl."

"And she was your roommate," Star added, realizing the gravity of the situation.

"Well, that's another problem," Theresa agreed. "So, I decided I'd put off Manatee for the foreseeable future. But you know how Mother is. He said, 'Not this time, young lady. You're fired. Get out of this dump and go to school before you're too old and stupid to learn anything.' " Theresa began crying again. "And then he said, 'You know, Theri, those tits won't last forever.' "

"That's not true," Star said, coming to her defense. "Those implants I got you are top-of-the-line. They'll outlast all of us."

"I know it," Theresa wailed. "He meant I was getting too old."

"No, he didn't, sweetie," Star soothed, knowing that irony was not the only reason that their former employer was called Mother. "He wants you to get out of there and make something of yourself, and he's right."

"But school doesn't start till this fall, and even if I do go, I was counting on the summer tourist season at Mother's to help me afford it."

"Well, Theresa, today may just be your lucky day," Star said, leaping up to avoid a section of scaffolding that came crashing down the stairs after escaping from some unseen source that she searched the upper hall to discover.

It was the perfect plan.

Theresa would come out and work as Star's assistant on the movie. And Star would be able to hang on to her sanity with her fingernails as she shot her first major motion picture, dealt with being a newlywed, and was dissected on the daily news.

Even better, it worked out that Theresa could bring her current boyfriend, JC, along. Jimi was in the market for a trainer, and Juan Carlo was one of Miami's hottest fitness consultants, working with Miami's elite as well as plenty of Hollywood's A-list while they visited their Miami places. Jimi had always thought himself too skinny and was determined to start bulking up that summer, a goal JC assured Jimi was within his grasp in just a few quick sessions.

Star thought Jimi looked fine. The only part of his body that she might conceivably have wanted larger was plenty big enough, and no amount of exercising was ever going to change that.

Jimi and Star were devoted to one another. They were inseparable: eating every meal together, working out together,

taking on each and every task as a team. They were enthusias-
tically wading into redoing the house, shopping together for
each plant that was going into making over the grounds of the
Malibu house from sand and rocks into a garden worthy of
their personal Eden—Jimiville, as Star had taken to calling it.
To Star's surprise, Jimi was very knowledgeable about horti-
culture, knowing the names, often even the Latin ones, of
every plant they saw and considered.

He seemed possessed of some magical properties where
plants were concerned.

But as Star's career and the work on the film took more
and more of her time, Jimi switched his focus, and husband
and wife were inseparable, either on the set or in meetings or
in preparation for her role as the first female action adventure
hero. Since Cannes, their visibility was up and they stuck
more closely together than ever.

Because of her own athletic prowess, not to mention her
complete moviemaking naïveté, Star decided to do most of
her stunt work herself. She began frequenting the firing
ranges and became competent with all manner of guns; she
found the power arousing. She took martial arts training and
boned up on her old gymnastics skills. It was fun and exhila-
rating to discover that she still had it in her.

One afternoon, after a costume fitting at the soundstages
where most of the interiors were to be shot, she ran into the
executive producer, Steph, and some of the other more minor
executives on the project. "How's it going?" Steph asked in
greeting as they passed. In answer, Star did a standing back-
flip, shook his hand, and went on her way. Their applause accompanied her exit, which she made with a bow.

Jimi helped out where he could.

One of the many stunts that Star had elected to do, at least in part, was to ride a motorcycle. Star felt that since her character rode, learning was a part of understanding her role, and it sounded like fun. The stunt coordinator arranged for her to go to a Westside Harley dealership to take out the kind of bike she would be riding in the film for a test-drive to "get the feel of it." Jimi insisted on accompanying her, but when the time for her lesson arrived, he was delayed by negotiations over a possible new Fools Brigade project.

Figuring it was no big deal, and actually quite delighted by the opportunity, Star kept the appointment. Arriving at the dealership dressed in a pair of cutoffs, a tube top, heels, and a rhinestone-studded necklace that said FOXY in bold block letters, she felt she had mastered the most important part of successful motorcycling: costuming. "What else would a biker chick wear, right?" she said in response to the appreciative whistles she got from her "instructors" at the dealership.

As with most things in her life, it simply never occurred to Star that she couldn't ride a motorcycle. So she did. The instructor explained the basics. Star kicked the bike into life and took the Sportster for a spin.

Jimi roared up to the dealership riding his own bike complete with illegal ape hangers about a half hour after Star's departure, demanding to know where she was. "What the hell do you mean, she already left?" his voice echoed through the tile-and-glass enclosure that housed the brightly colored, chrome-encrusted crotch rockets.

"Well, she seemed to know what she was doing," the salesman shrugged. "She said she just wanted to get the feel of the bike and so we let her go."

"How long ago?" Jimi said, panic beginning to creep into his voice.

"Half an hour? Forty-five minutes?"

"If anything's happened to her, I'll come back here and take you and this whole place apart," Jimi said with such frightening quiet that the salesman stepped back even though Jimi had not advanced on him.

"Look, man . . ." he began, holding his hands up in surrender.

"Which way did she go?"

"Toward the beach." The man paled as he began to realize the possible consequences, with or without Jimi's threats, if anything happened to Star.

Jimi took his bike and zigzagged up and down the streets that radiated from the dealership. Eventually he caught up to Star and fell in beside her. She felt happy and free as they made their way back to the dealership. As they pulled back in, Star popped the clutch and the bike fell on her painfully, burning her leg on the hot engine exhaust pipe.

"Fuck, you made me nervous," Star said to Jimi. "I was doing fine. Fuck!"

Like an overprotective parent's, Jimi's help didn't always make things better.

Making movies is like watching paint dry. You set up for hours, then shoot for a relatively few minutes, then set up some more. And work on a house *is* watching paint dry, and theirs was drying even more slowly than anticipated. The combination was maddening. "You're just trying to do too much, Star," Jimi bellowed, when there was to be yet another delay while the tile people did yet another acid wash to remove the yellowed finish on the tiles in the enormous main hallway and staircase.

"Jimi," Star sighed, trying to make peace while she got ready for her next shot. "We agreed this had to be done, remember? And we can't get back in the house if we can't get in the front door or use the stairs. Try to be patient."

"I'll be patient in my own house," Jimi groused, slouching on the trailer's sofa.

The soundstages where the shoot was to take place were a long way from the beach communities where both their houses were located. Star rented an apartment in the ultrahip area off Sunset Boulevard. The idea was to bring them closer to the set and, she hoped, make it easier on both during the renovation.

Despite the fact that they owned two homes and were renting an apartment, Star and Jimi ended up living in a hotel that was closer to the shoot. It was fun and reminded them of when they'd first met.

Above and beyond the tension of the shoot and the remodeling, the news of the body in Lake Havasu had hit the news. Though no one had thought to link the two, husband and wife were even more on edge—and inseparable. And what with principal photography beginning on the movie, Jimi became still more security conscious, still more protective of Star.

But neither had any experience with moviemaking, so they got off to a rocky start.

The opening of the film was envisioned as a dance sequence in which Star's character performed her acrobatic choreography swinging from a "live" electrical cable suspended above the heads of the crowd in a cross between a postapocalyptic strip club and the Thunderdome. Special effects wizards had labored for days to make it appear that electricity issued from Star's fingertips, showering the audience and her scantily clad body with sparks each time she came in contact with the metal framework surrounding the stage. It was genius. Not only would it capitalize on the film's voluptuous star, it made the point that her character was impervious to, and an excellent conductor of, high voltage, hence her name, Hy Voltz.

Star's costume for the number was little more than an unlaced corset that partially exposed her breasts, a "problem" made worse by all the swinging. She looked amazing and Jimi couldn't resist. They were barricaded in Star's trailer until the director went ballistic.

Steph arrived on the set and explained to Jimi that Star would have to pay hundreds of thousands of dollars for the lost shoot unless they got the shot that day.

And so rather than an eight-hour shoot starting in the morning, it turned out to be an eleven-hour shoot that didn't even get started until eight o'clock at night.

"Hello," Star answered groggily.

"Star?"

"Theresa?" she said, not yet realizing that it was time to return to the set. "What is it? What time—"

"I'm downstairs, are you ready?"

"I'm, um, not yet," Star lied, dragging herself partly out of bed as she tried to act as if she'd been up longer than just the length of their conversation. "Could you come up?"

"JC's with me, do you want us to come up?"

"No, you just wait right there. I'll be down as soon as I'm ready." Star clicked off the phone and threw it in the other direction as she rolled over, snuggled up against Jimi, and went back to sleep.

"Star and Rockstar Boy Toy Turn Movie Set into Mayhem."

"Star Wood Leigh Fined Thousands for Production Delays."

"Jimi Deed's Wild Man Act Overshadows *Hy Voltz* Production."

It didn't take long for the rumors to turn into headlines.

The articles about how difficult Star was to work with began to appear by the end of the first week of shooting. The days and the shoots ran long, and the time she insisted on with Jimi made them longer. Star paid the price. Tired and exhausted trying to please the director, the producers, and Jimi, she was miserable and unhappy with her work.

Finally, almost by accident, Star hit on the solution.

It happened one day about a week into the shoot. Missy, Billy, Skip, and Theresa were buzzing around the trailer. Jimi and JC were just outside on the workout equipment the studio had provided for her to keep in shape during the demanding shoot. Jimi's workout schedule was showing remarkable results, and JC's reputation in Hollywood was growing as well.

Star was back for a costume change and touch-up on her makeup and had just begun the arduous process of getting out of her costume. It was no small achievement, given that just her lace-up gloves took about twenty minutes to put on. The series of corsets that comprised her costumes were even more tedious and time-consuming to remove, even more so since they had learned the hard way that due to Star's low blood pressure, if they unlaced her too quickly, she fainted.

"I just don't get it," Billy said, exasperated with a knot in the laces of Star's glove. "How the hell are superheroes supposed to do all the amazing stuff they do in these impossible outfits?"

"Really," Skip agreed, ruminatively combing out Star's hair. "Can you imagine having a huge fight with half a dozen bad guys wearing a cape? How could that possibly help?"

"Or chase villains in these shoes?" Missy agreed, wrestling off one of Star's stiletto-heeled, thigh-high, black-leather, lace-up boots.

"Or outsmart the evil geniuses with this updo," Star added, laughing along. " 'Cause you know . . ." she only had to begin.

"I can hardly think with all this hair," everyone chimed in.

"Where's the party?" Jimi said, coming into the trailer just as Star was coming out of the outfit. "You boys had better be gay, in here with my wife's tits hanging out."

"We could prove it to you," Skip said from under a wickedly arched brow.

"No, that won't be necessary," Jimi said, holding up both hands in surrender. "I'll take your word for it."

"Where's the fun in that?" Billy said, tapping his chin with the rubber tip of a prop knife that he'd taken from the sheath in Star's glove.

There was a knock at the door.

"Miss Leigh? Five minutes."

"My wife's fucking name is Deed," Jimi shouted in reply. "And it's gonna take longer than five minutes. Could everyone excuse us?"

"Great," Skip said, taking a seat on the workout bench. "Go tell your masters," he said nastily to the production assistant. The kid ran off.

"And could you bring back some lattes?" Billy called after him.

Jimi and Star began trashing the inside of the trailer—their third since the shoot had begun.

Jimi buried his face in her breasts, tweaking one and then the other nipple with his teeth as she tore at his clothes. They collapsed onto the floor, still clutching each other; Star shoved his Levi's down with her feet, her legs wrapped around him. And then he was inside her, and he began slamming Star around the trailer as the two took their tension out on each other. It was like the rough sex they both liked—biting, clawing, and slam-fucking each other against the walls, on all the furniture, and finally against the door of the trailer.

She caught his lip between her teeth and actually drew blood as he pinned her against the frail metal door and drove himself into her with all his force in each impassioned thrust. Rather than catching a rhythm, he would pull himself almost all the way out and then throw himself against her to find new depths to her and her passion.

The little group just outside silently regarded the door straining at its hinges.

"You think it's gonna blow?" Theresa asked mischievously.

"Should we do something?" Missy wondered aloud, unable to look away. "I mean, do you think they're all right?"

"Are you kidding?" Billy laughed.

"I wouldn't mind doing that," Skip snorted.

"I wouldn't mind it if you *could* do that," Billy said, laughing harder.

"I wonder if we can get the trailer next," JC said, grinning, taking Theresa's hand.

"Is everything okay?" Steph inquired, approaching the trailer warily.

"Oh, God!" Star's scream rang out from inside the trailer, accompanied by their violent pounding against the door.

"Should we do something?"

"You got a cigarette they can bum afterwards?" Skip asked with a knowing smile.

"Fuck yeah," Jimi shouted, loud enough to be heard back inside the soundstage. "Baby, baby . . . all . . . fuck!"

"Oh," Steph said. "I heard there was trouble. When do you think they'll be done?"

"That sounded like the end to me," Billy said, trying not to laugh.

"Well, I mean . . . ," Steph began.

"Come on, JC," Jimi said, emerging from the trailer. "Let's go get some supplies for tonight." He stumbled out of the trailer, smiling at everyone, climbed into his Testarossa, lit a cigarette, and left.

"Shit," Star said, walking out the door of the trailer. "I'll need an hour-and-a-half shower."

"Got it," Steph said, departing.

It was so simple.

Star had a new secret weapon. Well, it wasn't that new, but she had a new strategy for using it.

The real challenge became keeping Jimi happy and her hair, makeup, and costumes intact for the next scene. Star joked she was going to write a book of "safe" sex tips—positions to maximize pleasure while preserving hair and makeup. It was a strange peace and there were still delays, to keep the production consistently and very publicly a week behind schedule. But it kept everyone happy at least, but wary of the next delay as the production moved forward.

And so it was, with everyone lulled into a false sense of security, that the fateful day arrived.

Star was really thin and exhausted and kept going fueled on adrenaline and coffee. Jimi was there at her side all the time, but that only meant their sex life was vigorous and more active. Star didn't mind so much, except that she was trying to make a movie.

The day that everything changed was a particularly physically challenging one for Star. She was doing most of her stunt work. The day's stunt was one that might well have been given over to the professionals. It was a judgment call, but whatever the verdict, it was the most strenuous stunt work Star had done to that point on the shoot.

The shot called for Star, captured by the movie's villains, to be hung upside down and hoisted several stories into the air to participate in a fistfight with men on an elevated catwalk.

"And wearing a rubber bodice, high heels, and enough hair spray to hold up a Dolly Parton tour," Skip said, shaking his head in disapproval as he helped her get ready. "It's too much. Your stunt people should be doing this."

"It ain't fittin'. It just ain't fittin'," Billy said in his best Hattie McDaniel.

"Fiddle-dee-dee," Star said, sawing the air with an imaginary fan.

"It ain't fittin'."

"Star, you okay to do this, babe?" Jimi asked, distracted. "I'm good if you're good, but if not . . ."

"No, I'm fine," Star said, pleased by his show of interest, but not wanting to risk shutting down the production. "It'll be fine."

"Okay, then," Jimi said, edging toward the door. "It's just, well, JC and I need to go get some cigarettes."

"You boys run on," she said, knowing that his absence would speed up what was already promising to be a long day.

"Cool," he said, leaning in and smearing her makeup with a substantive good-bye kiss. "Sorry Billy," he added sheepishly when he saw what he'd done.

"Well, that move's not going in the book," Billy snorted, only slightly amused.

Heading out the door, Jimi closed it behind him.

All anyone knew that day was that Jimi had left the set and Star was ready on time and the shoot began on schedule. Skip hid his eyes as Star was strapped onto the steel beam and hoisted high above the studio floor. Once she achieved the desired height, a trapeze swing was lowered from the ceiling so that Star could sit upright between setups until they needed her. It was somewhat more comfortable, but not a lot, and it required Star to swing backward, grab the ropes, and hoist herself onto the bar, where she sat with her legs more or less straight in front of her, still lashed to the I beam for the sequence.

It was hideous.

And it was the only comfort available to her in a long, long day of shooting. She'd slip off the swing, they'd get a couple of shots of her fighting, swinging, and hanging upside down as she met the enemy on the steel catwalk across from her. Then she'd perch on the steel bar of the trapeze swing and sip lukewarm coffee through a straw. And then they'd film a bit more.

Finally, she was finding a use for the gymnastics training she'd had from the time she was nine years old.

It was getting done, but it was difficult and exhausting.

They had been at it for several hours when, in the middle of one of the fight sequences, Star began screaming and writhing, taking out two of her opponents and almost knocking a third off the catwalk.

There was a moment of uncertainty. It was a fight sequence and it seemed that Star might either be out of control or trying to dial up the action.

Skip's lips disappeared and his mouth became a line between his nose and his jaw as he watched the action and tried to keep quiet. Billy squeezed his hand.

"Cut," the director called. It had looked great and he was glad they'd gotten it, but it wasn't on the storyboards, so he wasn't even sure they could use it. "That was amazing, Star, but save your energy. Let's try it again, from one, and just the movements we've discussed."

Star hung limply from the I beam.

"Star?" the director called through the bullhorn he was using to direct the sequence. "You ready?"

No response.

"I think she's out," one of the players called down from the catwalk.

"Oh, God," Skip said, leaping to his feet. "Get her down from there now."

The crew, uncertain, were slow to react, as Skip, not the director, had issued the directive.

"Cut her down, cut her down, cut her fucking down," Skip began screaming, near hysteria when no one responded to his earlier plea.

Billy rushed out to her and caught her in his arms as she was lowered from the ceiling. The grips began untying the lashings that held her ankles to the I beam, but Skip grabbed a box cutter and slashed through the bindings and safety straps.

Once she was freed, Billy and others carried her to the trailer, where they laid her out on the sofa.

Missy rubbed Star's wrists with ice as Billy checked her head for blood.

A number of the crew and some of the cast gathered outside Star's trailer door to find out what was going on. Theresa tried to reach Jimi. As it was, she only got both his and JC's voice mail.

Initially, it was thought that Star had hit her head on the railing and knocked herself out, but there was no bump or blood or other obvious sign. Star moaned as she slipped marginally into consciousness. "Mom?" she groaned. "I didn't start it, I swear."

Slowly, Missy began to unlace the rubber bodice, and Star sat up, screamed out in pain, and passed out again.

"What is going on?" Skip demanded, rising and storming to the door. "Where is an ambulance?"

"It's complicated," the shop steward said with a shrug.

"No, it isn't," Skip said. "It's 911. How hard is that?"

"Well, the insurance guys are unclear on whose responsibility it is," Steph explained, covering the mouthpiece of his cell.

"Are you kidding me with that?" Skip snorted. "Well, I'm not sure that it makes any difference whose fucking responsibility—"

There was familiar tire-squealing in the near distance, and a hush fell over the group.

"Thank God," Skip said, folding his arms.

Jimi drove the car up to the trailer at full speed, knocking over a catering table and some lighting equipment that had been in his way. Without a word he leaped from the car, stormed into the trailer, swept Star into his arms, and carried her out where JC helped him get her into the tiny sports car.

The first of three ambulances arrived just as Jimi was pulling away; two followed the car to the hospital, carrying friends and crew, as did the insurance van.

As always, Jimi's reaction was unexpected. Suddenly serious and quiet, he pumped the doctors for information, was at Star's side as much as they would allow him, and even sometimes when they wouldn't. When he wasn't at her side, he was just outside whatever door she was behind, sitting on the floor if no chair was available. And then only when he was too tired to pace.

"You really do love her, don't you," Billy said, arriving with an order from Starbucks to fuel the little group huddled in the waiting area.

"Dude," Jimi said, a couple of tears escaping in a puff of

what might have been a laugh, "what would you do if it was Skip?"

Billy was so touched and overwrought that he hugged Jimi.

"That may be the nicest thing you've ever said to me," Billy snuffled, breaking the hug abruptly and getting back to the coffee.

"Don't let it get around," Jimi said quietly, glad of the comfort. He was truly worried about Star. And he felt guilty for not being there when she'd needed him.

"Mr. Deed?" the doctor said, emerging from the room. "She's awake and she's asking for you."

Without a word Jimi rushed past the doctor and into the room. Kneeling beside the bed, he put his arms around Star, more or less lying across her and the bed.

"Jimi," she said quietly, stroking his hair. "Get off of me, you're hurting me, babe."

"Oh, sorry," he said, sitting up, afraid to touch her at all.

She took his hand and kissed it.

"As long as you two are here," the doctor said, closing the door and following Jimi into the room, "I've got some news about Mrs. Deed's condition."

"So, what's up, Doc?" Star asked with a little giggle, unable to resist the line.

"Is it serious?" Jimi said, the color draining from his face, feeling as though he might fall.

"Well, yes," the doctor said evenly. "Star had an ovarian cyst about the size of a grapefruit, which burst. There was a loss of blood and drop in blood pressure."

"And a lot of pain," Star put in.

"Yes, and everything looks good," the doctor went on.

"The bleeding is stopped and we're running some tests, but we're optimistic. We'll take care of the surgical correction through the belly button, and she should be up and around soon."

"Oh, that's great, Doc," Jimi said, shifting nervously from one foot to the other.

Star only sighed, too tired for much more.

"The bad news is, you miscarried," the doctor concluded solemnly.

"Miscarried?" Jimi repeated, disbelieving.

"You mean I was—" Star's tears cut her off.

"Pregnant." The doctor nodded. "But not for very long."

Jimi held Star until she fell asleep, the realization of what they'd lost hitting them again and again.

4

once upon a time

 Inquiries from the film's producers about Star's return to the set arrived at the hospital within hours. She was too stunned to reply.

As soon as the doctors gave Star the all clear, Jimi sneaked her out the back door of the hospital with the laundry and into Star's Range Rover. Jimi had arranged for Theresa and JC to park the room-sized ride by the loading dock, thinking it would be more comfortable for Star than his cramped sports coupe. JC brought Jimi's car around to the front door of the hospital, and the press cued up to capture the moment. The ploy was pretty successful and they thought they were home free as they made their way to hide out at their unfinished beachfront home.

They didn't talk much. Jimi didn't know what to say and Star was too tired to speak. She took his hand as he drove toward home down the familiar stretch of Pacific Coast Highway, PCH as it's better known to the locals, wedged between the beach on one side and the sheer rock face of the mountains into which the road was carved.

"Thanks for getting me out of there," she sighed, curling up in her seat.

"Nothing to it," he said, raising her hand to his lips and kissing it gently. "I'm just glad you're okay."

A dark Ford Explorer darted in front of them without warning, and Jimi swerved, nearly plastering their car into the man-made cliff that ran along the shoulder, before rebounding back onto the highway. He flipped off the driver just in time to get his picture taken by the paparazzi inside.

The Explorer played a dangerous game of cat and mouse with the Range Rover in the four lanes of busy traffic on a winding and unforgiving roadway that offered little margin for error. Jimi tried to outrun the carload of paparazzi, but they caught up and cut them off again and again.

Star was screaming and crying, overwrought from an emotional day and the terror of the chase. Jimi too was screaming and overwrought, but his emotions took a more violent turn as he shouted profanities and picked up the speed of the chase.

Finally, patience ran out. On his last pass to gain the lead, he cut in front of the photographers' car, forcing them off the road, where they hit a parked car and the stone cliff wall before crumpling to a rest. Just as quickly, Jimi had stopped the Range Rover and was running toward them with a tire iron in his hand, Star close behind. The stalkers, unable to get their car restarted, rolled up their windows and locked their doors as they braced for attack.

Star began trying to kick in the driver's door as Jimi began smashing every piece of glass on the car—the headlights, the mirror, the taillights.

"We love you, Star!" the car's occupants screamed in their defense.

"Fuck you, you assholes!" she shouted in her blind rage. "You almost killed us. Fuck you!"

As the windshield shattered into a spiderweb of broken glass, the car's occupants' dog jumped up on the dashboard and began barking in loyal defense of his indefensible masters.

"Jimi, stop, there's a dog!" Star screamed, leaping back from the car where she had been trying to break the driver's window.

It was an act of will, and he took a couple of swipes, denting the car's hood, before he gave it up entirely, but Jimi let it go. Together the two raced away, frightened more by their own rage than by the accident.

Afraid of retaliation for the incident and on the run from the relentless film producers, they returned briefly to the hotel in Pasadena to get a few things and plan a getaway.

But it was not to be.

Still shaken from the experience on PCH, they headed for the hotel bar to get a drink to settle their nerves. One quiet drink was all they managed.

Jimi's cell rang.

"It's JC," he said, checking the phone. "I'm going to take this one and find out what's going on."

"Okay, I'm going to the ladies'," Star said. Sliding out of

the booth where they had enjoyed a fleeting moment of privacy, she knocked her purse on the ground and leaned over to pick it up.

"Nice ass," said a guy sitting with his family at a nearby table.

"What did you say?" Jimi said, standing suddenly at the man's table, almost before it seemed possible.

"What?" The guy looked up, startled by Jimi's appearance out of nowhere.

"What did you say to my wife?" Jimi demanded, raking everything off the man's table, covering everyone there with fresh guacamole dip—the house specialty.

"Take it easy," the guy said, standing and leaping back from the flying debris.

There were screams as other people fled the bar.

"Jimi, let it go, it doesn't matter to me," Star said quietly, taking his arm.

"It matters to me." Jimi shook her off. "That's my wife, you stupid motherfucker. Apologize."

"You want *me* to apologize?" the man asked in amazement.

And Jimi, cell phone still in his hand from the conversation he'd been having when it had all started, decked the guy, dislocating two fingers, knocking the guy unconscious, and disconnecting the call.

The *Tits* was a 152-foot yacht belonging to zillionaire concert promoter turned record executive Missouri Harris, MO to his friends. He'd made a fortune developing trendy record labels and then unloading them at the top of the market onto slow-moving corporate media behemoths just before the trend went bust.

It was just the sort of yacht you'd expect a rock promoter to have. Mirrored ceilings, marble Jacuzzis, and leopard-skin everything, it made the merely vulgar seem commonplace. It also made for the perfect hiding place for Star and Jimi. On the run from angry paparazzi, the producers, and the authorities, their business and their pictures plastered on the covers of everything in print in most languages around the world, the middle of the Pacific Ocean was just about the only place left where they still might find a little peace. Even then, it was not a sure thing. But at least when the time came, they would see them coming.

So, it was a good thing that Jimi was one of the intimates who called Mr. Harris MO. The two had worked together early in Jimi's career when MO had produced the *Hell in a Handbasket* tour when Fools Brigade had opened for the Prince of Darkness himself, Sidney Melbourne. Jimi, Sid, and MO had gotten into so many scrapes with the authorities during the first leg of the tour that MO sent Fools Brigade into the studio to record a new album he financed.

It not only resulted in a platinum album, it was the beginning of a lifelong friendship that was their lifesaver that Fourth of July weekend.

Besieged in their hotel, Jimi and Star emerged in hoodies, hats, and dark glasses, dove into a waiting limo, and led the paparazzi on merry chase through Old Town before revealing in the parking lot at Huntington Gardens that they were in fact Theresa and JC. The stunt almost got Theresa fired from the production, but covered Jimi and Star's escape.

By the time the ruse was revealed, Jimi and Star were on a

motor launch taking them out for a little much-needed R&R on the borrowed over-the-top yacht. Star was unaware of their destination, and Jimi insisted that she wear a blindfold until the *Tits* was in sight.

"You bought me a boat? It's huge," Star squealed as they drew closer to the three-story behemoth sitting placidly on choppy waters, too big and heavy to be jostled by the roiling water.

"Star," Jimi chided shyly, "you don't have to keep telling me."

She splashed him with water from over the side, and the two were soaked by the time they boarded.

"Let's get out of these wet things," Jimi said, kicking off his shoes and pulling his collared shirt, still buttoned, over his head.

Star joined in, and to the surprise of the astonished crew, the two shucked their clothes in a spirited game of chase. It wasn't anything the crew of the wild party yacht hadn't seen before, they just didn't usually see it so soon. Heedless of the staff, their romp wound them up naked and sprawled on a couple of the sumptuous chaises on the top-level sundeck.

"Um, yes, excuse me, sir," the chief attendant said, politely averting his eyes. "The captain would like to know your pleasure, and I wonder if I might offer any refreshment?"

"Tell the captain we don't want to see land or another boat for a week," Jimi shouted joyously. "And we need champagne right away."

"Very good, sir," the attendant said with a small bow. "I'm Albere, if you need anything; pick up any phone you see. Otherwise, the crew will stay in quarters to afford you your privacy."

"Perfect," Star said, wallowing in the faux-leopard-skin cushions. "This fur had better be fake."

"Absolutely," Jimi replied—hoping.

The world searched frantically for them over the next five days, but Star and Jimi stayed out of sight, wandering the polished mahogany decks nude—or nearly—eating when they felt like it, feasting on caviar, lobsters, and crab washed down with buckets of champagne and making love every time the mood struck them.

As always, their time on the run gave them the chance to remember that they always had each other, and that anything was possible.

Jimi was looking for more sunscreen when he happened on the video camera that had haphazardly been tossed into their luggage when they'd scrambled to escape from their hotel room.

"Smile," he said, waking Star from her nap as she sunbathed nude on the deck off the master cabin. "I love you, babe."

"Jimi," Star moaned. "What's up?"

"I just love you, you complaining?"

"Never." She laughed, taking "little Jimi" in hand, bringing him to full attention, then swallowing him whole.

Jimi fell back onto one of the fur-covered chaises as Star climbed on top of him, her head bobbing in and out of the increasingly erratic shot.

"Here, my turn," he said, lacing his fingers into her hair and pulling her up for air as he handed her the camera.

She howled like a savage, tossing her feet into the air as he began crawling menacingly over her body, his face moving closer and closer to the lens. He growled seductively, then swept her into the air. He plunged himself inside her as he carried her across the deck, bringing her to rest on the marble surface of the outdoor edition of the room's three bars. Glassware and bottles tumbled everywhere as he began to sprint into the home stretch.

Jimi took the camera and zoomed in with a porn aficionado's eye and a surgeon's anatomical expertise to capture in detail their most intimate contact as they joined as one again and again. It was a strange and heady experience for him as he had the feeling he was appearing in the porno and watching it at the same time.

For her part Star was too lost in the actual reality of the moment to be worried about the virtual one. She felt great for a change and was reveling in being fully present in the moment as Jimi's video-enhanced excitement translated into a focus and intensity that took Star along for the ride. She writhed on the cool marble surface, enjoying the feel of her own body as she dragged her hands over her own skin, relishing each little touch.

The sight of Star playing with her own breasts and nipples along with the sight of his own cock pistoning in and out, kicked Jimi's pornographic VR experience up a notch and incited a riot of feeling that played havoc over his body. His excitement only drove him on, and they shouted out endearments as they destroyed the bar and reached the end of their private show. Jimi fell back, exhausted and drained by the moment, their third so far that day, still looking through the lens of the camera he seemed to have forgotten he still had glued to his face.

"That was a-fucking-mazing, babe!" he howled at that cloudless blue sky above them.

"Yeah, baby, it was great," she said, dragging herself off the bar and onto the chaise beside him. "Only, promise me something."

"Anything," he said, sitting up and framing her face in the viewfinder.

"No more camera," she said, reaching out and switching it off.

Paradise and the *Tits* were lost all too soon.

As they were anchored just south of Catalina and surprisingly close to the world that clamored for them, a small fishing boat drew inconspicuously near. Star was swimming nude in the water, and Jimi was, despite their agreement, getting just a few more shots. He'd stopped filming their lovemaking, but he couldn't resist the shots of her perfect, tanned skin flashing at the surface of the warm, choppy water from which he himself had only just emerged. What he didn't know was that Star had sneaked shots of his skinny-dipping before she'd jumped in to join him.

The fishing boat was one of many that had lazily drifted by on that perfect July afternoon. They paid no more attention to it than they had to those earlier. No one knew that Star and Jimi were on board, let alone drifting off the coast of Catalina. Star was still in the water when the smaller boat was put over the side of the fishing vessel and the occupants rowed themselves toward the gangway from which Star and Jimi had been diving.

"Hey," the tanned and weather-beaten man called from under his wide-brimmed hat.

"What's up?" Jimi called genially.

"Just a delivery" came the reply from under the hat.

For her part, Star continued discreetly treading the water, as it was the only thing she was wearing. Jimi left his towel draped around his shoulders, more curious than concerned about their visitors.

As the rowboat reached the gangway, the man removed his hat respectfully and bowed his head in greeting.

"Jimi Deed?" he asked politely.

"Yep," Jimi answered warily.

"For you." The man extended his hand and pushed a long manila envelope toward Jimi.

Clearly this was just the messenger. Jimi figured rightly that the boat and its crew would likely earn more for finding them and delivering the mysterious envelope than they would in a whole week of good fishing.

"Thanks," Jimi said, taking the envelope.

The man tipped his hat politely and, his job happily completed, rowed away with his silent companions.

Jimi regarded the unopened and unmarked envelope for a moment.

"What is it?" Star asked, swimming nearer.

"We may already have won ten million dollars," Jimi said, laughing.

"Don't open it," she said, hoisting herself onto the little, white, expanded metal landing just above the water level at the base of the gangway.

"I don't supposed I really have to," he said, smiling at her sadly.

"No, I guess not," Star said, leaning over and kissing him gently. "Thanks for doing this. I really needed it."

"I'll tell the captain to head for home," he said, drawing her body against his and holding her just a moment more.

It was just as well that they didn't open the envelope. It contained legal documents and prefiling papers along with a letter, which more clearly stated the threat to sue Star for $100 million if she did not return to the set forthwith and recommence shooting.

They took their time getting back up the coast and didn't call until they got back to port in Los Angeles. Star had had the break she needed, and she knew full well that the studio would rather have her finish their film than enjoin them in their threatened lawsuit, so everyone made nice on her return. The trailer was filled with flowers and greetings and notes of sympathy.

JC and Theresa were there to meet them.

For Star, the excitement of making a movie was completely gone, squeezed out of her. Only a shapeless and empty film remained. All that was left was showing up at dawn, trying to get enough footage in the can to cut together into a movie before they ran out of time and money. It left a bad taste in her mouth.

Worse still, the shooting schedules for *Lifeguards* and *Hammer Time* had begun, and so her production schedule became impossibly difficult. Star's final two weeks on *Hy Voltz* took three as she started work on the two television shows.

She enjoyed seeing her friends and put up with what she had to, to get the movie done. After the heartless response to her illness, she didn't really care anymore, letting Jimi take control.

Jimi worked with the producer to make sure Star got enough rest and breaks. They worked to accommodate their Star, who, for her part, had little idea that any of it was even going on. It just seemed to her that despite their being more pressed for time, she had more time to do things like eat or take an afternoon nap or just spend time with Jimi.

By the time the shoot was finished, there were no new friends; only the people Star had been close to before the production, like Billy, Skip, and Missy, was she close to afterward. The producers, the director, and the principals never worked with her again. In fact, after the wrap party on the last day of shooting, they only ever saw one another once—at the premiere.

Her movie career had begun with more promise and fanfare than *Gone with the Wind,* and it ended, at least for the time being, almost unnoticed by any, save those who were merely relieved to be done.

"Not with a bang but a whimper," she said to Jimi as they removed the last of their personal stuff from the trailer to return to their still-unfinished home.

"So this is the way the world ends." Jimi smirked. "I thought there would be more, you know, smoke."

She kissed him for knowing the poem, and the tires of the Testarossa squealed out of that particular parking lot for the last time. "Let's get the fuck out of here. I hope I never make another movie."

5

wild horses

"Which script is it gonna be today?" Stan Merman asked, holding up two scripts as he entered Star's trailer. "Romance or just friends? We can't do it if he's here, but if she doesn't get a little action soon, her fans are going to desert us." He threw himself on the sofa in disgust.

"Well, you've got yourself on the horns of quite the little dilemma there, Stan," Skip said, looking up from his copy of *Variety* with a wicked smile. "I was just reading that you're the executive producer on the number one syndicated television show in the world. You don't seem all that powerful to me."

"Is he coming today or not?" Stan sighed.

The trouble had begun almost as soon as shooting ended

on *Hy Voltz*. Jimi had moved into Star's trailer on the *Lifeguards* lot, and nothing had ever been the same. He'd been a minor disruption the year before when he was flirting with Star, but now that she was Mrs. Deed, he had taken up residence.

So, despite Stan's success, he still got butterflies each day on his way to work as he wondered whether Jimi would be waiting for him.

Star's romance with costar Rufus Forrest was common knowledge. And her romance with costar Antony Cravatta to those who had been able to read for more than two years. Jimi fell into both categories, which meant he'd forbidden Star to be alone in a scene with either man.

Now, Jimi had no actual authority to forbid anything. But Jimi had never had any difficulty getting exactly what he wanted. The set of *Hy Voltz* had taught him how to manage on set and the producers on *Lifeguards* were no match.

For openers, the show filmed outside, so disrupting the shoot was child's play. An afternoon of cutting wheelies in the parking lot with his Ferrari could virtually bring production to a halt. Not to mention throwing a party, cranking up the music, renting a helicopter, inviting over a motorcycle gang for a beer bust, or just simply refusing to allow anyone access to his wife.

In a matter of weeks, both Star's exes had become strangers and were rarely even scheduled to shoot on days when Star was on the set. Ruf was actually kind of pleased about the situation. He was still smarting from Star's unceremonious wedding to the unruly rock star, whose constant presence was a painful reminder of the love he'd lost. For his part, Ant kept count of his pages, and so long as the producers met his arbitrary quota of screen time, he hardly noticed anything else that happened on the show, let alone after "cut" was called.

The only problem was the fans. Star's character, BeeGee, was the show's most popular, and the viewers made it more than clear that they were interested in whomever BeeGee was interested in. Stan didn't really care what the fans wanted, but he cared what the syndicators who bought and sold the show thought, and they only cared what the fans wanted, since audience, not art nor on-set acrimony, was their solitary concern.

That made it Stan's problem.

His solution: Operation Swedish Meatball. Named by Skip and Billy for the show's newest cast member, Sven Erickson, the unpleasant nickname was the kindest part of the covert operation. It began with a disinformation campaign to convince Jimi that Sven was gay. He wasn't, but Jimi was all but oblivious to having Skip and Billy as intimates in Star's life, hence Stan's twisted plan. To that end, step two involved convincing Skip and Billy, for huge concessions, to become confederates in making Jimi, and to some degree Star, believe that Sven was just one of the girls. The final and most complicated component of the ludicrous top-secret scheme was crafting two different scripts for the show, one that included increasingly romantic moments for Star and Sven, and a second that gave no hint there was anything going on.

Jimi was only ever allowed to see the sanitized scripts, and the romance was shot only when he was not expected on the set. So Operation Swedish Meatball remained largely untested. The trouble was, no one ever knew for certain when Jimi was going to be on the set.

"He's not coming," Missy said, laying out the makeup. She was an unindicted coconspirator in Operation Swedish Meatball. She understood the problem, but wasn't crazy about the level of deception necessary.

"How do you know?" Stan asked, hopeful for the first time that morning.

"Well, you did not hear it from me," Missy sighed, debating her truest loyalty to Star and then deciding the best course. "He's supposed to be meeting with someone from a new label and a couple of guys from the band about possibly a new project."

"God, who's the patron saint of musicians?" Stan sighed, leaning forward in an unspoken prayer that Jimi would have to go away on tour. "We need to make an offering or get a medal or whatever it is you do with saints to get them on your side."

"Your support is touching," Skip said with a smirk. "Perhaps you want the patron saint of cynical aspiration."

"I'd perform a tribal war dance at the start of each take if I thought it would help," Stan declared.

"You'd do what?" Star asked, puzzled by Stan's odd behavior.

"Just a figure of speech," Stan said, happily handing her the romance script. "I gotta go talk to Sven. See you on the set."

"What was all that about?" Star asked the little group waiting for her.

"Maybe he got religion." Billy shrugged, taking her bag and leading her to the chair. "You ready to get started or do you need a minute?"

"No, I'm good to go," Star said, shedding the habitual

sweatshirt jacket and falling into the chair. "I'm already exhausted and I haven't even started working yet."

"Want a mocha?" Billy asked, patting the large and largely unused heap of brass and copper fittings. "I think I've figured out how to use this thing."

"Billy, no one wants another incident," Skip warned, sampling Star's hair tentatively, contemplating the next steps.

"Yeah, someone could really get hurt," Missy agreed, popping some moist towels into the microwave. "That milk gets pretty hot, not to mention the steam."

"Plus, remember that thing we saw on the news about that coffee bar in Sherman Oaks?" Skip said, shaking a warning comb in Billy's direction. "The whole thing could just blow."

"I saw that," Missy said, programming the machine. "They found pieces of the roof in Tarzana."

"You should probably just wait until Jimi gets here," Star agreed, remembering how long it had taken to get the chocolate syrup out of everything in the trailer the last time Billy had tried to operate the espresso machine.

End of conversation.

"Jimi's coming?" Missy said, looking up from the spinning towels and then realizing and feeling instantly guilty. "I thought he had the meeting with the record people."

"It wasn't a real label," Star said sadly. "It turned out to be one of those infomercial compilation deals. So it really didn't involve the band. The agent went."

"Oh," Missy said, ignoring the reminder bell on the microwave as she stared out the door after Stan. "Well."

"Are you okay, Missy?" Star asked, puzzled by her curious behavior.

"She was dropped on her head as a child," Skip whispered into Star's ear. "Let's get started."

Hair and makeup for *Lifeguards* was mostly about upkeep and maintenance. Skip got her hair up a bit and Billy got the pink lips, lashes, and eyeliner on her. The rest of the time the three took turns freshening her up as the sand, wind, and water destroyed their work, though it mostly fell to Missy.

Jimi came in just as Star was getting ready to go over the day's pages.

"Hey, babe," he said, leaning down to kiss her on the top of the head. "What's up?"

"Hey, sweetie," Star said, reaching up to stroke his face as she leafed through the pages. "How was your morning?"

"Kinda boring," he said, stuffing his hands in his pockets. "Waited for the tile guy. Met up with some of my boys, but they had stuff. Thought I could hang with you," he suggested, taking a chair next to her.

Missy and Skip moved nearer the door.

"I'll tell you what you can do," Billy said, taking his hand and dragging him away. "You can teach me to work this coffee machine. You're the only one anyone trusts to work it, and sometimes I want espresso when you're not here."

"Billy, my man," Jimi said, in his element, "there's nothing to it."

By the time everyone had their favorite, the tension had dissolved. Star looked over the day's pages while Missy worrid how to let Stan know the pages weren't safe or get Jimi to leave. "So what are you up to this afternoon?" Star asked, sipping her mocha.

"Nada," he said, taking his espresso straight with a twist

of lemon. "Thought I'd just hang. What are you shooting today?"

"Some dialogue scenes at the lifeguard stand with Sven," Star said.

"Oh, Sthven," Jimi lisped, making a joke of it with Skip and Billy.

They laughed nervously.

"What's that about?" Star asked, thinking she was cautioning Jimi about making fun of Skip and Billy.

"Just a little joke between me and your boys," Jimi chuckled with Skip and Billy.

"Really?" Star asked, eyebrows raised. "What's the joke?"

"Guy stuff," Skip said, wrinkling his nose dismissively.

"Yeah, guy stuff," Billy echoed.

"Guy stuff?" Star asked incredulously. "That the three of *you* have in common?"

"Yep," Jimi said smugly.

Before the conversation could progress any further, Stan arrived with Sven and the episode's director. "Star, are you . . . Oh," he trailed off. "Jimi. Hi. You're . . . here."

"Yeah, thought I'd come by, check in," Jimi said, giving Stan an intentionally complicated handshake just for the fun of making him look uncool. "Sven, you and Star are at bat today. Your hair looks really nice."

"Thanks." Sven was always a bit put off by Jimi's manner toward him, but unable to put his finger on just why. He turned to check his hair in the mirror.

Jimi swapped a look with Skip, rolling his eyes behind Sven's back as he primped.

Skip let a snort of laughter escape.

"Well, it looks like you're busy," Stan said, shoving the director back through the door. "Come on, Sven, we'll come back—"

"Stick around," Jimi said, putting his arm around Sven's waist and guiding him chivalrously into a chair. "We were using the new espresso maker you got for the trailer, Stan. Billy makes a really mean latte. What'll you have?"

"That'd be great," Sven said, a little flustered by Jimi's familiarity, but taking it as a sign of generosity. He was new to the show and so had no experience of Jimi. "That'd give us a chance to talk before we start shooting."

"Well, I've got to get back to the set," the director said, rushing for the door.

"I'd better go with you," Stan said, following hurriedly.

"No, wait, guys," Sven called after them. "They're in the middle of setup and they'll come for you as soon as they're ready. They know where we are. I'd really like the chance to go over this before we shoot it."

"I'm not thinking we're going to have time," the director said evasively.

"Yeah, we're running way behind," Stan agreed, again pushing for the door.

"What?" Sven asked, completely confused. "But the whole reason we came over here—"

"Was to let Star know that we wouldn't have time for the scene today," the director said, riding over him.

"So we're not going to get the chance to do the make-out scene?"

Icy silence.

Stan and the director, their backs to the room, froze in the doorway.

Skip examined his copy of *Variety* very closely as Billy bus-
ied himself with the lattes.

The only sound was of steam escaping as Billy heated the
milk.

"Don't worry, Sven," Jimi said, breaking the silence and
patting him on the shoulder. "It's just like kissing a guy."

Even the sound of escaping steam stopped.

"Well, I mean, I know it's impersonal, but that's just the
point," Sven said. Completely misinterpreting Jimi's mean-
ing, Sven rose and spoke to the director, who was forced to
turn back. "I'd like to take the time to do what we can to
bring some life into it. It's the first time for these two characters, it's a little unmotivated, and I think it's important."

Still no one spoke.

"Well, Star always says that she just imagines that she's
kissing her husband," Jimi added, trying to be helpful. "You
just do the same."

"That's absolutely right, Jimi," Stan said triumphantly,
turning back into the room, as Operation Swedish Meatball
succeeded beyond his wildest dreams. "Good advice. Don't
you think, Brock?" He gave the director an elbow.

"Right," Brock said. "Just pretend you're kissing your
husband. Transference is a powerful way to bring, um, reality
to a situation when there's, uh, no time for preparation."

"Transference, that's the ticket," Jimi said, passing Sven
the latte from Billy's inert hand and giving him an affectionate
little pat on the ass. "Just as long as you don't imagine that
you're kissing her husband," Jimi concluded with a laugh.

It started small but everyone laughed. Almost none for the
same reasons, but it was hearty bordering on hysterical.

Star laughed along, though she didn't really think it was

that funny; she was relieved and mystified that Jimi was taking it all so well. Perhaps wisely, she decided simply to leave well enough alone.

While Operation Swedish Meatball was under way on the work front, Star had been at work on a secret plan of her own. To make a more solid commitment to their life together, she'd decided to make getting the house ready priority one. It was a great idea, except that, like it or not. Star already had at least two other priorities—shooting two television shows a week.

That meant, in the midst of the shoots, Star was having to meet with decorators and contractors to approve samples, colors, plans, and changes. Star found herself with more to do than ever. But with the added demands of keeping up with the house, she was even more overloaded. For the first time, she resorted to some of the pills a bud of Jimi's had recommended in the final days of *Hy Voltz* to pep her up once in a while. Not every day, but when her schedule got too much.

Not only did she feel that she could get more done, she felt more organized somehow. She could sit in the tub with a yellow legal pad and plan out a week's worth of work on the house, then get on the phone, get it all delegated, then sleep it off and get back to work. It was like magic. And magic can be so tempting.

For the time being, it was working. Even their fear and anxiety over Cabo subsided.

"Honey," Jimi called to her one rare evening when she'd returned home at a reasonable hour. "Come here and look at this."

"What?" she called back from the kitchen, where she was making herself a smoothie. "What is it?" She walked into the den licking the honey off her finger, still carrying the jar. "You want a smoothie?"

"Look at this." He pointed at the screen.

"Oh, Jimi," Star said irritably. "You dragged me in here to look at porn? Whatever they're doing, I've seen it, or done it, or whatever." She turned to go.

"No, wait," Jimi said excitedly. "That's not it. Look at that guy there. With the nipple ring."

"The one who obviously dyes his hair?" Star asked, turning back, squinting her eyes and folding her arms.

"Oh, yeah, I guess you're right." He chuckled. "You notice anything else about him?"

"Aside from the obvious similarities to every man on earth?" Star said, hungry for her smoothie.

"Not just that," Jimi urged, taking her arm and leading her nearer to the huge screen she was having no difficulty seeing. "Look at his face."

"His face?" Star snorted, looking. "That's a novelty."

"Doesn't he look kind of like—"

"Oh my God!" Star said, sitting on the edge of the coffee table and covering her mouth. "It's the plumber."

"I knew it," Jimi howled, throwing himself onto the sofa beside her. "I thought it was."

"It's totally him."

The video and the smoothies were quickly forgotten, though not the honey. Star and Jimi loved honey. So much so that they had devised a game they called simply Honey. They took turns. Each would take the jar and put a spoonful of honey on his or her own body. The object was for the other to

lick off the honey. They had discovered that you could lick
and lick and lick and the honey would still be where you put
it, so a couple of spoonfuls could go a really long way. Their
plumber proved quite inspirational, and they used nearly half
a jar.

Their porn star plumber was not the only interesting dis-
covery that the renovation produced. Getting a permit for ad-
ditions, Star was asked to sign some papers about the
ownership of the house, about them and previous owners.
She discovered that the house had once belonged to Vincent
Ewer, the star of one of her all-time favorite movies, *Stolen
Love*. It was the story of a man who while robbing a woman's
home discovers her most private fantasies and then pretends
to be the woman's ideal in order to win her love. But once he
has that love, he begins to reveal his true self, and he is not at
all the man she fell in love with.

But illusions were not the immediate trouble. Reality was
causing Star far more problems.

Hy Voltz's holiday premiere was looming large. On the
surface it was a joyous event, a big studio premiere of Star's
first film. There was every reason to celebrate her big moment. Yet, in truth, the experience had left her with so many
unpleasant memories it was hard to be excited, let alone celebratory.

On the plus side, a piece of music Jimi had written had
been selected as the title theme, and it was something for him.
More than anything else, she was happy about the opportunity to promote the sound track and Jimi's work. Jimi too
seemed pleased about the event.

It was their first red carpet walk together. That is, it was
the first time they had actually invited the paparazzi to take

their picture together. The opening was held at the old, historic Chinese Theater on Hollywood Boulevard, the site of all those famous handprints and footprints in the cement out front. Star had not been to the Chinese since she'd first arrived in Hollywood and taken the irresistible trip over to see.

So returning to the spot for the opening of her first film was more than a little significant to her. Of course, she was wearing a lace-up rubber outfit, huge hair, and major eyeliner. Jimi had combed his unruly hair and slicked it back. In his tuxedo he looked more like a 1920s matinee idol than a wild man rock star, and it was all Star could do to let him out of the back of the limo as Lito drove them to the event.

"Later," she said, stealing one last kiss as they pulled up to the entry for the carpet walk.

"It's a date," he said, copping a squeaky feel.

The door flew open and the world rushed up to meet them.

The photographers were quickly sated with couple shots and soon began screaming out for Star alone.

Star was torn. It was work. She was there to draw as much attention to the event as possible. The best way for her to do that was to pose for the photos and do the interviews on the carpet. But fuck them, she decided, clutching Jimi's arm, she would take pictures only with Jimi, and too bad for a movie that had treated them both so shabbily.

When they got inside, she was held up by the producers, and Jimi went to get them something to drink. Jimi was well on the way to plastered by the time she caught up to him, though where he'd gotten enough to drink that fast she wasn't sure. The party wasn't until after. So, drunk in the car on the way home, he had canceled their date by passing out on the way inside and slept on the floor in the front hall.

The film fared much better than anyone expected, rocketing to number one.

The critics didn't agree, but to everyone's surprise—including Star and Jimi—the public couldn't get enough of *Hy Voltz*, which quickly became the highest-grossing film of the year. Even the sound track shot up the charts, with Jimi's theme song getting constant airplay.

It was as if Star couldn't make a mistake. But the increased scrutiny only served to heighten her fears that someone was going to find out what they'd done, which only drove the two of them more deeply into seclusion and—irony of ironies—only increased the paparazzi's appetite.

The only answer was escape of a different kind.

6

oh me, oh my

Jimi seemed happier. In the midst of the chaos of their home renovation he'd somehow managed to get the garage studio up and running. While there was nothing official yet, he'd been having a high old time jamming with his buds on tunes new and old. He even set up a little production company he called Jimiville after the name Star had given the house.

Star was pleased that Jimi was spending more time with his work, but between the two of them the party never stopped. There were always friends over and plenty of good times, but it was starting to take its toll on Star. Often, there were still people up from the night before when she left for work at 5 A.M.

Star was working two production jobs, and her hours did

not match those on the unwritten party invitations. So, in the credit column, Jimi was more occupied, leaving her on her own on the set. On the debit side, Star was catching up on her sleep in her trailer, her only refuge from the Hollywood Scene Stealers taking over her life.

The combination was wearing her down, but she wasn't sure how to fix it. If things got too quiet the paranoia and anxiety kicked in. Not to mention that she was actually having a great deal of fun when she didn't have an early call the next day.

Operation Swedish Meatball continued to work, as well, and even when Jimi was on the set, he was less jealous and suspicious of Star and her costar. Their on-screen romance was flourishing, and even the tabloid rumors of an offscreen romance between her and Sven only made Jimi laugh. Star was unaware of the hoax that was responsible for Jimi's change of attitude and just chalked it up to their party-like-a-rock-star lifestyle.

It was a tiring but good time. The only real sour note seemed only a little sharp at the time.

The party moved to Star's trailer as well. She regularly returned from the set to circumstances that to call unprofessional would be a massive understatement. Loud music, naked groupies, and more than one of the show's staff injured. One of the wardrobe ladies ended up getting divorced over a particularly spicy afternoon.

It meant that Billy, Skip, and Missy were almost constantly on set to look after Star's hair and makeup and to escape the goings-on in the trailer.

But it also strained Operation Swedish Meatball to the breaking point.

The romance between Star's and Sven's characters was really heating up. "When will BeeGee and Casey do it?" the tabloids and the fan magazines wanted to know. The romance had progressed well beyond the moonlight-kiss stage, but hadn't quite made it to the bedroom. Clearly, what had started as a little on-the-job flirtation between the two lifeguards was barreling toward the bedroom.

Jimi remained oblivious, even going so far as to try to fix Sven up with a record promoter who Jimi knew batted for Sven's team. Skip headed off the disaster and assured Jimi that Sven was seeing someone. Fortunately, that someone's name was Samantha, and Sven always called her Sam.

The double play saved the day temporarily, but ultimately doomed the game.

Jimi could ask about Sam and Sven could mention her without raising much suspicion, but only because Jimi and Sven didn't really talk much—until they discovered a shared fondness for that peculiarly L.A. obsession, the Lakers.

"We should have Sven and his partner over for game night sometime once the season starts," Jimi suggested to a distracted Star. "Or maybe we could all go to a game."

"Oh, I don't think so," Star said, only half-considering it as she checked herself in the trailer's makeup mirror following a quick bathroom break between takes. "Is Sven starting a business?"

"I don't know." Jimi shrugged. "Why do you ask?"

"You said his *partner.*"

"Oh, well, what's the right term?" Jimi turned his palms skyward. *"Lover, significant other?"*

"Aren't you formal?" Star eyed him in the mirror.

"Okay, Sam then." Jimi shrugged. "We never do anything with your friends. I thought it would be nice."

"That's sweet, honey, but really, we're not that close." She gave him a quick kiss as she headed out the door. "Anyway, I'd rather keep it that way. I feel like everyone here knows too much of my business as it is."

Sven was such a big Lakers fan and the series was doing so well that he treated himself to two courtside season tickets to the Lakers. At the price of a luxury sport coupe, the tickets were a celebrity indulgence.

For reasons defying logic outside the balance sheet, with no football team, the Lakers became L.A.'s official home team, attracting a veritable who's who of Hollywood royalty. The courtside seats are always filled with faces of those even more famous than the world champion team they come to watch. As a result, the cameras present are as likely to be focused on the stands as on the court.

And the cameras were at the ready when Sven took Sam to inaugurate his seats. Sven had already earned a spot on everyone's most-beautiful-people list, so when he showed up at the game with his girlfriend, the photos were an easy sale for the season-tipoff coverage. When Jimi spotted his beloved Lakers on the cover of *USA Today* and picked it up to get the highlights of the game, he also saw Sven's beloved Sam.

At first he looked at the guy on Sven's right, smiled, and thought what a nice-looking couple they made. But as he read and reread the caption, it became clear that *Sam* was short for *Samantha* and that Jimi had been played. He kept questioning it as he went over it in his mind. Had he simply been mistaken? Had he gotten the wrong impression?

Feeling hurt, deceived, and betrayed, Jimi blamed the only

two people who were only guilty of having amazing onscreen chemistry—Star and Sven. He also leaped to the conclusion that they must really have had something to hide to perpetrate such a massive deception. He jumped into the Ferrari and tore off to the set to have a word with his wife.

Lulled into a false sense of security, no one at *Lifeguards* reacted to the sound of squealing tires in the parking lot with anything other than mild annoyance. At worst they'd either have to retake the shot without the racket or loop it by having those in the scene rerecord their dialogue by lip-synching to get the noise out of the ruined take.

"Cut," Brock called irritably, preferring to retake the scene as he had notes anyway. "Okay, when the demolition derby is done up there, let's try it again. And this time, Sven, as you take her hand, I want you to be more tentative."

"Tentative," Sven repeated in a way that Brock knew meant Sven had no idea what the director was talking about.

"Look at her face like you've asked her a question," Brock went on, to avoid making his actor look foolish. "Will she come back to your apartment with you or not? That is unanswered here, and the viewers won't know what she's decided until the next scene with the two of you in the sack."

"I'll tell you what she's decided!" Jimi shouted from behind the camera crew, stalking forward awkwardly across the sand. "She's decided to come with me."

The crew immediately began acting busy to avoid seeming to watch the action that was unfolding between Star and Jimi.

"Jimi?" Star said. "What's wrong?"

"I just saw the pictures of Sam in *USA Today,*" Jimi said, grasping Star's hand firmly to drag her away from the rest of the cast.

Sven was not only baffled and confused, but since Sam was his girlfriend, he felt oddly responsible.

"Sam's picture?" Star asked, clueless. "Have you been drinking?" she asked quietly.

"I'm sober," Jimi hissed.

"I'm missing something here," Star said quietly, still unsure what they were talking about. "I'm guilty of Sam's pictures? Baby, I'm worried about you."

"I'm not crazy!" Jimi shouted. "Although I was crazy to trust you in the first place, considering how we got together. How do you think it makes me feel to be deceived like this?"

"Is something wrong?" Sven asked absurdly, walking dangerously close to the ticking time bomb.

"I have no idea," Star confessed.

"Don't play innocent with me," Jimi bellowed, drawing back as if to take a swing at Sven as he came within striking distance. "Don't forget, I know the truth."

"Just what do you think I'm guilty of?" Star asked carefully.

"Like you don't know," Jimi growled disgustedly. "Do I have to spell it out for you?"

"Well, I'm not a very good speller." Star shrugged. "But I'll take whatever clues you've got."

"Sam is Sven's girlfriend," Jimi said as though he'd discovered the Holy Grail.

Star and Sven only stared at him expectantly, still waiting for it.

"That's it?" Star said finally when Jimi said no more.

"You owe me a hundred dollars," Billy said surreptitiously to Skip as Skip moved in to start the salvage operation.

"That's lunch," he called as he took Sven's elbow. "We need to do something with your hair."

A much relieved crew dispersed as they all but ran away from the setup.

"My hair?" Sven said, reaching information overload, what with Jimi's odd behavior and Brock's whole new "tentative" concept. He wondered why Jimi felt so strongly about Sam. Was he jealous? Was Jimi gay or bi or what was going on? Sven was in his trailer before he thought to ask any of these questions and soon became distracted with the touchups for the scene.

Star was not so lucky. Left standing on the beach to deal with Jimi's over-the-top reaction to something she knew nothing about, she tried once more to calm him and to figure out what he was talking about.

"Why are you so upset about Sven's girlfriend?" Star asked gently in the hopes of not setting him off again.

"You're fucking him, aren't you?" Jimi demanded.

"Why does the news that he has a girlfriend make you think I'm fucking him?" Star said, looking for a place to sit down.

"Are you?"

"Of course not." Star made her way toward the folding chairs just off camera.

"Then why all the lies?" Jimi said, grabbing her shoulder and spinning her back to face him.

"What lies?"

"Something's up. I'll figure it out." Jimi clenched his fists and made a noise that caused Star's blood to run cold. It reminded her of other men in her life. Star knew all too well this was the sound you hear before you get hit. Instinctively, she flinched, but instead of her, Jimi went after the folding chairs and coolers under the canopy in the break area.

"This innocent thing just makes it worse, Star," Jimi wailed, waving his finger in her face, tears of rage in his eyes. "Sven is not gay and you know it."

"Yeah, I do," Star said, sitting at last on one of the ruined coolers. "Did you think he was?"

"Don't act innocent," Jimi said, kicking at what was left of the craft services table. "The game is over, Star." He trampled potato chips and cookies under his boots. "Do you hear me? Over."

What had just happened? Star wondered as she picked up one of the Perriers out of the sand and opened it. Jimi's moods had always been unpredictable, but this one seemed to come completely out of nowhere. She worried that all the parties were catching up with them and that maybe something worse was going on. But most of all, she worried that the man she loved more than anything else in the world was way more upset with her than he'd ever been before. They had to trust each other.

They had to stay together.

She smiled as the answer came to her—a celebration of him. His birthday was coming up and it was the perfect excuse to throw him a party that would show him in ways that she knew he could understand just how much she loved him.

She wandered back toward the trailer as she began planning the extravaganza.

The show wrapped for the day, and when they resumed, there was a whole new script. Needless to say, the on-screen romance was derailed, however temporarily. Instead of their going back to Casey's place, they rewrote the script to have BeeGee spot a swimmer in distress and drop Casey's hand to run to the rescue. The answer to the tentative question turned out to be no, and the whole thing was posed as a tease. BeeGee thinks they should call it quits because the distraction at work endangers the lives of those they protect and serve. Casey still thinks they should get together or they'll be too distracted to do their jobs in the first place.

It was pure Velveeta, but the audience loved it and the show scored another ratings bonanza. But then, their audience really did love Velveeta.

At least that went smoothly.

"Fuck no. I just saw *Extra* zooming in on your kiss with Sven and I'm not coming with you," Jimi said, snatching his hand from hers as she pleaded with him, sobbing.

"But, Jimi, you have to," Star wailed, her voice echoing in their tennis-court-sized master bath.

She sat on the edge of the marble tub that might easily seat five, but was built just for two. It was where she had done most of the planning for the night that Jimi was threatening to ruin, because it was one of the few places where he would leave her alone. She was determined it was truly going to be a surprise party.

Following Jimi's strange overreaction on the set, he had been constantly at her side, watching her as if she were trying to escape. She did everything to try to reassure him, but it was to no avail. He saw malice in her every action and read deceit into her every word.

A suggestion that they go to a party or an event together

was met with questions of "Why?" and "Who's going to be there?" He could never seem to believe that it was only him that she wanted. So they'd stay home and he'd accuse her of being ashamed to be seen out with him.

She'd pinned her hopes on a surprise birthday party and hoped for the best.

It was the most elaborate thing she'd ever done or imagined doing in her life. She'd always loved the circus and had actually trained with Cirque du Soleil, so she was able to convince them to perform at the party. What she didn't know was that Jimi had checked up on her and found out she was lying when she'd told him she was going to the set or to a costume fitting to keep the party preparations secret.

Over one hundred performers were to entertain at a party with only twenty-five guests. She had hired a huge ranch on which to set up three massive circus-sized tents and had a full-scale light-up entry sign built to proclaim the fantasyland she had constructed in his honor—Jimiville. Beyond, a Ferris wheel and a merry-go-round played their haunting and seductive carnival music, and their lights brightened the wilderness that surrounded them. But the beacon would go unheeded unless she could change Jimi's mind.

The party was to be a private funfair, planted in the desert soil just for Jimi's pleasure. But because he'd become jealous and suspicious of all the sneaking around Star had had to do to put it all together, he was refusing to do the only thing he had to do to make the night a success.

Star had told him there was going to be a costume party for his birthday, but that was all she'd told him. She needed him to put on his crown and get in the car. That was it.

All her planning, time, and effort—not to mention the

hundreds of thousands of dollars—were about to go to waste. She felt helpless. She felt despair. And then she felt the fury of hell blaze bright in her chest. Her tears vanished, and she opened the bathroom door with a bang.

"Jimi," she shouted with enough threat to let him know he'd better answer.

"What?" he yelled back from what he called their rumpus room. He was lying on a massive two-man chaise that Star had chosen because it reminded her of the big chaise on the *Tits*. The use they had made of the new chaise had earned the little sitting room its raucous nickname.

"As I see it, you have two choices," Star said, standing firmly in the doorway, hands on hips.

"Oh, do I?" Jimi said.

"You can either get up, get dressed, and come with me to see for yourself why this is so important to me. You can divorce me tomorrow if it's not a good enough reason," Star said, waving one finger and then raising a second without waiting for a reply. "Or, you can sit right there and play video games. I don't know what to say to you anymore."

Twenty-eight minutes later, Lito held the door for Jimi as he belligerently climbed into the back of the car in full costume.

"Star, I'm warning you—"

"Not one word," she said with such force that Jimi actually stopped talking. "You can yell at me all the way home and I won't argue a bit. But on the way, not one word."

He was so angry that he actually remained silent, arms folded, teeth grinding.

Slowly his mood began to change.

First, at the restaurant he thought they were going to, he

met a group of twenty or so of his closest friends, all done up like characters from a Fellini film. They were already loaded onto a tour bus, filled with enough food and drink served by costumed midgets to be a party all on its own.

But his mood shifted from puzzled and bemused to awestruck as the bus rounded the corner on the dark mountain road and the huge JIMIVILLE sign illuminated the night and the glow of the funfair beyond came into view.

As they stepped off the bus, led by Jimi and Star, little people dressed as pawns unfurled a red carpet across the grass to meet their feet. The guests were greeted by naked dancers who tumbled across the lawn in a strange contortionist's dance.

An ice cream man pedaled his cart across their path ringing his bell.

"Welcome to Jimiville," Star announced, declaring the party officially begun.

It was a night of wild abandon and simple pleasures, like free rides on the Bavarian swings that spun the guests high into the air, and more sophisticated treats such as the laser projectors that beamed erotic shadows of groups having sex inside the tents. Topless models wearing painted-on clothes strolled among the guests with drinks and hors d'oeuvres.

Of course the music was amazing, and many of the famous musicians who were guests at the party joined in.

The action stopped throughout Jimiville at one point when a huge cannon drawn by naked men painted gold was brought to the center of the festivities. A hush fell over the crowd as a performer made up to be a very old man walked slowly through the gathering, dragging a huge ladder with the help of a band of the small people who were working the party. He leaned the ladder against the opening of the cannon and loaded himself into it. Then the little people drew away the ladder and lit the fuse with a torch.

With a wave of greeting to the crowd, the human cannon-ball slipped into the barrel. Moments later he was out again, fired over the heads of the crowd, over the tent and out of sight.

The music resumed and soon the revelers were back up to full speed.

The party reached a fever pitch with a frenetic dance number in which naked women were spun on a huge latex canvas while being slathered with paint by the hands of the guests and the other dancers who decorated them, smearing paint and glitter over naked flesh as the girls were spun faster and faster in time to the music.

The finale, a tribute to their wedding, came in the form of a company of Fat Elvis Impersonators singing "Volare" as they waved huge dildos at the wasted, painted, glittered crowd.

The Mighty Mouse cake was worn by the server.

And in an impassioned speech in which he said how much he loved his wife, Jimi pledged his undying love and devotion before, too drunk and heaven knew what else to stand any longer, he fell off the stage.

Full and under the influence, the crowd settled in to listen to the music. Jimi snuggled up next to Star, warm, content, and fortunately uninjured from his fall, all the jealousy and acrimony forgotten for that moment, and for good, Star hoped. When no one could eat one more bite or drink one more drink, the night was split by the peal of the bell on the ice cream cart as it twinkled by for the third and final time.

Star smiled, the perfect party was complete.

As if on cue, sirens intruded on the peaceful moment. A few guests were alarmed until they realized that a whole fleet of ambulances were lining up at the gate to take everyone home. A sign on the Jimiville bid farewell wih the message YOU'RE BEING VIDEOTAPED to the painted and glittered crowd.

"I love you, Jimi," Star said, taking his hand. "You know that? Just you."

"I love you too," Jimi said.

She wasn't sure her plan had worked or that he'd even re-member it all. But it was one hell of a party.

7

can't you see?

 "Look, Star," Stan said, catching up to her in the parking lot as she was leaving the set one day. "We can't keep this up."

"Well, there's always Viagra." Star giggled.

"I'm serious," Stan said, trying to be stern and failing miserably.

"I am too," Star said with a firm nod that made him smile.

He put a paternal arm around her shoulder as he walked her to her car. "It's like this. I need to get this shot and you need to deal with Jimi. I know that it makes Jimi crazy, but we have to get these two characters together."

"I'll see what I can come up with," she said as she vaulted up behind the wheel of her SUV. "Maybe we can take him out in the woods and leave him there. By the time he finds the gingerbread house or the three bears' porridge, we'll have the show in the can for the year."

"Thanks, Star." Stan waved as she backed out.

She smiled and waved as the window closed between them. She had no idea what to do. And she didn't have time to think about it. She had to get across town for *Hammer Time,* then meet her brother, Hank, who was coming out for his first visit now that the big Malibu house was finished and she had a place for him to stay.

Hank's trip was perfectly timed. Star had been invited to a party at the home of R&B music star Jean Soames. It was the sort of thing Jimi wouldn't be caught dead at, but Hank, who was no R&B fan, couldn't have cared less, as it was a Hollywood Party.

After *Hammer Time,* Star had just enough time to pick up Hank at "Lax," as she still called it.

"Who are you now, the tour guide?" Hank laughed as she pointed out the blimp field on the way up PCH as they headed toward home.

"No, I'm just your big sister and I'm older and smarter than you, dumb ass. Don't act lame at this party tonight, now."

"Don't worry about me," Hank snorted. "I've been living in the thriving metropolis of Florida City, I'll have you know."

The Soames house did not disappoint. Star's first stop in L.A. had been the French-château-styled Mann Castle, which was tough to top. But the Jean Soames place was pretty impressive, and Star was certain that it more than topped anything on Hank's regular party list.

It was one of those loosely referred to "architectural" L.A. houses. A cross between adobe mission and ultramodern, the place was all blinding-white stucco, blue glass, and water. Flat-roofed and stacked like building blocks, the house was behind a high wall sitting on a ledge on the hill overlooking West Hollywood, where Star had lived when she'd come to town.

"Look," she said, pointing from the hillside view as they walked down the drive to the front door. "There's the Bel Age. That's the hotel where I stayed when I first came to town."

"Hello," an extremely attractive young man, wearing little more than a smile, greeted them at the front door. "Everyone's out by the pool."

"Thanks," Star said flirtatiously. "Where are you headed?"

"I'm just here to answer the door." He smiled graciously. "Let me know if there's anything else you need."

"Okay," she said, heading across the large, mostly glass living room. Skylights made the all-white room glow in the late-afternoon sun. The glass curtain wall that comprised one entire side of the room opened onto a startling blue-tile infinity pool that floated like a sapphire in the blaze of sunset.

"Star," Jean called, spotting her and throwing his arms open wide in greeting. He made his way across the blue-tiled patio pursued by two young men wearing shorts with suspenders over their shaved and polished chests. "And who is this little confection you've brought?"

"Jean, this is my little brother, Hank. "Hank, this is Jean Soames."

"How do you do, sir," Hank said, taking Jean's hand. "It's an honor."

"My pleasure." Jean took Hank's hand in both of his. "I've always been very partial to little brothers. And these are O'Neil and Bartok, my little brothers, tonight anyway. This is—"

"Oh, Star Wood Leigh," one of the two gushed, taking Star's hand. "I'm a huge fan."

"I'm an air conditioner," Star replied, laughing at her own joke.

"I'm a big fan too," said the other one, giggling along with her.

"Now, boys," Jean said, giving both their tightly clad backsides a smack. "No starfucking. Well, not yet, anyway."

"I'm sorry, just so very pleased to meet you," one said.

"Likewise," his bookend concurred.

"Why don't you get them some drinks while I get Star and her little brother situated in the gazebo?"

"He doesn't look that little to me," the talkative one said, earning another smack.

Drink orders were taken. Jean, Hank, and Star made their way slowly to the gazebo on the far side of the pool overlooking West Hollywood below, and much of Los Angeles and even Long Beach beyond. They were delayed as they stopped to greet a who's who of Hollywood from the music industry and otherwise.

"There certainly are a lot of good-looking guys here," Star said once they were situated and Jean had left them to find out what had become of their drinks.

Hank snorted with laughter.

A number of beautiful women were present, but they were getting surprisingly little attention.

Star and Hank laughed pretty much through the whole party.

Perhaps the best thing that happened at the party was that

Star met avant-garde photographer Eric Marmont and his protegée. She had admired his off-beat style and vision, and the two instantly connected. While Hank was busy winning an impromptu limbo contest, Star and Eric were busy planning their spread for *Blab,* the edgy magazine which Warhol once edited. Star would pose as the corpses in a series of famous murders. They called it "want to chalk about it."

Though neither artist nor model realized it at the time, it was the beginning of a life-long partnership.

Star loved having Hank out for a visit; she kept finding reasons for him to stay a little longer. So, when he confided he'd like to stay on, Star was more than happy to help him get started. He moved into her old place, as she'd not gotten around to selling it yet. Actually, she hadn't tried very hard, as she enjoyed having her own little getaway when Jimi or work or whatever got to be too much. There was room for Hank at the house, but he was getting under Jimi's nails a bit, plus Hank had limited their sexual exploration and conquest of the house and all its rooms and flat surfaces. More to the point, Star thought Hank would do better with a little independence. He promised to find work and get a place of his own as soon as possible, but there was no rush as far as Star was concerned.

It was nice to have Hank around to remind her who she was and where she came from. And what was really important.

There were so many things to be valued in Hollywood that it was hard to keep account. Was it the awards or the money or the fame or the attention or the looks or the career? The checklist on a Hollywood scorecard was endless enough to keep the richest and most beautiful people hungry and motivated. No matter how spectacular the life—and whole television networks were devoted to describing the spectacular lives of the city's most glittering inhabitants—someone always seemed to have it better. So, having Hank in her life was like having an anchor to keep her in port when she was buffeted by the winds of outrageous fortune.

Though she didn't know it and couldn't have predicted it, a squall was shaping up.

She had given careful consideration to the *Lifeguards* dilemma. She wanted to be honest with Jimi, but he wanted to hear only what he wanted to hear.

In the end, Hank's down-home sensibilities won the day.

He overheard a phone conversation Star had with Theresa and picked up enough to figure out what was going on.

"You want a beer?" he called to her after she'd hung up.

"Root beer," she called back.

"Here you go," he said, cracking one for her, his own long-neck tucked under his arm. "You know, it's none of my business . . ."

"I know it isn't," she said, afraid of what was coming.

"All's you really have to do is make arrangements for him to be somewhere else when you shoot the scenes. Just make sure that he's not there."

"Isn't that deceptive?"

"Maybe." Hank shrugged, taking a pull off his beer.

Perhaps the most original idea had come from her costar Sven. Though he was still as in the dark about the Swedish Meatball conspiracy as Star, he was much better informed about the whole situation since Jimi's big scene at the shoot.

"Why don't we just get it over with," he suggested, his sparkling blue eyes glinting at her from his top-ten-most-beautiful face.

Star laughed it off, but the irony of the situation was not lost on her. She was actually being persecuted for something she wasn't doing, even though she easily could have . . . and it would hardly have been unpleasant. It had crossed her mind, but Sven was just a little too clean-cut for her tastes.

Hank was working as an extra on *Hammer Time*. In fact, like many newcomers to Hollywood he got his union membership card doing walk-on parts. And like all but about 5 percent of the members of SAG, he barely made enough to cover gas to the shoots, let alone to support himself.

On this particular day he was hanging around Star's dressing room at the end of a long production day. Star was giving him a ride home, as he did not yet have a car, and they talked as she got ready to leave. She did not have the kind of personal crew on *Hammer Time* that she did on *Lifeguards,* so it was just the two of them as she got out of makeup and costume on her own.

"Have you heard from Mom?" she asked, still waiting to hear back from her mother. She had suspected that her father was just not passing the messages along, at first, anyway. But too many were unreturned.

"Nah," Hank said, leafing through a magazine and not really paying attention.

"When was the last time she called you?" Star put her costume on the rack for the wardrobe lady to pick up.

"Not exactly sure." Hank looked up from a spread on NASCAR drivers.

"Hank, be serious," Star said irritably as she sat at the makeup table to survey what, if any, of Billy's work she wanted to take off before heading home. She frequently got her makeup done by her personal crew on *Lifeguards* before coming to the *Hammer Time* set, where she was at the mercy of the general cast crew—they were good, they just weren't Skip, Billy, and Missy.

"I am serious," Hank said, going back to his magazine. "And I kind of prefer it that way. She's always bossing me about something."

"I just wanted her advice," Star explained.

It was an unreasonable but manageable level of stress.

And then the world just completely went out of control.

Star had called her mother once again, and was surprised when her grandmother Gitta answered the phone.

"When will they be back?" Star asked, confused as to why Mama Gitta was there if her parents weren't home.

"Oh, I don't rightly know," Brigitta said in a singsong kind of way she had when she was nervous.

"Where have they gone?" Star said, growing tired of the runaround and determined to track her mom down.

"Well, that's the thing," her grandma said evasively.

"What's the thing? What's going on there?" Star said, getting anxious. "Are they all right, is everything okay?"

"Well," the old woman said, drawing it out, clearly deciding how to answer, "Star, your mom's in the hospital. She's had another attack."

"*Another* attack?" Star shrieked, unaware of any attacks.

"She can't walk at all anymore." Brigitta sighed sadly. "And the doctors say that without the surgery she never will again, and even then . . ."

It was more than Star could take.

Her mother's illness gave Star something to focus on at a time when she needed it most.

The couple, already the darlings or the target, depending

on how you looked at it, of every tabloid and paparazzi, and they followed Star to Cedar Sinai Hospital in Beverly Hills, where Star had her mother transported to get her the best specialists and find out what could be done.

Much to Lucille's—Star's mother's—dismay, her arrival at the hospital made the evening news. "I've never been on TV or had my picture in the paper in my life," she said disgustedly as she was wheeled into the hospital. "And they wait until I've got two weeks' worth of bed head, I'm strapped to a gurney, and have tubes sticking out of my nose."

"Is this what you have to do to make it in Hollywood nowadays?" Lucille joked through her oxygen mask.

"I don't know," Star said, taking her hand. "I do know it's the first time I got you out here for a visit."

The two women laughed until they cried.

Lucille never said, but she was plenty scared. And Star was overwrought and terrified over the developments surrounding her mom's health.

She turned her full attention to her mother's condition. It was serious and life-threatening. Her mom had lost the ability to walk because her circulatory system was so devastated by her years of chain-smoking. She simply didn't have the strength.

Star had always kidded that she was a committed second-hand smoker. She had never even tried smoking herself, but her mom and many of Star's boyfriends over the years were big-time smokers.

Her mom's problem had a surgical solution, but it was invasive and risky. However, the alternative was for her mom to spend the remainder of her brief life strapped to an oxygen tank, never to walk again.

There was also the cost, and Lucille had no insurance. For the first time, Star was truly grateful for her success. She simply wrote the hospital a check for the hundreds of thousands needed for the procedure.

And so, the surgery was scheduled, but it was far from a sure thing.

Star wanted to commit her time and resources full-time to taking care of her mom.

"This is another fine mess you've gotten me into, young lady," Lucille called to her daughter as she was wheeled off to surgery, delirious from all the medications they'd given her for the procedure.

"I'll be right here waiting for you," Star said, trying to act brave, but not doing a very good job of it as she walked alongside the gurney wheeling through the halls of the hospital. "You get better, you hear? I can't do this without you."

Lucille reached out and took her daughter's hand.

"You can do anything you want," Lucille said, giving a little squeeze. "Remember, it's your choice who you are. I'll be watching, whatever happens. I love you, Star."

Their hands separated as they reached the operating room doors and Star was left behind.

"You just get well, old woman," Star said, releasing her mother's hand and blowing a kiss after her. "I love you, Mom," she called, waving as Lucille passed through the swinging double doors into the land of authorized personnel only. The tears came as soon as her mom was out of sight. Once she felt she didn't need to be strong for her mother, Star collapsed onto the cold tile outside the OR doors.

8

no excuses

Lucille's funeral was a small family affair in the mainland cemetery just north of her home on Arcady Key. The bereaved were outnumbered four to one by members of the media.

Star was too devastated to notice the hyenas. All she could think of were her mother's final words.

"Remember, it's your choice who you are. I'll be watching, whatever happens."

The events of the past few months just kept playing over and over in her head. If only she could take them back. If only she could undo it all.

As they made their way to the cars after the graveside service, a photographer who must have slipped past security and hidden in a tree in the cemetery, dropped out of the branches into their path, shouting at them to "look this way," "give us a wave good-bye to mama." Blind with rage, Rick went after the man, catching him by the ankles as he tried to make his getaway over the fence, and dragged him facedown across the lawn and down the drive to the main gates.

"Dad, stop, you really need to stop!" Star shouted, trying to bring her father to his senses, but understanding his rage.

"The hell with that," Richard said, holding the flailing man up by his ankles. "Jimi, come open this goddamned gate and I'll give them a good-bye picture."

"I'm with you, Rick," Jimi said, dragging open the cemetery gates that had been kept closed to prevent just such intrusions.

As the broad metal panels rolled to one side, the press surged forward, stepping back as (to the edification of those present, not to mention newspaper buyers around the world) Star's father pitched the man down the drive, smashed his camera and tossed what remained of it after him.

"Leave my family alone," he said, waving an appropriately Neanderthal fist as the gates closed like a great steel curtain on his world debut performance.

Jimi gave him a high five of approval, which the press captured as the gates ground shut. Star was both upset and pleased. She was horrified that her mother's funeral had come to this, but how else could they react?

Sorry, Mom, but fuck them, she thought. To hell with the consequences.

"Tell me what's the difference between that man in the tree and anyone else in the world breaking in here?" her father asked, genuinely.

"He had a camera around his neck," Star shrugged.

"So that's the only difference between a stalker and a re-porter?" her father asked incredulously.

"Apparently," Star said, patting her father on the shoulder.

"Well, that's crazy." Rick wagged his finger. "I'll tell you, Star, you say the word, I make one phone call, and they just start disappearing."

Star and Jimi shared a knowing look behind her father's back.

"Jimi," Star said as they dragged the heavy-duty garbage bag through darkness.

"I couldn't agree with you more," Jimi said as they emerged in the darkness from the bushes onto the fairway of the unfinished golf course. "But they just won't leave us alone."

"That's not what I meant," Star sighed.

"Come on," he urged her. "Our flight leaves in an hour."

Star wondered if her mom was watching.

"Okay, on three," Jimi said, picking up one end and di-recting Star to get the other. "One, two, three."

The heavy bag splashed into the water, bubbling at the sur-face for a moment before it sank. There was another splash and then a couple more from the other side of the murky water hazard.

"What's that?" Star hissed, again horrified that they would be found out.

"The gators will be eating good tonight," Jimi chuckled as he took Star's hand and they made their way back to their rental car.

Things were just not the same when they got back to L.A.

The work was the same, the shows were the same, the twenty-four-hour party was the same, but something inside had shifted. It was as if she had been nearsighted and suddenly put on a new pair of glasses. The harsh new clarity made the world ugly and unbearable.

She would sit with Mutley in her room, in his favorite chair. He could stare out to sea for hours at a point beyond the horizon that only he seemed to see.

"What is it, boy?" Star said, snuggling up to him. "What's out there?"

Mostly, she just missed her mom, their conversations, her slightly cracked advice that always turned out exactly right. But life, flavorless as it had become, did not allow her much time for mourning.

Their personal life was not what it had been, either. Star was tired and exhausted most of the time, and Jimi was more and more frequently drunk to the point of passing out. If they went out, they were hounded by the press, which made him furious, which meant that he'd get so drunk that it didn't matter anymore. Some nights, he'd just pass out in the car and Star would leave him there to sleep it off. On his not-so-good nights, he'd bring his plans for revenge, belligerence, and anger into the house. The stress of it all was hurting their relationship.

Still, the sex, when it happened, was as fiery as ever, and Star preferred getting him to stay home rather than go out to play. She became quite the provocateur, surprising him wearing only a string of pearls or Gucci lingerie, or showing up in the bedroom with a whip.

One area that they had tried before and which they unsuccessfully tried again brought Star to seek expert advice.

"Missy," Star said one day when the Fab Four, as the little team called themselves, were alone in the trailer. "Would you go find Sven and tell him that I'd like to run the scene with him, if he has a chance?"

"Okay, sure," Missy agreed suspiciously, since no one on *Lifeguards* ever ran scenes. She was technically Billy's assistant and responsible for on-set makeup continuity, and Star was respectful of that, though occasionally she'd ask her for a favor. Missy gave Billy a questioning look.

"It's okay," Billy said, shooting Missy a you-got-me look behind Star's back. "I'll be fine. It's an easy morning."

"Thanks, Missy," Star said, "I really appreciate it."

Missy figured she'd get the dirt from Billy later, so she went with a knowing smile.

"No problem, Star," she called, leaving the trailer.

"Okay, what was that about?" Skip asked, taking the pins from his mouth.

"Well, I need to get you guys' *advice* about something," Star said tentatively, not sure of how to bring it up.

"Our advice?" Billy questioned, more suspicious still. "We do your hair and makeup."

"How do you fuck up the ass?" she blurted, unable to think of a more politically correct way to ask. "Give me details."

"What?" Billy laughed.

"Well," Skip snorted. "I guess you have come up with one other area where we might have a little insight."

"A little?" Billy was getting progressively more amused. "I gotta know, what is it that you want to know? *Do* we?"

"Well, really, *how* do you?" Star asked sheepishly. "I kinda figured from some of your jokes that . . . that you do. Jimi wants to, so I figured I'd come to the experts."

"Then you'll want to talk to Billy," Skip said archly.

"Hey!" Billy exclaimed.

"Well, I just figure you're going to have the experience she'll need in this arrangement," Skip said, raising his shoulders practically to his ears. "I could maybe advise Jimi."

"So, you're the boy?" Star asked Skip, delighted to talk about someone's sex life other than her own.

"We're both boys," Billy snorted.

"Well, he's the boy and I'm the man," Skip said, earning a crack with a wet towel.

"Okay," Star said, rolling her eyes. "If everyone in the entire world gets to talk about my sex life, you two can talk about yours in the privacy of the trailer without turning into a couple of thirteen-year-olds."

"All right," Billy said, sobering up. "It's called bottom and top." He pointed at himself and then Skip.

"Or passive and active," Skip said, pointing at Billy and then himself.

"Too clinical," Billy said, wrinkling his nose. "Pitcher and catcher."

"I like that one," Star said. "It sounds fun, like a game."

"Well, then, Miss Star," Skip said, taking her hand, "meet Billy, the biggest catcher in the league."

Billy threw the wet towel over Skip's head.

Star's phone rang with the opening strains of "Can't You See," and she checked the number. "It's the lawyer. Excuse me a minute."

Star listened, then rolled her eyes as he explained the latest lawsuit, this one from a producer who claimed she backed out of a film she'd merely read the script for. "Tell him to take a number," she sighed, before turning back to Billy.

"All right, what do you want to know?" he asked, taking the makeup chair beside hers.

"Well, like everything," Star said, throwing up her hands.

"It requires preparation and practice," Billy said. "Straight boys and tops live in the delusion of spontaneity."

"Oh, please," Skip said, waving the conversation away.

"He just wanted to stick it in, right?" Billy said, not looking at Skip at all.

"Pretty much." Star nodded, then sipped her coffee.

"Typical," Billy sniped, folding his arms. "Well, first off, some bad news. Being a girl, you're never going to enjoy butt sex quite as much as boys do. It's a design thing."

"Boys are designed for butt sex?" Star said, her eyes widening.

"Surprising, huh?" Billy said with a little grin.

"You know, you hear it's unnatural."

"Not a bit. You remember the little hint I gave you about the come-hither finger up the chute during blow jobs?" Billy asked seriously. "Well, that's Mr. Prostate you're tickling. Only boys have them, and they get really tickled during butt sex. Not every guy wants to, but it's the same for all boys."

"Me, for instance," Skip said, raising his hand.

"Yeah, we all got that, butch," Billy said with an exasperated sigh. "But for boys who do, there's plenty of good reason built right in."

"It's all part of God's plan," Skip said derisively.

"Don't mock." Billy raised a warning finger. "I could have a really bad headache for a few months."

"It's a beautiful thing, Star," Skip said sincerely.

"But not for girls?" Star questioned.

"I didn't say that." Billy patted her hand. "Plenty of girls like it too, as I understand it. It's just a question of technique and personal preference. Straight boys and tops alike can learn a little thing called the reach-around."

"A hand job?" Star asked.

"During," Billy said, giving Skip a meaningful look. "It can go a long way toward improving the experience for both parties by motivating the catcher."

"Got it," Star said. "Jimi never minds that."

"Lucky girl," Billy said, rolling his eyes. "Now, the rest is all about preparation."

"Stretching exercises?" Star asked. "My mom was big on Kegel exercises, where you spread your legs and sit on the floor and try to suck up the carpet."

"You should show Billy how to do those," Skip teased.

"Douche," Billy said, pointedly ignoring him.

"Back there?"

"Yeah, you can get little enema bottles all ready to go at the drugstore. They're pretty self-explanatory and they're reusable with plain warm water. Just a tip, though. You do not have to lie on the floor and pull your leg up to your chest like it shows on the diagram."

"Though that's an excellent position for getting started later," Skip mused.

"Well, yeah, that's actually true," Billy agreed after first looking for and not finding an argument. "But the best way to begin, as with all things sexual, is with a little foreplay. If you're all nice and clean, and some people shave too, it's a matter of taste."

"Well, you all remember how they had to glue it on to give me pussy hair," Star said, breaking up at the memory.

"Oh, that's right," Skip said, cackling. "I remember that. It was so hideous. Marsten is so weird about that."

"And that poor little guy," Billy said, recalling the beard maker. "I felt bad for him, but he was such a professional."

"Anyway," Star said, riding over the digression, "shaving won't be a big issue for me."

"Right," Billy said. "And Jimi, he's good about oral sex in general?"

"I married him, didn't I?" Star said with laughter.

"Well, the same technique applies here, and, girl," Billy said, taking her hand, "it'll make you scream."

Skip nodded his head and put his fingers in his ears.

"Then he works in a lubed-up finger, and then two to get the lube in and the idea started. This is the part where having a prostate comes in handy, so you'll have to find your own ways to improvise," Billy said, not entirely sure of the mechanics involved. "And then the big show. Now, you can actually practice beforehand with your own fingers or with a dildo."

"Practice?" Skip snorted. "Is that what we're calling it now?"

"Or a vibrator if you've got one," Billy went on, pretending not to hear.

"If?" Star laughed. "One?"

"Okay, well, just get him to go slow at first," Billy forged ahead. "Easy in and then wait. You can breathe or even push like you would if you were, you know, using those muscles down there ordinarily, but the main thing is just to relax. It's not going to injure you; the pain is just because you're not used to it. Once you relax and get going, it all changes. And with a good reach-around or, better still, if you're facing just a plain old hand job, you'll forget that it ever bothered you in the first place."

"Aw, what a touching mother/daughter moment," Skip said, batting his eyes foolishly.

"You make fun," Billy said, "but I can't remember a single complaint."

"If I can add something," Skip said, putting an arm around Billy in a sideways hug, "Jimi'll love it if you kind of squeeze your cheeks together."

"Like you're trying to hold a fart." Billy nodded with an embarrassed shrug.

"Oh my God!" Star shrieked with laughter.

"When he's pulling, not pushing," Skip added, reaching over and holding up Billy's hand by a diamond-and-sapphire ring. "Trust me on this one, he'll really, really love it."

"Is that how I got that ring?" Billy asked, startled and unsure exactly how to react.

"It sure didn't hurt," Skip said with a knowing smile.

Star got a diamond necklace a week later.

Maybe it was just a coincidence.

9

nobody's fault

Going out to celebrate had seemed like a good idea at the time.

The nightclub Ka Mano, in fact, partly belonged to Star, so she would have some measure of control over the situation. She had been out of the house only to go to work and to court, and Jimi didn't have a gig, so he had been pacing the confines of Jimiville like a caged cat. They had indulged in their singular recreation until they had worn each other raw. Even with Skip and Billy's tip and their own wild imagination there was only so much they could do.

So they arranged an Ecstasy party to shake off the mood with sweat, love, and rock and roll.

She wore a rubber dress, so naturally the party declared

her the dominatrix. She had everyone skip into the bar past the phalanx of photographers banked there in anticipation of the moment. Even Jimi didn't get upset, as they were already rolling on X and too busy being ridiculous to care what the press did or said. Once inside, she decreed that it was topless night, but with a twist. The men would go topless and entertain the women. The decree soon became unenforceable, but not before most every man in the place had shed his shirt.

Along with the X, which made the most of all the exposed flesh, their neighbor Enoch had brought enough speed to keep the celebration in high gear, virtually indefinitely. With a bottomless bar tab and Star the owner there to keep the place open as long as they cared to play, it became quite a night.

Mack Wraith, a musician friend, was the first to start dancing on the tables, which he did most ably, including a glassware-shattering finale that cleared the table. Star did backflips, wiping out once or twice on the wet tables in heels.

Jimi hit Star's black rubber bodice with a cigarette and it exploded, rolling up her body like a window shade. Women throughout the club, long since closed to the public, followed her lead.

As the party made its way back out to the car in the early-morning hours, a photographer ran into Star's breast, his lights blinding her. She looked back as Jimi grabbed the stooped man by his camera, yanking him forward with the strap still securely around the photographer's neck. As the photog struggled, Jimi began spinning him around like some wild dervish, trying to wrench the camera free. Eventually it slipped over the photographer's head, and Jimi raised it into the air and smashed it to the pavement like Moses and the tablets. The photographer took a dive and rolled down a steep hill. It might have ended there, but one of the photographers pulled a canister of pepper spray from his pocket and sprayed Jimi and Star in the face.

It was like gasoline on a fire.

As Mack, Enoch, and Lito tried to help a wailing Star into the back of the Escalade, Jimi charged, taking their attacker down and pounding his head onto the carpeted pavement. Jimi was completely out of control, and as the photographer's colleagues merely watched and got the sexy shots, Jimi took out weeks of rage. Here was an enemy he could find and face. One neck he could twist. One battle he could win. Mack and Enoch dragged him off the bloody man and had to wrestle and fight with Jimi to get him into the car.

Star too was out of control, screaming over and over again for everyone to "fuck off." The press went wild, and the entire event was caught on tape, launching a weekly television series on the cable entertainment channel featuring unflattering candid moments of famous people provoked by the paparazzi.

After their escape from the nightclub riot, Star's and Jimi's eyes still burning from the spray, they pulled over into a residential yard and borrowed the sleeping owner's hose to wash it off.

The incident further served to unite the two against the world outside. "Everyone sucks but us" became their motto.

Perhaps the only ray of sunshine was a benefit concert in New York that Star's favorite cause, the Brotherhood for Animals Gaining Legal Equality—B.A.G.L.E.—was hosting. Jimi's band was to play along with a host of ultrafamous rock icons. Star could not have been happier about it.

Billy and Skip were not fooled.

"So," Billy teased, "your pet charity is having a concert on the other side of the country?"

"And it just happens to be on the very same night that you're shooting the big love scene with Casey?" Skip said, clicking his tongue. "Star and Sven are sitting in a tree . . ."

"K-I-S-S-I-N-G," the two chanted together. "First comes love, then comes divorce, then comes Jimi with his day in court."

"Funny," Star said, not amused by the joke nor admitting any complicity in the scheduling of the concert.

"I'm sorry, honey," Billy said, patting the back of her hand indulgently. "Not feeling well?"

"How's your head?" Skip asked, an exaggerated expression of concern on his face as he leaned down next to her, their cheeks almost touching.

"Well, I haven't had any complaints yet," Star said, cracking up.

In honor of the momentous reunion of Fools Brigade for the big concert, there was to be a big do out at Jimiville. It was Jimi's deal and Star decided she would let him plan it.

She would only be a guest at this party.

She had a shoot the day of the festivities and had planned to drop in with some friends from work and join the evening in progress. The shoot ran late and her work friends bowed out, so by the time she returned home the party was well under way. Fueled by the usual better living through chemistry, the party made out-of-hand seem like a Sunday-school social.

The front hallway was filled with people in varying states of undress, seated on the steps and hanging over the banister above. Those who weren't making out were watching a couple of kids with guitars doing their own variations on whatever was blaring on the house sound system. As Star made her way past the miniconcert, which was no small task, she found the living room filled with a pack of Hollywood Scene Stealers and every manner of vice. You name it and you had only to look behind a few pieces of furniture to find it, from all-but-full-on sex to every recreational application of most every substance known to man. The speed freaks were grinding their jaws, dancing, playing some kind of game, and talking all at the same time. The potheads were either smoking or eating or giggling or some combination of the three. The heroin chics were nodding out. And the cokeheads were talking as fast at they could, mostly to the nod-outs and potheads, who were not really listening but not interrupting. The drunks were mostly fighting among themselves.

Not spotting Jimi right away, Star climbed the kitchen stairs up to her room, which, along with every other bedroom and bathroom, was in use by couples horny from all the mood generators downstairs. She threw everyone out of her bedroom and locked the door against further intruders. She wanted to be mad, but she'd known whom she was married to when she told him he was in charge of the party.

Tired, Star opened the door to her bathroom. All she wanted was to clean up a bit from a strenuous day at the beach and try to catch a second wind so she could join the mayhem already in progress downstairs. She paused as she heard the all-too-familiar noise of what sounded like at least two couples doing she knew exactly what. One of them was her brother, Hank, who was snorting coke off the ass of one of the girls.

"Unh-huh," Star cleared her throat without looking too closely. "Excuse me."

There was a small scream, some scrambling, and then JC,

Hank, and Theresa emerged with two other young women wearing Star's best bath towels.

"Hi, Sis." Hank grinned, his face flushed and his pupils dilated.

"Hi, Hank, Theresa," Star grinned back. Her little brother was growing up. "You kids need to find a new playroom."

"Yeah, sure," JC agreed, hustling everyone toward the door. "See you downstairs, Star." Theresa grinned.

"There's a sauna off the changing rooms by the pool," Star said, amazed that it was her house she was talking about.

"Sure thing, thanks," JC called over his shoulder, pulling the door closed behind them.

It reopened as another small group poked their heads in, looking for a space.

"Occupied," Star said, crossing to relock the door.

"May we join you?" an attractive young surfer with shaggy blond hair asked, his treacherously beautiful blue eyes locking with hers.

"Private party," she said, pushing the door closed and turning the latch. But if she hadn't been a married lady, she'd surely have yanked blue eyes inside before she'd locked the door. She had to laugh at herself as she looked out the back window and saw the orgy that was evolving in the pool and hot tub. She'd have to point blue eyes out to Jimi later.

She was still laughing to herself as she headed for the privacy of her bathroom. She smiled as she remembered how Roberto, whom she'd worked with on the Cabo shoot, had become so sexually obsessed with Jimi that he'd broken into the house one night when he knew Star was working late and Jimi was alone. Creeping into that very room, he had awakened Jimi with promises of the best blow job he'd ever had.

As always, Jimi woke up horny and ready to go, so with a shrug he agreed and the deal was struck. The comforter was tossed aside and Roberto moved in to close the deal when Jimi spotted the braces on Roberto's teeth.

"Whoa, tiger," Jimi said, pulling the comforter back up to cover his hard-on.

"What's wrong?" Roberto asked, still panting with excitement.

"Dude, head's head but those braces might tear my shit up," Jimi said giving his intruder a friendly pat on the shoulder before turning over and going back to sleep.

She had to laugh and she had to love him. It wasn't that he was a married man, it wasn't the blow job from another guy, and it wasn't even the breaking and entering that put her man off. It was the braces. She laughed and thought again about blue eyes and wondered what Jimmy would say; after all, it was a party.

After the shower she put the dogs away out of concern for what they might pick up off the floor, and went in search of Jimi.

When she finally found him, he was in the studio at the keyboard with Fools Brigade doing what he loved best. Star would have liked to think it was second best, but she doubted it and that was okay. She sat and listened and watched for a while. He looked so happy and complete.

Darien and Joshua, bass and guitar, had been in high school with Jimi. Fools Brigade had started in Jimi's parents' garage, and they were still playing, as they had back when Jimi's father had enclosed and soundproofed the carport in self-defense. Vic, the drummer, had joined them a bit later, after they'd quit school to follow their dream to the Sunset Strip music scene and follow in the footsteps of their idols.

They were grown men now and had reached an age when most men in their field were either dead from the excesses of the life or slipping into obscurity. Some few, if they were smart, lived on the investments made during their salad days. Some, like the Stones, stayed on to become legends. And some just refused to leave the stage, even though the audience had long departed. You never knew which it was until you were being voted into the hall of fame or a made into a punch line.

Which it turned out to be hardly mattered at that moment.

Star knew how happy Jimi looked pounding out their old hits, his drink untouched and melting, his hands busy. What she didn't know was that playing together was all that was still possible for the group. Whether or not they'd been on-stage too long, they had been together too long, and the minute they stopped playing, they started fighting. But Star couldn't tell by looking. She only saw Jimi's joy as his fingers found the familiar keys. Eventually she went and joined him on the bench, resting her head on his shoulder as he played on into the night.

When they finally took a break, he kissed her and before she could say anything at all and put her at ease. "I have no idea who all these people are," he said quietly into her ear. "I invited about twenty or thirty of the usual suspects, and this is who showed up. They had to have the gate code to get in, so it was an inside job. I'm thinking Hank and JC?"

"Or Theresa; I caught them upstairs in our bathroom." She grinned, nodding. "I didn't know they were that close."

"The candy man is everybody's best friend," Jimi said knowingly. "I think they knew each other from back home. Or maybe they just had that in common."

"Yeah, well, there's way, way too much candy in this

house," Star said, just strongly enough to let him know she wanted to turn down the volume.

"I'll do a little housecleaning," Jimi said, kissing her forehead. "You amuse the band, but remember, you're *my* groupie."

She smiled as he slipped away. He could be such a good guy.

"Okay," Jimi said, waving his arms like a traffic cop. "Mom's home, time to go."

"Who needs a drink?" Star asked, turning back to the more intimate inside crowd in the studio.

Jimi got it down nearer to the originally intended group and their "plus ones," which was still fifty or so, and the odd straggler who'd turn up or regain consciousness in some forgotten room or cranny of the house and wander back into the party. Hank, Theresa, and JC were not around, but Star figured that with Hank's house just down the road they'd moved the little party from her bathroom to the privacy of Hank's bachelor crib.

The band played for a while, then headed out to the pool, where Jimi served dinner off the grill built into the natural rock that they'd used to frame the pool. Dinner wasn't served until around one in the morning, but no one seemed to care.

Star knew she should get to bed for work the next day, but it was turning out to be such a magical night, and they were already home and safe. It was a relief to have a good time when nothing could go wrong.

Eventually, the fact that they were no longer eighteen-year-old rock warriors took its toll, and the professional musicians and their plus ones and twos began to drift away for the evening. As Star and Jimi were closing the gates behind the last of the guests, and Mutley made one last check of the bushes before following them upstairs to his place in the chair at the foot of the bed, the house phone began to ring.

"Who can that be?" Star wondered. It was almost morning.

"I'll go," Jimi said, trotting across the lawn.

Jimi didn't come back out or call her, so she figured that it must have been someone from the party who'd forgotten something, otherwise it was too late for anyone in that hemisphere to be phoning. She had a nice walk around the big yard with Mutley, then headed inside, where she found Jimi, still on the phone, looking grave and writing away.

"What?" Star said, surprised to see that Jimi was still up, let alone still on the phone. "What is it?"

"Hank's in jail."

"What?" Star said, genuinely not comprehending.

Jimi might as well have said "The Martians have taken Washington." It just didn't make sense, didn't fit somehow.

"He was arrested for dealing drugs," Jimi said, holding his hand over the mouthpiece. "I woke up the lawyer and I'm on hold to see what we can do about bail tonight."

"Hank, my brother?" Star asked, her brow knit. "It's a mistake." She slid down the wall and sat on the floor. How was it possible?

Their lawyer arranged for Hank to sit out the night in an office at the police station where he'd been brought after his arrest, then be taken directly to be arraigned, without ever having to actually be in jail.

As it turned out, the arraignment never happened. The lawyer met with Hank in the police chief's office to get an idea what they were up against. Star went along to see if she could talk to her brother and find out what had happened.

The sun was just rising as she and the lawyer were admitted to see Hank in the sterile, no-frills office.

"Hank," she said, throwing her arms wide.

"Star, I'm so glad to see you," he said, falling between her arms, his head on her shoulder. It had been a long time since the old days when he'd come to her frightened by a storm or a bully or one of their parents' fights. They held each other for a bit.

"Are you okay?" she asked intently, holding him at arm's length to look at him and see for herself.

"Yeah, I'm fine," he sighed. "Considering."

"Then what the hell happened?" she demanded, smacking him sharply on the shoulder. "You scared the hell out of me."

"It was an accident," he pleaded.

"An accident?" she asked incredulously. "You were accidentally dealing drugs?"

"I was not dealing drugs," he said indignantly. "JC was dealing drugs. I was just in the car when he ran into the back of the police cruiser."

"He ran into a police car?" Star said, the hint of a smile beginning to crack her stony expression.

Hank nodded.

"With a carload of drugs?"

"Pretty much."

"Well, thank God Theresa wasn't with you," Star said, strangely relieved by the way things were unfolding.

They held each other and laughed.

10

the light

By the time Hank made bail, the press had not only convicted Hank of being a West Coast drug kingpin, despite no charges ever being filed, they'd also "discovered" that Star was a heroin addict. True, she had been more adventurous about "experimenting" since she and Jimi had gotten together. True, some of those experiments were extensive enough to have qualified as FDA studies. But not only was she not a heroin addict, she'd never even tried it.

Star heard the news of her alarming addiction while listening to the radio in her car one morning on the way to work. This curious and unexpected fact about herself came to her with the aid of Andy Callas. Star had tuned him in to let Andy do the talking on the way to the set.

"And did you see this thing about Star Deed?"

"Who?" said Jai, the woman who worked with Andy on the air.

"Star Leigh. Okay, Jai, it's time to let that go. She changed her name, okay?"

"That's just wrong, Andy."

"Hey, I don't make the rules."

"Star has certainly been in the news a lot lately."

"Too bad about her brother's getting arrested and all," Andy said, clearly not aware of the charges having been dropped. "He's a drug dealer, apparently, and now I see in this morning's papers that she's a heroin addict."

"That really is a shame. Do you think that's true?" Jai asked, knowing when to tee her boss up so he could drive it home.

"Yeah, well, I'll tell you," Andy said pensively, "if she is, she's the healthiest-looking heroin addict I have ever seen."

Star turned off the radio.

"Well, what's next?" she said to Mutley as they arrived for another brutal day of running in the sand. "Come on, boy."

She liked being able to take her old pal with her to the set from time to time. She didn't do it every day since he had a yard of his own, but she loved the extra affection and company.

"We heard," said Billy as she followed Mutley into the trailer. "You okay?"

"Glad I look healthy," she moaned, falling into the chair. "When is it ever enough?"

"We figured that you'd be pretty upset. How's Jimi taking it?" Skip asked.

"I don't know if he's heard," Star said. "He doesn't usually listen to Andy."

"It was in the trades and the tabloids too." Skip pointed at the papers on the couch.

"Oh, God," Star whined as she read the headlines. "FORMER ROADIE SUES FOOLS BRIGADE. This is the sue-me state."

"Hello," Billy called, wiggling his fingers in a little wave as he held up his hands. "Skip and I have opted not to sue you in favor of writing a really vicious tell-all book after your career tanks."

"You two," Star said, pinching his cheek affectionately. "You are true Hollywood friends."

"So, you didn't know?" Skip said, whipping up some magic chemicals to tame the roots he'd spotted as Star had first slumped into the chair that morning.

"About this lawsuit?" Star said, pointing at the paper. "First I heard of it."

"Well, then what was it you were talking about?" Skip said, setting the bowl of dangerous chemicals aside and adjusting her posture as he put a plastic cape around her.

"I'm a heroin addict."

"Oh. Yeah, that does sound pretty awful," Skip teased. "So put some down below too. Here's an extra teaspoon to make sure the carpet matches the drapes." He handed her the bowl of bleach.

She was shooting a scene with the show's star, Foster that morning. As head lifeguard, his character frequently offered guidance and sage advice to his little grasshoppers. Despite his serious character, being in a scene with him was a rollercoaster ride, though Star loved him just the same. He'd been the brains behind the show and she looked up to him.

Typically, he'd do his part of the shoot and leave. The person "sharing" the screen with him acted to a piece of tape on a stick at Foster's eye level with someone else reading Foster's dialogue. The only thing more nerve-racking was when Foster actually stayed to do the scene, as Star was experiencing that morning. While he was on the set with her, he was also talking on two cell phones between his lines and during hers, making bets on horse races. It was amazing how he could manage both at once.

The sun went behind a cloud and the director called cut on the scene. It was a big cloud, and Star took the opportunity to call Mutley over and take a little walk on the beach.

She paused to look out over the water. The ocean always made her feel in perspective somehow. It was so vast and so eternal and so unfathomable. Standing at the water's edge, she could see herself the right size. Not bigger-than-life, as on the *Hy Voltz* movie screen, but tiny and powerless in the face of how big life really was.

For the first time in a long time, the two creases disappeared from between her eyes. Her spider sense was tingling and she knew just what to do. The sun came out from behind the cloud and she raced back to the setup to finish the scene.

"Cut. Excellent, Star," Brock said, seeming genuinely surprised. Oftentimes the call was "If it's in focus, print it." But there had been a new life to Star's performance.

"Thanks, Brock, am I done?" she asked genially.

"Check the schedule, but as far as I know," Brock said, giving her a little wave. "Okay, people, we've got two more setups this afternoon. Let's act like we care!" he shouted to the crew, clapping his hands.

"Come on, Mutley," Star said, racing back to the car.

For the first time in a long time she knew just what to do. She wasn't a victim. She had a choice and she was willing to make it.

Star ran past the trailer, waving to Billy and Skip, who were working on their tans on lounge chairs outside. "I'll see you tomorrow," she called, rushing to the car.

"But, Star," Billy called, sitting up. "The suit."

She looked down, realizing she was still wearing the navy blue one-piece she'd made famous. "I'll bring it back tomorrow."

Star raced Mutley back to the car and climbed behind the wheel. She knew just how to handle the new lawsuit as well as their standoff with the press, and couldn't wait to tell Jimi.

The roadie in question had been injured in an accident at one of the stops on the band's last tour. Rather than take care of him, the guys replaced him and didn't help him out with his bills. Ironically, he'd sued only when he saw the announcement of the new concert date, figuring that if the band was getting back together, there would have to be money involved.

By comparison to the rest, it was just a nuisance lawsuit, but it was the straw that broke the camel's back.

"Jimi!" she shouted, running in the front door like George Bailey returning home after waking from his dark vision. Mutley barked joyously as he followed her in. "Jimi, are you home?"

"Out here, babe," he called from the room they called their office, really just part of the laundry room where they kept their files. Jimi was sitting at the desk talking on the phone when she found him, his feet up on the edge of the old metal monstrosity she'd found at a secondhand furniture store and had refurbished.

"Jimi, I know what to do," Star said excitedly. "I figured it all out today."

"I'm on with the lawyer," he said, covering the mouthpiece. "I don't know if you heard, but there's a lawsuit."

"Isn't it great? I know just what to do. Hang up."

"What?" Jimi said, confused by her enthusiasm. He was still in the old mood, the one she knew how to fix. "Can't it wait?"

"Hey," Star said, grabbing the phone. "McBride? It's Star. How are you? . . . Well, you should take a break. Get some lunch. Charge it to us. Take the afternoon off. It's a beautiful day for a walk on the beach. It would be a shame to waste it in Century City. We'll call you later. . . . Great, bye."

She hung up the phone and climbed onto Jimi's lap, straddling him as she planted a big kiss right on him. He responded by wrapping his arms around her.

"I love this solution," he said in a sleepy, deep voice, drunk with his passion.

"No, no." Star sat up. "This isn't it. That's just the kind of Hi-honey-I'm-home kiss you should be getting from me every day. We're newlyweds, for fuck sake."

"We sure are." He nuzzled her, not quite ready to talk.

"Jimi, Jimi." She took his face in her hands. "I know just what to do. I know just how to handle all this."

"Okay, what is it?" he sighed.

"Surrender," Star said with a shrug. "We don't have to fight."

"What are you talking about?"

"I mean it. This roadie who's suing? He's right. You should pay his medical bills. And you can. So settle it. I think we should settle it all."

"What about the rest of it?" he said, sitting up.

"I can't hide and fight anymore." Star threw her arms into the air. "I can't. I'm done. What difference does it make anymore? My life is worth more than this. Our life is worth more than this. I cannot, will not spend it fighting with people I don't even want to talk to. Don't you see? In a hundred years, who'll care?"

"Yeah, I see," Jimi said, a smile spreading across his face. "I do see. You're right." His mood was rising to match hers.

"You know what we should do?" Star said mischievously, taking his hand and rising from her seat on his lap.

"Yes," he said.

11

the bitch is back

The trip to Paris was perfectly timed. The freedom of surrender had reinvigorated her life with Jimi. He was in love with her and his music, so her life got better. *Hammer Time* continued to dominate the ratings, and *Lifeguards* was the number one syndicated show in the world. Her career was fine.

Hank was working on *Hammer Time,* making work connections and staying away from the other kind. He was even dating Theresa—a little weird, Star thought, but whatever.

As if she needed a prize for having such a great life, Star was being given a humanitarian award for her service in the cause of animal rights through B.A.G.L.E. And the frosting on that cake was that the award was being presented in Paris.

It was the perfect opportunity for a romantic getaway for two. Star had never been, and their schedules allowed for a little time following the ceremony to discover the legendary city of love together.

The sprinkle on the frosting was that Star was to receive the award from rock legend Sir Andrew Manchester, one of her favorite musicians and a longtime supporter of the animal rights cause. It was the first time the award, named after Sir Andrew's late wife, had ever been presented.

The trip even timed out perfectly with Star's production schedule, though to be honest, she had wheedled, begged, pleaded, and bullied anyone who could help create the time for her departure. The big, top-secret, season finale with Sven was up on her return, and Jimi's New York concert was happening almost simultaneously. Star and Jimi were thinking of taking the summer off to be with each other after a pretty rocky first year. But they both hoped that the concert would jump-start Jimi's career, so their summer plans were filed under wait and see.

A few days in Paris at the George V and an award from Drew Manchester at the Tuileries for being kind to animals was the dream weekend getaway for a girl from Arcady Key.

The trip began with an adventure. They left Hank to look after things, and Lito got them to the airport. Because the purpose of the trip was so visible, their departure was far from secret. They were amazed as throngs of screaming fans descended on her and Jimi.

Breathless with fear, they stood frozen as the mob closed in on them.

"Run," Jimi whispered urgently into her ear at the last moment.

Star turned to look at him and caught the spirit of his grin. It wasn't running to get away, it was a game of chase.

She grinned back.

It was on.

They took off running down the long, tiled passageway into the depths of LAX. The mob was surprised at first, and that gave Star and Jimi a bit of a lead, but it wasn't much. Screaming with delight, the dozens who had somehow gotten on the other side of security took off after them. It turned out that many of their pursuers had actually purchased tickets with no intention of flying, just to be in the terminal with Star and Jimi.

They gave their pursuers quite a run for their money, turning over brochure racks and dropping things in their pursuers' path, managing to get just far enough ahead following a sharp turn that they had time out of sight to hide behind an idle ticket desk. The hardest part of not getting caught was not laughing. Eventually, they got to the first-class cabin of their flight and took their seats.

Seated across the aisle from them was Star's rather intimate acquaintance Randy Pizarro. She had not seen him since she'd escaped from his clutches and his bedroom, giving him the slip by hiding in the guest bathroom.

Star laughed at the private joke between them.

The flight to Paris was long and uneventful. They had dinner and a bit too much champagne, then passed out with the help of a little Ambien. They woke up refreshed and completely out of sync with Paris time.

The press and the crowds were there in force for their arrival, but the security was ready for it. The event planners had escorts and a car there to see them smoothly through customs and into the country.

The director of B.A.G.L.E., Mike Dean, met them at the hotel and saw them to their suite, all the while briefing them on their itinerary. Star didn't know him well, but Mike had a mischievous quality that appealed to her. He was tall and wickedly good-looking with a Southern gentleman's charm that Star felt right at home with. Yet she had learned from their few conversations that he was quite the party boy. They quickly discovered that they had everything in common and that both were big punk fans, as well as animal lovers. They didn't get to spend much time together in Paris, but Star decided to change that situation at the earliest opportunity.

There was a lot to do in their short visit, but thankfully she and Jimi had a little time on their own after Mike dropped them off at the Louis Quatorze Suite. It was exquisite and romantic and the two were glad to have some quality time alone.

They made the most of it.

Their clothes were soon strewn from the front door, across the sitting room, past the blazing fireplace, like a path to the bed.

Star knew how sensitive his nipples were and that rubbing his chest and tugging at his nipple rings while she went down on him drove him nuts and pushed him toward the brink. He had to fight his way back, unwilling for it to end too quickly.

Jimi had brought a Chinese basket in his suitcase, a canvas sling that supported one partner at waist level for easy access when you fuck standing up. They made full use of it that afternoon. The mysterious holes in the ceiling of their room left the staff at the grand old hotel wondering.

All too soon, their serenity was shattered by two familiar voices.

"Hi, kids, how's the show going?" Skip called, letting himself and Billy into the main room.

"Cut," Billy called. "That's a wrap."

"Hi, boys," Jimi said, coming into the room in one of the sumptuous white terry robes the hotel supplied. "She'll be right with you, we just got out of the shower."

"Thanks, Jimi," Skip said, setting out his things on the marquetry table covered with inlaid roses. "And, um, your cock is out."

"Oh, sorry." Jimi grabbed his robe and pulled it more tightly together.

Billy grinned. "Don't worry, we're professionals. We've seen more naked people than most doctors."

"I guess that is a hazard of your job," Jimi said sheepishly.

"Our job?" Skip said, putting his hands on his hips as he considered. "I guess we do see a lot of naked people at work, too."

"Now that you mention it," Billy agreed, nodding.

"Don't pick on Jimi," Star said, coming in bundled in a similar robe. "In fact, if there's time, Skip, maybe you can do something fun with his hair while I'm in makeup."

Jimi looked less than thrilled at the prospect.

"Now who's picking on him?" Billy teased.

"She's a remarkable woman of many talents who has worked tirelessly with B.A.G.L.E. and other animal rights groups to raise public awareness not only of problems but of solutions," Sir Andrew said from the microphone in front of a crowd of people Star had only imagined seeing in person. And now she was not only one of them, but they were there to honor her.

"But don't take my word for it," he went on with the introduction. "I could hardly describe it all. We have a most revealing video. Not that kind of video," he said, riding over the gentle laughter as Star and Jimi shared a nervous glance.

As Star watched along with everyone else, tears came into her eyes. She was proud of herself for making it there. It all seemed worth it somehow. She could see how much her crazy life had meant in the fight for a cause that she'd been rolling pennies for since her childhood.

The applause and the chunk of crystal etched with her name that Drew handed her paled next to the look of pride on Jimi's face as he rose to applaud her.

"I feel like I'm accepting this award on behalf of the people who do the real work," Star said, trying not to cry. "If what I do can help draw attention to their work, then I guess I've helped a little. There's a lot more to be done and we all have to get involved. But tonight, I pay tribute to all those people around the world who are truly making a difference. Thank you."

It was simple and eloquent and very Star. Never one to take all the glory nor to neglect to give credit where it was due, her words went out around the world, beating her home—though not by as much as she'd originally planned.

Hank had gone out to Star and Jimi's house to watch them on the big screen, and his discoveries there would ultimately bring her Paris trip to an early conclusion and change their lives forever.

After the event, Star and Jimi were piled into a car with Mike, Sir Andrew, and his wife, Blanche, for a short ride to a small after party in Star's honor.

She could not have been more thrilled. She had thought that she was only going to get to see Drew onstage when he gave her the award, but they had actually spent some time together and even got to meet his activist wife, Blanche, whose cruelty-free fashion line Star was wearing that evening. Jimi's first opportunity to meet the rock legend and his wife was in the car, where Mike made introductions.

After the banquet in her honor, they returned to the hotel, where Star picked up a message from Hank.

Jimi hit the bed as soon as they got back and left Star dialing the phone. He found her, hours later, still in the gown she'd been in the night before, unable to speak or stop crying.

Jimi had brought along some speed to get them past the jet lag, and they'd gotten pretty motivated before the festivities. To avoid any potentially embarrassing questions, instead of calling a doctor in a strange country, he called Skip and Billy, who were staying in somewhat less grand quarters down the hall.

"Star, darling," Billy said, kneeling beside her. She only clutched him and sobbed harder in reply.

"Did anything happen tonight that might have upset her?" Skip asked, trying to get some sense of the situation. She had seemed almost joyful only a few hours earlier when they were getting her ready.

"Not really," Jimi said, baffled by the outburst.

The two looked on helplessly as Billy held her in his arms and rocked her gently for a bit, until she fell asleep.

"Here," he whispered to Jimi and Skip. "Help me get her to bed. Maybe if she gets some sleep . . ."

When Jimi lifted her, Billy discovered the note on the tearstained carpet where she'd lain.

"Oh, God," he said softly as he read. "I think I know what's wrong."

"What is it?" Skip asked, looking back over.

"It's a message from Hank."

" 'My North, my South, my East and West,' " Star read to the small group gathered in rows of gold cane catering chairs in the big living room at Jimiville. " 'My working week and my Sunday rest. My noon, my midnight, my talk, my song; I thought that love would last forever: I was wrong.' "

Jimi stood sullenly in the back of the room, arms folded as she read the words from a small book of W. H. Auden.

" 'The stars are not wanted now: put out every one.' " She continued reaching out to touch the simple stone urn, glinting in the afternoon sun. " 'Pack up the moon and dismantle the sun; pour away the ocean and sweep up the wood. For nothing now can ever come to any good.' " She concluded her reading and collapsed into tears once again. She had read the same verse at her mother's funeral only weeks before.

Theresa took her hand and helped her to a chair.

Jimi went outside; he couldn't stand it any longer. He bummed a smoke from someone's driver.

Star had been in tears pretty much since he'd found her in their hotel room in Paris. They'd left early, cutting their trip short and returning home to make arrangements. But other than planning for that afternoon, Star had completely withdrawn. She would not eat, she couldn't sleep, save for the few moments when exhaustion overcame her and she dozed, only to wake up screaming.

Jimi had tried to comfort her, but she continued to push him away. He even sheltered her, not telling her about the strange and unnerving phone call from *Scum* magazine offering to buy their sex videos which he knew were still locked away in the safe.

He stomped out the cigarette, and as he returned, saw that the gathering was getting ready to make a move. Star clutched the urn to her breast as the somber little party made their way out to the cars. Jimi fell in behind, riding in silence with Star, the only sound the sobs that accompanied her periodic tears.

They arrived at the marina and boarded the chartered yacht that would take them up the coast to their final destination. Food and drink were served in the main cabin of the luxury cruiser, but Star stood alone at the prow of the ship, caressing the urn as if the act could bring her closer. Jimi fought to contain his anger over the whole farcical afternoon. In a way, he was glad Star did not want him now, because he was too angry with her, with her abandonment, to allow her her grief.

They sailed up the coast for a while, viewing the city from a rarely seen perspective. Despite having one of the busiest harbors in the world, Los Angeles has no real reputation as a seaport and is rarely depicted that way. Whereas New York is always shown from across the river or harbor or from the Atlantic, Los Angeles is almost never shown from the water. It made for an unfamiliar experience for those aboard. Things looked oddly familiar, but they could just as easily have been sailing past a foreign city.

Eventually, the boat pulled even with their house and the captain killed the engines. Star rose and walked to the rail, her black dress billowing in the stiff breeze. She upended the urn and allowed the wind to take the ashes and spread them over the water.

"Good-bye, old friend," Star said softly as she watched the ashes disappear. "You always did want to swim out here; I thought you might like to see it now."

She dropped the urn and sank to her knees, holding on to the railing to keep from falling overboard herself.

Theresa rushed forward to help her. "There, there," she said, stroking Star's hair back out of her face. "It's over now, time to go home."

"It won't be home without Mutley," Star said, dissolving into tears once again.

The guests paid their respects at the slip.

Hank took Theresa to his place while Jimi and Star returned home alone together for the first time since Paris. They rode in silence for a bit. He sighed deeply, unable to think of anything to do or say.

"Don't you care that Mutley is dead?" Her accusation broke the icy silence between them.

"Don't you care that I'm alive?"

"What does this have to do with you?" Star asked bitterly.

"Exactly," he snapped. "You have shut me out. You care more about that damn dog than you do about me."

"Is that all you can think about?" Star's tears came again as she struggled not to let go.

"Stop being such a soap opera queen," he sighed, looking out the window.

"Don't you get it?" she demanded, pounding his shoulder as the tears threatened to take her voice. "He was all alone. I left him here all by himself and he died alone. It's my fault he's dead."

"What are you talking about?"

"I feel like there is a curse on us," Star said, nearly hysterical. "Ever since Cabo. It's like fate wants to punish us for enjoying our lives after doing such horrible things. I just wanted to have a little fun, and first Mom and now Mutley is dead."

She cried all the way back to the house, into bed, and off to sleep that night.

When she finally woke up, alone in their room, she looked to the chair where Mutley used to sleep in the hope that it had only been a bad dream. She arose, opened the curtains, and sat in Mutley's chair, staring out to sea as he had so often. She gazed toward the spot where she'd sprinkled his ashes. And that's where Jimi found her when he came home that afternoon.

"Okay," he said. "That's it. You're coming with me."

"I don't feel like it."

"Star, break's over. You've got to get back to the set in two days, and I'm leaving for New York in the morning. Life's in session. Put on a sweatshirt and some jeans or something, but I need for you to come with me."

They regarded each other a moment.

She got up listlessly, went into the dressing room, and found some sweats. "Okay," she said, emerging.

She followed him wordlessly downstairs and got in the car beside him without questioning where they were going.

The weather was beginning to warm up as spring took hold, and she looked out the window and watched the wildflowers on the banks alongside PCH blur past. After about a half hour's drive, Jimi pulled into the lot by the offices of Mutley's vet.

"Why are we here?" Star asked.

"For the truth." Jimi got out and went around to open Star's door for her. Reluctantly, she took his hand and followed him across the cracked asphalt of the lot.

They went inside and Jimi let the receptionist know they had arrived for their appointment. Star took a seat and looked around at the lobby, filled with pets and their owners. Bandages, the humiliating "Elizabethan" plastic collars, and worried faces filled the room. Star thought that she might have to leave. Her feelings were just too strong.

"Jimi?" the doctor said from the doorway. "Star, good to see you. Come on back."

"What are we doing here?" Star asked Jimi angrily once they were in the little hallway that led from the lobby to the examination rooms. The sounds of dogs yapping and the occasional wail of a cat brought the space alive with pain.

Jimi didn't answer. He took her hand and led her along as they followed the doctor into his office at the end of the hall. The small, warm space was filled with pictures of the doctor, from his youth to the present day, each with him in the company of a series of Weimaraners. Ribbons and diplomas told the story of a love affair that had become a career for the sprightly, curly-haired little man before them.

"Doc, tell Star what you told me," Jimi said.

"It was a heart attack, Star," the doctor said. "And judging from the way that Hank found Mutley, he was asleep when it happened. It was massive and almost instantaneous. He never even woke up. We should all die such a peaceful death."

"But if I'd been there," Star said, crying angrily, "I could have done something. I could have helped him. He wouldn't have been alone."

"No, Star," the doctor said, comforting her. "There was nothing you could have done. If you'd been there, you probably wouldn't even have known. He lay down to go to sleep and never got up again. He was an old dog and it was his time. And you and I have no say in such things. It's as much a part of life as birth."

Her tears stopped after a few minutes.

She looked into the doctor's eyes and around the room at the pictures of the succession of Weimaraners that had filled the doctor's life. She realized how many times he must have had to say good-bye.

She looked at Jimi. He gave her a nod. It wasn't what she'd wanted, but it was what he could give her. It might even have been what she needed. She didn't feel great, but she did see that feeling responsible wasn't loving to Mutley anymore than she already did.

"Time to go on," she said, rising and pushing past him. She took the doctor's hand as they left. "Thanks."

"Do what I do," he said with a sad smile. "Take some time and then get another one. There's a puppy out there that needs to love you just as much as Mutley did."

She smiled at the idea.

Jimi started the car and they drove for a bit in silence.

"Thank you," she said, patting the back of his hand as it rested on the gearshift.

His lips disappeared in a tight smile. It was all he had for her, whether or not it was enough.

12

lovely day

It was one of those perfect L.A. mornings.

The cool breeze blew in early off the Pacific and the clouds dissolved into a clear blue springtime sky. The light was inspiring and the view clear and crisp, as if the whole city had suddenly snapped into focus.

They had awakened from a night of lovemaking and felt as clear and focused as the morning outside their widow. Jimi made them an extraspecial "breakfast," as they would be separated for the first time since that night in Cabo. He was off to New York for the concert and she would join him after she wrapped shooting on *Lifeguards*.

It was a fresh new start, Star thought to herself as she showered and got ready to go to the set. Her mom's last words came back to her once again. "Remember, it's your choice who you are."

Jimi was packing, getting ready for his trip when she came out of the bathroom.

"Jimi," she said, coming up behind him and hugging him from the back. "I was saving it as a surprise, but I can't wait. There's something I want to tell you."

"What is it, babe?" he said, turning to take her in his arms.

The doorbell rang.

"Who is that?" Jimi said. "The car's not supposed to be here for another hour."

"Don't go," Star said, her spider sense on full alert.

"Who is it?" Star whispered as Jimi tried to peer around the edge of the curtains in one of the front bedrooms.

"It's the police," Jimi said, drawing back suddenly from the window.

"Maybe it's nothing," Star suggested as the two rushed to the back of the house.

"There's four at the door and the street out front looks like the parking lot at the sheriff's station." He looked out back and saw the uniformed officers encircling the house.

"How did they get in?" Star said, wondering that the police were inside the gates. "No one has the code but you and me and . . ."

"Hank."

"Not my own brother," Star said, shaking her head in disbelief.

"Did you give them the code?"

She shook her head.

"Well neither did I," he said.

"What are we going to do?" Star said, as the tension of the past months built to the breaking point.

"Come with me," he said, taking her hand.

The officer rang the bell for a third time, but still no answer.

"Maybe they're still asleep," his partner said, standing back from the door, his gun drawn.

"What's happening?" the captain's voice crackled through the officer's walkie-talkie.

"No answer," the officer replied. "Maybe they're still asleep. The brother said they were partiers. What's the next step?"

Before the captain had a chance to answer, the black Ferrari burst through the garage door, the wood panels exploding into splinters as the high-performance projectile rocketed down the drive, through the open gate, and down the street before any of the police on the scene had a chance to draw their service revolvers.

"Woo-hoo," Star screamed as they tore up the canyon road, the police nowhere in sight. "Let's go again."

Jimi laughed in spite of the tension. He knew she was trying to cheer him up.

"Whatever happens, babe, it's been the best ride of my life," he said, taking her hand.

She kissed his knuckles.

"Where to?" he asked her as they rocketed toward Mulholland Drive, the legendary road that snaked along the ridge of the mountains that formed the northern border of the Los Angeles basin.

"Mexico," she said with a shrug. "And then, who knows?"

"You got it," he said, passing a car and nearly running an oncoming truck off a cliff as he continued to pick up speed.

Both were unaware that overhead the police they thought they'd left behind had taken to the air to keep them in sight. Unfortunately, the police weren't the only ones who'd taken up the chase.

"And this just in," Kurt Blanche said, reaching up to touch his earpiece in disbelief. "Police are involved in a high-speed chase in the canyon roads up from Malibu. And . . . are we sure?" he said, looking to the booth for further confirmation as L.A. was waking up to his morning news break-in on the network's morning talk show. "Okay, we have confirmation, the fugitives being pursued are Star Wood Leigh and Jimi Deed, though it's unclear yet why the police want them. We'll keep you posted as the story develops.

By the time Kurt had finished the weather, he was co-anchoring the national news with New York. News helicopters had joined the chase along with those from the L.A.P.D. and Sheriff's Department.

Dozens of radio cars, police helicopters, as well as at least one chopper for each of the networks, had taken up the high-speed pursuit. Morning traffic reports took up the story and thousands, bound for work, called in sick from their cars and headed in the direction of the chase. Traffic arteries in and around the beach began to shut down as the curious poured into the area to get a closer look.

Across the country, work came to a standstill as people clustered in front of any available television set to see what would happen next. In fact, most everyone in the country knew about the chase before Star and Jimi did.

"So, do you think we should take the 405?" Jimi asked, running the light and making the turn onto Mulholland at full speed as cars spun out of control to avoid hitting them. "Traffic may not be as bad southbound."

"I don't know," Star said, trying to find something to listen to on the disc changer. "The 405 is always a nightmare."

Bill Withers's "Lovely Day" came out of nowhere and she had to laugh at the irony. In so many ways, it really was a lovely day.

"What is this doing on here?" she giggled.

"I like all kinds of music," Jimi said, reaching over to try to change the disc. He hit the wrong button, and the radio came on instead.

"The occupants of the car appear to be Star Wood Leigh and husband, Jimi Deed," the announcer was saying.

"Fuck you, dude, her fucking last name is Deed!" Jimi shouted, taking up the gun in his lap and firing a shot at the radio but only blowing off the glove compartment door.

"Jimi, be careful with that," Star said, turning up the volume for details.

"Police are closing in on the couple as they make their way

toward the 405 on Mulholland Drive. Motorists are asked to avoid the area, as they are believed to be armed and dangerous."

Jimi turned the wheel and spun the car, dangerously close to flipping it as he reversed course at such high speed and almost immediately rode head-on into a wall of police cars coming straight for them.

"Jimi, there's something I should tell you!" Star screamed when it looked as though they were about to be plastered across the grille of an oncoming prowl car.

But at the last second, he turned onto a small paved road that swept them rapidly up into the hills above and momentarily away from their pursuers.

"Hang on a second, babe," he said, maneuvering the car into the hills without losing speed.

"Okay," she said, not wanting to distract him as they narrowly escaped death on each turn.

"Evidence has been uncovered linking the couple to the deaths of a series of photographers known in the entertainment business as paparazzi," Kurt said earnestly to his viewers as voice-over to the airborne cameras following Star and Jimi's progress into the hills. "The deaths in this country, Mexico, and possibly Paris had previously been thought to be unrelated, but . . ."

"Hold on, Kurt," Cathy, the New York anchor, broke in. "I'm getting word that we have just acquired exclusive video that links the couple to the crimes. So we're going to cut away to that for a moment and then we'll come back to our live coverage of the Star chase."

The chase squeezed into the corner of the frame as the

scene from the balcony at the El Presidente suite in Cabo San
Lucas filled the screen.

"On three? One, two, three."

Their nudity had been digitally masked but the murder
was shown on national television. Cathy was mistaken about
one thing, the footage was far from exclusive. Hank and
Theresa had dubbed off as many copies as they could that
night, and while he was working with the police, she had been
putting together their retirement fund, selling copies to every
network and news outlet in the world.

"I can't believe that," Star said, staring at the radio as they listened for the third time to the photographer's screams as he
plunged from their balcony. "How did they get the video?
The only person who had the combination for the safe besides
you and me was . . ."

"Hank," Jimi snarled, his knuckles turning white as he
clutched the steering wheel.

"Well, to be fair, Theresa knows too," Star said. "But then
she's dating . . ."

"Hank," Jimi said. "The rat fuck sold us out."

"You don't know that," Star said, trying vainly to defend
her beloved brother.

"We take you live to a press conference with Star Wood
Leigh's brother, Hank Leigh, as he reveals his tormented decision to turn in his own sister when he discovered evidence of
her despicable crimes."

"For the last time her last fucking name is Deed," Jimi
said, succeeding in blowing the radio out of the dashboard
with his Mauser Hsc.

"Look out!" Star screamed as she saw the metal barrier closing fast in front of the car.

Jimi braked too late.

As the world watched in horror, the little black sports coupe smashed through the barrier, hit the dirt road at the entrance to the small hilltop park, and disappeared into a cloud of dust.

For minutes, as newscasters the world over speculated, the fate of the two was not known as everyone waited for the dust to clear.

"According to park rangers there is a massive drop just a matter of yards from where the car broke through the barrier," Kurt was explaining for the cameras. "Unless they were able to stop in time, they could easily have plunged to their deaths over the cliff, ironically, just like the man believed to be their first victim. We have computer simulations of what that plunge might have looked like."

Hank was annoyed that their deaths had cut his news conference short, but the three movie offers he'd already had that morning went a long way toward helping him get over it. He still could not quite believe the strange series of events that had begun while he was sneaking a peek at the amateur home videos only the night before and landing him on the world stage before lunchtime.

L.A. was a long way from Arcady Key.

"Hello? Andy?"

"Star? Is that you?" Andy Callas said by way of welcome to his on-air guest as Star's voice crackled onto the airwaves of America's most listened to morning radio program. Always at the top of the charts, Andy's show went off the scale when every network and news service around the world went live with his broadcast so that Star spoke to the entire world at once from her cell phone as she and Jimi sat in Topanga State Park waiting for the dust to settle.

"Hi, Andy," Star said, her girlish voice strangely at odds with what the world had just discovered about her only moments before.

"Star, is there anything you'd like to say?"

"Yes," Star said, softly. "I just want to say first that those videotapes were our private property and they were stolen from our home. And secondly, that man broke into our hotel room and photographed us making love on our honeymoon. So, whatever action we took was in self-defense."

"He looked pretty defenseless hanging from that balcony," Andy said in his typical cut-to-the-bone style.

"That's how he broke into our room in the first place," Star said. "It's dangerous hanging from the sides of buildings."

"Anything you want to say to your fans?" Andy asked as he could see on the monitors that the dust was clearing and an army of police cars were closing on them.

"Yeah," Star sighed. "First, thank you for you support. And second, leave us alone."

"Thanks Star, for being on the show today," Andy said. "I hope we'll get the chance to talk to each other again."

"Yeah, me too, Andy," Star said. "Anything you want to say, Jimi?"

"Everyone sucks but us," Jimi's voice, cracking with laughter, came in from the background.

"I love you, babe," Jimi said, taking her hand and kissing it. "It's been the best with you, every, every minute."

"I love you, babe," Star said, kissing his hand, his chest, his neck, and then finding his mouth for a passionate moment, lost in each other once again.

"Jimi," Star said, her eyes brimming with tears. "I have to tell you something."

"No more words, babe," Jimi said, touching her lips to silence her. "No apologies. We've lived our lives full speed and that's how we'll go out."

Jimi stomped the accelerator and, as the world—which had just heard the declarations live via Star's still open cell phone call to Andy Callas—watched in horror, the Testarossa's tires spun in the dust and the car reached nearly 100 m.p.h. as they hurtled toward the cliff that they had chosen as their launching pad.

Unlike the rest of the world, what Jimi and Star could not see was the line of police cars rushing up to cut them off, robbing them of their dramatic final moment and their freedom to choose their own fate.

Jimi spun the car away from the intervening police cruisers to avoid a collision. Chaos ensued. Clouds of dust made it hard to see. Shots were fired, but it was unclear by whom. Star and Jimi leaped from the car to make a run for each other for one final embrace before the officers tore them apart.

"Star, Star!" Jimi screamed straining against the hands of half a dozen officers to get to her as she struggled to reach him.

"Jimi," Star shouted. "I love you, babe."

"I love you, babe."

The police began to jerk her around roughly in an effort to get cuffs on her, knocking her down briefly and then yanking her to her feet again. "Be careful," she screamed. "I'm pregnant."

"What?" Jimi says, going rigid for a moment and then turning into a wild man to try to get to her.

"I'm pregnant," she said tenderly as she was cuffed and led away.

"No!" Jimi screamed, losing control. As the adrenaline kicked in, his strength became almost superhuman, and he began tossing police officers aside like rag dolls. The officers responded in kind and began clubbing Jimi into submission, tackling him to the ground as Star watched in horror.

Despite the beating he was taking, Jimi would not give up his struggle to be at her side and broke free, charging toward Star and the officers surrounding her.

"Let her go!" he screamed, pulling the Mauser from his belt as he charged. "I love you, Star."

Armed and dangerous, the officers opened fire on Jimi.

"I love you, Jimi," Star screamed hysterically as a hail of bullets brought him down before her eyes. Hands restrained her as she tried to get to him when he fell. And a hand on her head as she was forced into the car and driven away. Star clutched her stomach to embrace and protect all that she had left of the man she loved.

"I love you, Jimi," she whispered. "I'll always love you."